LANDER ROCK CLIMBS | 2018

Steve Bechtel | Kyle Duba | Ben Sears

Vertical-Life
climbing app

DOWNLOAD THE APP
and unlock this guide

CODE

LANDER ROCK CLIMBS | 2018

Steve Bechtel | Kyle Duba | Ben Sears

ISBN 978-1-5323-7588-0

Cover Photo: Inge Perkins Climbing in the Little PoPo Agie
Photo: Ben Herndon

Climb Strong
134 Lincoln
Lander WY, 82520

steve@climbstrong.com

Lander
Chamber of Commerce
TOURISM ASSET
DEVELOPMENT

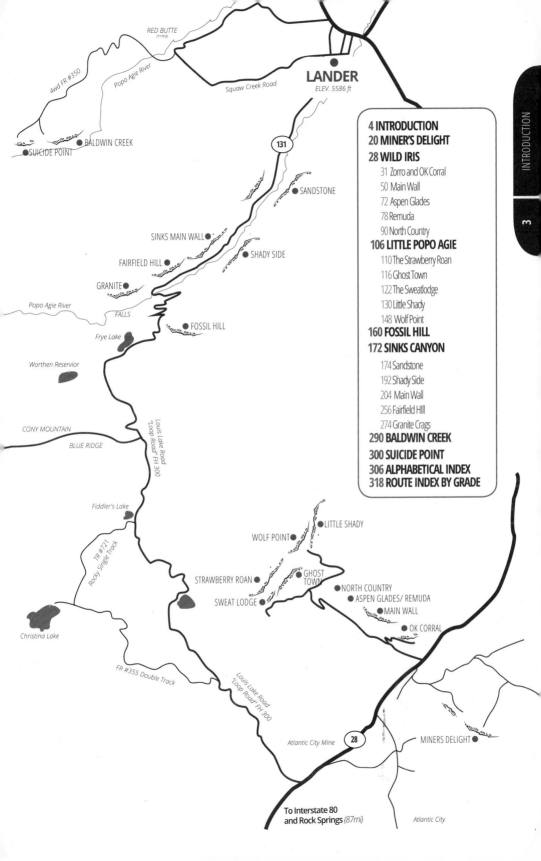

RED BUTTE
(7174 ft)

4wd FR #350

Popo Agie River

Squaw Creek Road

LANDER
ELEV. 5586 ft

SUICIDE POINT

BALDWIN CREEK

131

SANDSTONE

SINKS MAIN WALL

FAIRFIELD HILL

SHADY SIDE

GRANITE

Popo Agie River

FALLS

Frye Lake

FOSSIL HILL

Worthen Reservoir

CONY MOUNTAIN

BLUE RIDGE

Louis Lake Road "Loop Road" FH 300

Fiddler's Lake

TR #721
Rocky Single Track

WOLF POINT

LITTLE SHADY

STRAWBERRY ROAN

GHOST TOWN

SWEAT LODGE

NORTH COUNTRY

ASPEN GLADES/ REMUDA

MAIN WALL

OK CORRAL

Christina Lake

FR #355 Double Track

Louis Lake Road "Loop Road" FH 300

Atlantic City Mine

28

MINERS DELIGHT

To Interstate 80
and Rock Springs *(87mi)*

Atlantic City

WELCOME TO LANDER

In 1990, I was working at a climbing store in Laramie, Wyoming, and making weekend trips to Fremont Canyon to climb on the newly developed bolted routes in that area. Rumors kept spreading through town that Wyoming's famed Todd Skinner had returned to the state and had found a limestone climbing paradise near Lander. In our quest to climb the most and hardest routes we could find, it was a siren song too strong to resist. Within weeks, the trips to Fremont stopped and we were making the 3.5 hour drive to Lander most weekends.

At that time there were maybe 30 routes at the Wild Iris and an equal number at the Main Wall of Sinks. Each week, it seemed, another new line would get done and another new climber would show up to spend the season exploring and developing the crags. By 1995, many of us had moved to Lander full-time and there were more than 800 sport routes in the area. As I write this, nearly 30 years after my first day on the walls at Sinks Canyon, there are over 2000 routes in the immediate Lander area, and another 500 within a 90 minute drive.

With climbs on Granite, Dolomite, Sandstone, and even Quartzite, the Lander area offers challenges for climbers of all abilities. Once again we have done our best to give good recommendations, warn against dangerous climbs, and direct you to the newest and best climbs we have to offer.

The book you now hold is the second I have collaborated on with the talented Ben Sears and Kyle Duba. It has been a labor of love and we are very proud to record the history of this great sport in this great area. Please enjoy your time here.

-Steve Bechtel, April 2018

photo Kyle Duba

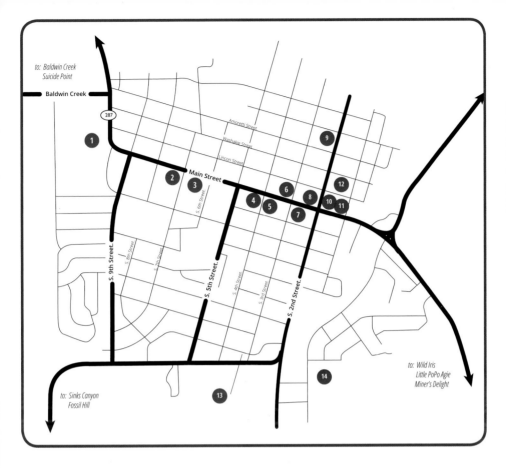

●1 Safeway
Grocrey Store

●2 Mr. D's
Mom and Pop Grocery Store

●3 Tony's Pizza
Pizza/Salads, Roof Patio

●4 Ken and Betty's
Ice cream

●5 Middle Fork
Breakfast/Brunch

●6 Crux Coffee
Coffee/Climbing Wall

●7 Lander Bake Shop
Coffee/Pastries/ Bagel Sandwitches

●8 Wild Iris
Camping/Climbing Gear

●9 Library
Books/Wifi

●10 Cowfish
American Cuisine

●11 Gannett Grill/ Lander Bar
Burgers/Salads/Beer

●12 Elemental
Climbing Gym

●13 City Park
Free 3 day camping!

●14 Hospital

photo Kyle Duba

RED CANYON

GETTING THERE

Lander is in the middle of the least populous state in the country. If you don't have a car, you're going to have a hard time getting to Lander and a hard time getting to the crags.

For climbers coming from other countries, it's best to fly into Denver (6 hours) or Salt Lake City (4.5 hours) and rent a car. If you are planning on climbing anywhere besides Wild Iris, Sinks, or Fossil Hill, you'll want a high-clearance vehicle. You can also fly to the small airport in Riverton (RIW) 28 miles away, but flights are limited and rental cars are not always available.

Driving here from nearby areas can be touchy in the winter, but the roads are generally clear except right after storms. See the overview map for details on which highway will get you here the fastest.

Detailed driving directions to the crags from Lander will be provided in each of the chapters, but you should note that some of the approaches require high clearance or 4-wheel drive vehicles.

ANY VEHICLE	HIGH CLEARANCE (Subaru Outback or equivalent)	4 WHEEL DRIVE
Sinks	Little Popo Agie	Baldwin Creek
Fossil Hill	Miner's Delight	Suicide Point
Wild Iris		

Yes, it can be difficult to access some of these crags, but if you're used to waiting in line at the base of popular routes and get tired of the typical crag "scene", this might be just the change of pace you need.

FRENCH	YDS	AUS
4	5.7	15
5a	5.8	16
5b	5.9	17
5c	5.10a	18
6a	5.10b	18
6a+	5.10c	19
6b	5.10d	20
6b+	5.11a	20
6c	5.11b	21
6c+	5.11c	22
7a	5.11d	23
7a+	5.12a	24
7b	5.12b	25
7b+	5.12c	26
7c	5.12d	27
7c+	5.13a	28
8a	5.13b	29
8a+	5.13c	30
8b	5.13d	31
8b+	5.14a	32
8c	5.14b	33
8c+	5.14c	34
9a	5.14d	35
9a+	5.15a	36
9b	5.15b	37
9b+	5.15c	38

USING THIS BOOK

○ white indicates 5.9 & Under

● green indicates 5.10

● blue indicates 5.11

● yellow indicates 5.12

● red indicates 5.13 & up

● black indicates Projects

+ indicates the route is an extension

🔗 indicates the route is a Link up

These symbols appear at the beginning of eatch section. They give a idea of what angles, approach time, and sun the wall gets.

 When Wall Gets Sun

 Approach Time

 Vertical Wall

 Slightly Overhanging

 Steep Walls

 Roof

 Rattle Snakes

 Rock Fall

 Season Fall

 Season Spring

 Season Winter

CLIMBING GEAR & GYM

Wild Iris Mountain Sports
is located at 166 Main Street. Widely regarded as one of the best climbing shops anywhere, Wild Iris has been a fixture of Lander climbing for over 25 years. They have a wide variety of gear and apparel, as well as good information on the Lander area and the Wind Rivers. *307- 332-4541: www.wildirisclimbing.com*

Elemental Performance + Fitness
is a block behind Wild Iris, at 134 Lincoln. This is Lander's climbing gym. Elemental also offers a full training facility and provides showers for $5. *307-332-0480 : www.lmntl.net*

NOLS Rocky Mountain Branch and The Gulch
are located at the corner of 5th and Lincoln streets. The RMB has a full gear shop and is a great place to get NOLS logowear and souvenirs. In the same building is Then-Gulch, which is probably the best source for backcountry food anywhere. They offer freeze-dried everything, great snack bars, bulk treats, and even detailed information on exactly how much a person needs per day in the mountains. *307-332-4784 : www.nols.edu*

CLIMBING GUIDES

Wind River Climbing Guides
(www.windriverclimbing.com)

Exum Guides
(www.exumguides.com)

Jackson Hole Mountain Guides
(www.jhmg.com), both based out of Jackson, WY, offer guiding services around Lander.

WATER

During the summer months, water is available at the Lander City Park and at the campgrounds in Sinks Canyon and near Atlantic City.

CAMPING & ACCOMMODATIONS

The City of Lander allows free camping in the city park with a three day limit. There are toilets, water, tables, and a really nice atmosphere.

There are three campgrounds in Sinks Canyon. The first two are developed, and have toilets and water. The third, on the left side of the road just past the University of Missouri Field Camp is free, with a pit toilet and no water.

Camping is also available at the Wild Iris near the OK Corral. This is free camping with a 14 day limit. There is a pit toilet, but no water available. Nice tent platforms have been erected by the Central Wyoming Climbers Alliance. There are also two campgrounds near Atlantic City, 3 miles southeast of Wild Iris. Both of these campgrounds have water and toilets.

Unimproved camping is available at other areas around Wild Iris, as well as at Fossil Hill, Baldwin Creek, Wolf Point, and near the Sweatlodge parking area. No services are available in these areas.

CLIMBING WITH KIDS

Lander is a very kid-friendly area, but some crags are better choices than others. Certain areas, such as the OK Corral, are obviously good choices. Areas such as Wolf Point are not only hard on kids, but downright dangerous. Of special note is that Sinks Main Wall features lots of poison ivy and many snakes in the summer months, but these are not a problem in the winter. Sinks Main Wall, however, is a major rockfall zone so be very careful where you set up camp with kids.

HISTORY

Check out the video Wind & Rattle Snakes by Kyle Duba on the history and future of the Lander Area. You can watch online at:
http://vimeo.com/kyleduba/windandrattlesnakes

LOCAL FOOD

Lander has great restaurants. Compared with most other Wyoming towns, we really lucked out. Most of these establishments are reasonably priced, and several are even owned by climbers!

●Gannett Grill and Lander Bar
are the main hangouts for rock climbers in Lander. The Gannett's patio can't be beat on summer evenings. Climber-owned. *126 Main.*

●The Middle Fork
The Middle Fork is the number one choice for breakfast and lunch. Their huevos scramble is hard to beat. Climber-owned. *351 Main.*

●El Sol de Mexico
El Sol de Mexico offers an authentic Mexican menu at reasonable prices. Takeout available. *453 Main.*

●The Cowfish
The Cowfish offers a full bar, seafood, and great bowl food. Their patio is great and adjoins the Gannett Grill deck. *148 Main.*

●The Lander Bake Shop
The Lander Bake Shop offers a full coffee shop, bagels, and treats. Great atmosphere. Climber-owned. *259 Main.*

●Tony's Pizza
Tony's Pizza has a full menu of salads, pasta, and pizza. *637 Main*

●China Garden
China Garden serves authentic Chinese cuisine. *162N 6th.*

●The Oxbow
The Oxbow is your classic bacon and eggs breakfast joint. *170 Main.*

●Thai Chef
Great Thai food, worth the wait. *975 Lincoln.*

●Pizza Hut, *670 E Main.*

●Subway *960 Main.*

●McDonalds, *235 McFarlane Dr.*

●Dairy Land, *977 Main*

●The Breadboard, *1350 Main.*

●Crux Coffee, *300 Main.*

●Starbucks (in Safeway), *1165 Main.*

photo Kyle Duba

Darren Flack

COWBOY KING 13c

photo Kyle Duba

REST DAY ACTIVITIES

Lander is a great place to climb, and a great place to not climb. Rest day activities can range from touring around town to driving the Loop Road, to a short hike in the mountains to a trip to Jackson Hole to get rid of your money. Listed below are our top five rest day activities:

●Spend a Day in Lander-

Lander is a town of about 7,000, with an area population around 10,000. Small by most standards, it's still a nice place to visit. For climbers with kids, City Park (4th and Fremont) is a must. The park offers a large playground, tennis courts, a long river walk, and plenty of grass. North Park (8th and Jefferson) also offers a play area, and features a good skate park. Disc Golf is available at 1320 Bishop Randall Drive, near the hospital.

The Fremont County Public Library is really nice, and is located at 2nd and Amoretti. The Lander Swimming Pool is at 9th and Sweetwater. This indoor pool offers lap swim, rec swim, and showers.

●Visit the Mines-

The area around South Pass is rich with history. The mining towns of South Pass City, Atlantic City, and Miner's Delight are just a short drive away from the Wild Iris area. Miner's Delight is a nice little ghost town and has been preserved as a BLM historical site. Established in the 1860s, there are still a couple dozen buildings standing and it has a really neat feel. You can find Miner's Delight about 5 miles north of Atlantic City.

The town of Atlantic City is still inhabited today and hosts (depending on the year and time of year) anywhere between one and three restaurants. The "Merc" is the classic restaurant here.

Just south of Atlantic City is South Pass City. Originally a stage station along the Oregon Trail, South Pass later became a gold mining boom town. At one point, there were several thousand people living in the area, and the town was considered as a potential site for Wyoming's capital.

●Ride a Bike-

Both road and mountain bikers have plenty to do around Lander. The mountain biking at nearby Johnny Behind the Rocks is well-maintained and outstanding, and the trails of Sinks Canyon and "The Bus" are also worthwhile. Check in at the Bike Mill (1st and Main) or Gannett Peak Sports (351 Main) for more information. There are a great many road rides to be done in the area, but the most challenging and most scenic is to ride to the end of the pavement above Sinks Canyon. This is a ride of about 20 miles each way from town with a big elevation gain and spectacular views. Both bike shops offer rentals.

photo Kyle Duba

photo Lindsey Stevens

●Visit Sinks Canyon-

OK, sure you've been to Sinks, but there's more to the canyon than the Killer Cave, hard guy. Your visit should include a stop at the Sinks Canyon Visitor Center, near where the Middle Fork of the Popo Agie River "sinks" into a cave. The staff are very friendly and work closely with local climbers, so enjoy your time there. After checking out the Sinks, you can take a short trail down-canyon to where the river rises again and check out the huge fish that have reached the end of the line.

Higher in the canyon, you'll find Bruce's parking area. A great day hike starts here and heads up-canyon to Popo Agie Falls. The hike is about a mile and a half, and the falls make a great water slide in the hot summer months.

If you feel compelled, the trail continues up the canyon and as far into the Wind Rivers as you care to walk. Sinks also hosts several shorter hiking trails and several miles of good mountain bike trails.

●Visit Sacagawea's Memorial-

About 15 miles northwest of Lander is the small town of Fort Washakie. Located on the Wind River Indian Reservation, the town is of significance for many historical reasons. Most interesting, though, is that it is the gravesite for the great Chief Washakie, and for Sacagawea, the young indian woman who acted as an interpreter and "diplomat" for the Lewis and Clark expedition in the early 1800s. Although her true grave is elsewhere (likely in the mountains to the west), the graveyard is an interesting and moving visit.

CRAG	MINER'S DELIGHT (p.30)	OK CORRAL/ ZORRO (p.30)	WILD IRIS MAIN WALL (p.30)	ASPEN GLADES (p.30)	REMUDA/ ERRATIC (p.30)	NORTH COUNTRY (p.30)	SWEAT LODGE (p.30)	WOLF PUP (p.30)
DRIVE TIME	45m	25m	25m	25m	25m	30m	40m	55m
WALK TIME	10m	5m	20m	20m	20-25m	15m	15m	10-35m
SUN	10AM-PM	10AM-PM	10AM-PM	10AM-PM	NONE	3PM-PM	10AM-PM	3PM-PM
APPROACH	Short, Flat	Short, Flat	Long, Flat	Long, Hilly	Long, Hilly	Short, Hilly	Long, Hilly	Short, Hilly
SNAKES	Beware!	-	-				Beware!	Beware!
POISION IVY	-	-	-	-	-	-	-	-
ROCK FALL	-	-	-	-	-	-	-	Beware!
KID FRIENDLY	★★	★★★	★★	★★	★★	★★	-	★
SEASONS	🍁	☀🍁	☀🍁	☀🍁	☀🍁	☀🍁	☀🍁	☀🍁
WALL ANGLE								
ROUTES	34	107	120	38	55	78	23	64
5.9 &-	○1	○29	○9	○0	○4	○4	○0	○8
5.10	●5	●25	●29	●9	●8	●13	●3	●10
5.11	●8	●32	●27	●13	●23	●26	●5	●15
5.12	●9	●18	●28	●13	●10	●27	●5	●13
5.13 &+	●3	●3	●27	●3	●7	●7	●9	●5
PROJECTS	●8	●0	●0	●0	●3	●1	●1	●13

	WOLF POINT (p.30)	FOSSIL HILL (p.30)	SAND STONE (p.30)	SHADY SIDE (p.30)	SINKS MAIN (p.30)	FAIRFIELD HILL (p.30)	GRANITE (p.30)	SUICIDE POINT (p.30)	BALDWIN CREEK (p.30)
🚗	55m	20m	10m	10m	10m	15m	15m	55m	45m
🚶	60m	15m	10m	10-15m	10m	30m	20m	5m	30m
☀	11AM-4PM	10AM-PM	10AM-PM	3PM-PM	11AM-PM	11AM-PM	11AM-PM	10AM-PM	10AM-PM
	Long, Hilly	Medium, Hilly	Medium, Hilly	Medium, Hilly	Medium, Hilly	Medium, Hilly	Medium, Hilly	Short, Hilly	Long, Hilly
snake	Beware!	-	Beware!	-	Beware!	Beware!		-	Beware!
	Yes	-	Yes	-	Yes	Yes	Yes	-	-
rockfall	Beware!		Beware!	Beware!	Beware!	Beware!	-	-	-
stars	-	★	-	★★	★★	-	-	-	-
seasons									
shapes									
	54	71	94	56	353	126	98	15	60
○	○0	○4	○31	○18	○40	○29	○29	○2	○0
●	●2	●8	●31	●9	●65	●35	●15	●1	●1
●	●7	●16	●18	●21	●85	●32	●21	●4	●9
●	●12	●22	●12	●6	●88	●22	●18	●6	●26
●	●24	●9	●0	●0	●67	●4	●10	●2	●17
●	●9	●12	●2	●2	●8	●4	●5	●0	●7

ESTABLISHING NEW ROUTES

Although there are now close to 3000 rock climbs in the greater Lander area, there are ample opportunities for establishing new ones. Not only are there lines to do at well-established crags, but there are entire cliffs throughout the area that have yet to be explored. With a mind toward keeping climbing safe and maintaining sustainable routes, we've teamed up with the Central Wyoming Climbers' Alliance to offer the following guide-lines for establishing new routes in this area:

● All climbs established on the Bighorn Dolomite should be protected exclusively with bolts. Although we are huge advocate of traditional protection where appropriate, the dolomite is an especially fragile stone and doesn't tend to hold gear well. Routes established on granite and sandstone should be protected as dictated by the climbing, using natural protection where available, but still with a mind toward safety.

● All bolts, hangers, and anchors should be stainless steel. Ideally, all routes would be equipped with glue-in bolts and anchors. If this is not possible, please use a minimum of ⅜" x 3 ½" stainless steel bolts.

● Bolts should be placed so as to keep climbers safe from groundfall. The first bolt should be no less than 8 feet off the ground and no more than 12. The second bolt should be about 4 feet higher, and then bolts should be 6-8 feet apart thereafter.

● All anchors should be stainless steel bolts with ring anchors or a pair of steel clip anchors. These can be steel carabiners or mussy hooks. Chains are not appropriate for anchoring purposes.

● Routes should be selected on whether or not they will add to the quality of the climbing at a crag. Squeeze jobs, excessively dirty routes, and poorly bolted climbs will degrade the crag's quality. We want your new route to be the best at the crag.

● Flakes and loose rock should be removed from the the route and the surrounding walls. It is not uncommon for climbers to wander off-route, so be aware of potentially hazardous rock on either side of your climb. Also be careful to clear the area above the anchors if dangerous rock exists there.

● If your route is over 30m (100 feet) in length, please let us know so we can indicate that in the guidebook. Although 70 and 80m ropes are common, 60m ropes are still the standard.

● Please place bolts such that a shorter leader can place quickdraws on lead. Do not bolt with the assumption that the draws will be hanging.

photo Sam Lightner

INTERNATIONAL CLIMBERS' **FESTIVAL**

Every year for over twenty years, climbers have gathered in Lander on the second weekend in July for the International Climbers' Festival. Now America's longest-running festival, the event features five days of food, entertainment, education, and service projects. The atmosphere at City Park can't be beat, and the evenings at the Lander Bar are legendary. For more information, go to www.climbersfestival.org.

CENTRAL WYOMING CLIMBERS ALLIANCE **& BOLTS**

The CWCA is the organization that represents climbers' interests in the Lander area. The organization works closely with land managers and volunteers to maintain routes, to improve trails, and to generally enhance the Lander climbing experience. The CWCA is consists of Bolt and Anchor Replacement and Youth Climbing. They have been replacing unsafe or worn anchors in Lander since 1993. This is a donation-funded initiative with the mission of keeping the anchors on Lander's crags updated, unobtrusive, and easy to use. The fund provides anchors and hardware for replacement of old anchors, and provides new hardware for new routes, to prevent the use of substandard equipment such as webbing or chains. Consider donating to CWCA at wyomingclimbers.org. Or you can visit the Wild Iris store and buy a gumball and drop a few bucks off for bolt replacement. If you do not regularly volunteer or establish climbs, the authors feel it is everyone's responsibility to help out financially. Be a part of the mission, not a burden. Although all three of us regularly help out with new routes in the area, a quarter of this book's royalties will be donated to bolt replacement through CWCA.

(ACKNOWLEDGEMENTS:)

The authors would like to thank the climbers of Lander for making this book, and the climbing it covers, possible. Over the years, hundreds of people have been involved in first ascents and crag development in this area. However, there are a few climbers that have given far more than their fair share to the climbing in Lander. The big names in Lander climbing will be seen throughout the book, but we'll list them here: Bob Branscomb, Tom Rangitsch, BJ Tilden, Greg Collins, Todd Skinner, and Paul Piana have all had a major impact on the climbing here. Other climbers who have been pivotal include Porter Jarrard, Sam Lightner Jr, Heidi Badaracco, Evan Horn, Vance White, Pete Absolon, Dave Doll, Jim Ratz, Kirk Billings, Scott Robertson ,Sue Miller, Mike Lilygren, Kristi Stouffer, John Hennings, Kyle Vassilopoulos, Zack Rudy, Matt Wendling, Rick Thompson, and Gary Wilmot, to name a few.

We also wish to acknowledge a long line of land managers who have worked with climbers to help make the crags better. For twenty-five years, managers from the National Forest Service, Sinks Canyon State Park, and the BLM have worked closely with local climbers to develop trails, replace worn anchors, and provide signage to help make the climbing experience better. Most recently, Jared Oakleaf of the BLM, Jamie Simonson of Sinks Canyon State Park, and Steve Schacht and Crosby Davidson of the USFS have repeatedly come to climbers and asked, "What can we do to help?" We couldn't ask for better people to work with.

photo Kyle Duba

IN **MEMORIAM** -

Climbing is unique in many ways but perhaps most of all because of the large amounts of time climbers spend together. There are long approaches, rests between pitches, and the ever-present trust that your partner will keep you safe. Over the years, many climbers have passed though our lives and have left an indelible mark. Part of reaching for the sky is the truth that some of us will fall. We've lost climbers to accident, to disease, to avalanche, and to more sinister fates. Without the climbers below, Lander climbing would not be what it is today.

●Todd Skinner

●Jim Ratz

●Pete Absolon

●Bobby Model

●Inge Perkins & Hayden Kennedy

MINERS DELIGHT

photo: Kyle Duba

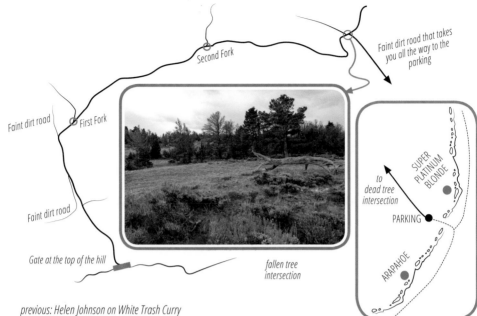

previous: Helen Johnson on White Trash Curry
photo: Kyle Duba

MINERS DELIGHT

This wonderful wall sits southeast of Wyoming 28, across the highway from Wild Iris. The cliff, easily visible from Limestone Mountain Road, has been developed for climbing since the early 1990s. This amazing cliff boasts only a few routes, with potential for hundreds more. Due to its south-facing aspect, it tends to be too hot in the summer, and is best as a fall crag. If you have a high-clearance vehicle, you can drive to within five minutes of the climbs. Some of Lander's best routes are at this cliff. Arapahoe, Yowzah, and Rattlesnake Tambourine are not to be missed.

There are two main sections of the cliff, separated by a break/pass, which happens to be right where you park. To the west of the parking is the Arapahoe sector, while the Super Platinum sector is to the east. Many climbers refer to the whole cliff as Super Platinum.

Directions from Lander: Drive Wyoming 28 south from Lander approximately 24 miles. Limestone Mountain Road turns right off the highway at this point. 0.2 miles further, you can take a left on a good dirt road. Follow this road around the hill and down into a little valley. After 0.9 miles, you'll pass a corral, and will stay left at the fork in the road. Stay on this rough two-track for another mile, climbing a steep hill that finishes with

some rough crawling before a gate. Open (and close) the gate, then continue east along the fenceline. After 0.8 miles, take the right fork, which leads you south and up over a small hill, through some trees and over another hill. After another 0.8 miles, the road passes a large fallen tree on the right (photo). Turn right on a faint road just after passing this tree. and follow this for a half-mile before reaching the parking area, near the cliffs and a buckrail fence that blocks the pass.

An alternate approach is possible by turning right 0.4 miles past the corral, and driving up a faint road to a parking area above a red sandstone cliffband. From here, you'll hike east for 40-50 minutes to reach the crag. This approach is possible with lower-clearance cars.

CLASSICS

— King Lazybones (p.25)

— The Undercling (p.24)
Arapahoe (p.23)

Yowzah (p.27)

Super Platinum Blonde (p.24)

1
5
8
9
3
8

10AM-PM

5m

Vertical

ARAPAHOE **WALL**

| 10AM-PM | 5m | Vertical |

(0) (1) (2) (1) (0) (7)

Routes are listed from right to left.

●1 ☐ Wounded Shin 10b ★
The leftmost route at the crag as of this writing. This is maybe 500 feet left of Arapahoe and takes the left wall in a big, left-facing dihedral. Start in an overhanging crack. *FA Dave Doll, 2006*

●2 ☐ KB Route (Open Project)
Leftmost route on the big clean face left of Arapahoe. This route starts on a small seam feature. *Equipped Kirk BIllings*

●3 ☐ KB Route (Open Project)
This project is maybe 15 feet right of the previous one, but is left of the big crack splitting the face. *Equipped Kirk Billings*

●4 ☐ PP Route (Open Project)
Right of the crack, there are two long projects. This is the left one. *Equipped Paul Piana*

●5 ☐ TS Route (Open Project)
The right one. *Equipped Todd Skinner*

●6 ☐ TS Route (Open Project)
This is a short climb on the low bulge left of Arapahoe. *Equipped Todd Skinner*

●7 ☐ Pickup Trucks and PBR 12a ★★
This climb starts in the wide crack left of Arapahoe, then takes the steep wall above. 90' *FA Evan Horn, 2011*

●8 ☐ Arapahoe 11d ★★★
This is the proud and very prominent arete/prow. Start in a slot to the right of the prow, then move up onto it and have a ball. For sure one of the top three 11d routes in Lander. *FA Paul Piana, 1994*

●9 ☐ TS Route (Open Project)
This climb follows the slabby face left of a cool overhang, 50 feet right of Arapahoe. *Equipped Todd Skinner*

●10 ☐ TS Route (Open Project)
Another Project, just right of the previous one. Maybe only two bolts have been placed. *Equipped Todd Skinner*

●11 ☐ Tonto's Revenge 11b ★
This climb takes the clean face to the right of the cool overhang, about 100 feet right of Arapahoe. *FA Dave Doll, 2006*

SUPER PLATINIUM
BLONDE

10AM-PM   5m   Vertical

(1) (4) (6) (8) (3) (1)

To reach the other routes at this crag, you walk east from the pass. About 200 yards from the parking area, you'll pass the wreckage of an airplane. The steep and clean wall near this wreckage will hold futuristic routes, and is named The Forsyth Wave in honor of the people who lost their lives in the plane wreck. The first routes described here are about 5 minutes east of the parking.

Routes are listed from right to left.

●1 ☐ **Walk that Relish 12a** ★★
This climb takes a slab to vertical wall to a 45 degree roof. Would be a classic if there weren't so many other great routes nearby. *FA Heidi Badaracco, 1994*

●2 ☐ **Super Platinum Blonde 13a** ★★
This climb takes a seam feature up the clean overhanging wall right of Walk that Relish. 50' *FA Paul Piana, 2005*

photo Kyle Duba **YOWZAH** 12a Helen Johnson

●3 ☐ **Red Right Hand 12b** ★
About 100 feet right of Super Platinum Blonde, this east-facing route starts on a small ledge. Big moves lead up the left margin of the wall. 45' *FA Steve Bechtel, 2005*

●4 ☐ **Abattoir Blues 13a** ★★
This route is just right of Red Right Hand, and starts in a seam just left of the big dihedral. Tricky moves on clean pockets. 45' *FA Steve Bechtel, 2005*

●5 ☐ **Tiger Sauce 11c** ★
This climb takes a slab to a cool bulge near the top. It's about 15 feet right of Abattoir Blues. *FA Paul Piana, 1994*

●6 ☐ **White Trash Curry 11a** ★
This route is about 50 feet right of Tiger Sauce. It tackles a slab with nice seams, then finishes in a leftward series of moves through a bulge. 70' *FA Dennis Vandenbos, 1996*

●7 ☐ **The Undercling 11a** ★★
This very cool route takes a corner crack to a roof, then traverses left under the roof to a vertical wall above. *FA Ellen Bechtel, 2005*

●8 ☐ Johnny Lee's Corner 12c ★
This route takes the same corner as The Undercling, but moves up and right through a crazy roof/dihedral. *FA Steve Bechtel, 2005*

●9 ☐ TS Route (Open Project)
This climb will take the rounded prow right of Johnny Lee's Corner. Anchors and a couple of bolts. *Equipped Todd Skinner*

●10 ☐ Anchovies 12a ★★
This is a cool seam and pocket climb on a vertical to overhanging wall. *FA Paul Piana, 1994*

●11 ☐ King Lazybones 10b ★★
This route takes a lieback flake left of the major corner. Short. *FA Steve Bechtel, 2005*

●12 ☐ Cracker Crumble 11b
This climb takes the leaning crack immediately right of King Lazybones. *FA Graham Kolb, 2011*

●13 ☐ Santa Cleopatra 11c
Start on the orange lichened flake 20 feet right of Cracker Crumble. *FA Heidi Badaracco, 1994*

RATTLESNAKE TAMBOURINE 12a

Taylor Spiegelberg

14 ☐ Totally Fully 13a ★
This climb takes a bulging wall behind a large pine tree about 400 feet right of Santa Cleopatra. It is near an area where a bunch of talus forces some scrambling as you move down the cliff trail. *FA Paul Piana, 1995*

15 ☐ Yowzah 12a ★★★
About 300 feet right of Totally Fully, this climb takes a vertical wall to a great 45 degree wall that faces east. If you like steep, juggy climbing, this is probably the best 12a in the area for you. 75' *FA Paul Piana, 1994*

16 ☐ Rattlesnake Tambourine 12a ★★★
About 50 feet right of Yowzah is a nice clean bulge. This climb takes the seam/flake that breaks the bulge. One of a kind. 50' *FA Paul Piana, 1994*

17 ☐ Last Year's Chili Queen 12c ★★
Another 150 feet down the cliff is a clean wall with small pockets. This climb takes the center of that wall.
FA Paul Piana, 2004

18 ☐ Someday I'll Have a Son Named Griffin 12a
100 feet right of Last Year's Chili Queen is a steep, right trending prow just right of a high roof. This is the climb.
FA Ty Mack, 1994

19 ☐ The Leather Nun 10b
This is a short, clean climb on an east-facing wall, about 100 feet right of the previous route.
FA Karn Piana, 1994

20 ☐ Fool's Gold 11b ★★
This climb is about another 150 feet down the wall. Just left of an obvious 3-foot squarecut roof. Slabby technical start into steep juggy goodness on a golden streaked wall. Graham thought it might be 5.9 when he first scoped it, but it turned out way steeper than it appeared...hence 'Fool's Gold.' *FA Graham Kolb, 2011*

21 ☐ The Midnight Oil 9 ★
This is the grey prow right of the squarecut roof. Mostly easy climbing with some thought-provoking reaches.
FA Graham Kolb, 2011

22 ☐ Lump of Coal 10a
Around to the right of The Midnight Oil, this is a pretty face on the left wall of the alcove. Doesn't climb all that well, though. *FA Graham Kolb, 2011*

23 ☐ Tire Iron 10b ★★
20 feet right of Lump of Coal. Climb a slabby wall past seams and flakes to juggy glory climbing on the over-hanging wall above. *FA Kyle Duba, 2011*

WILD IRIS

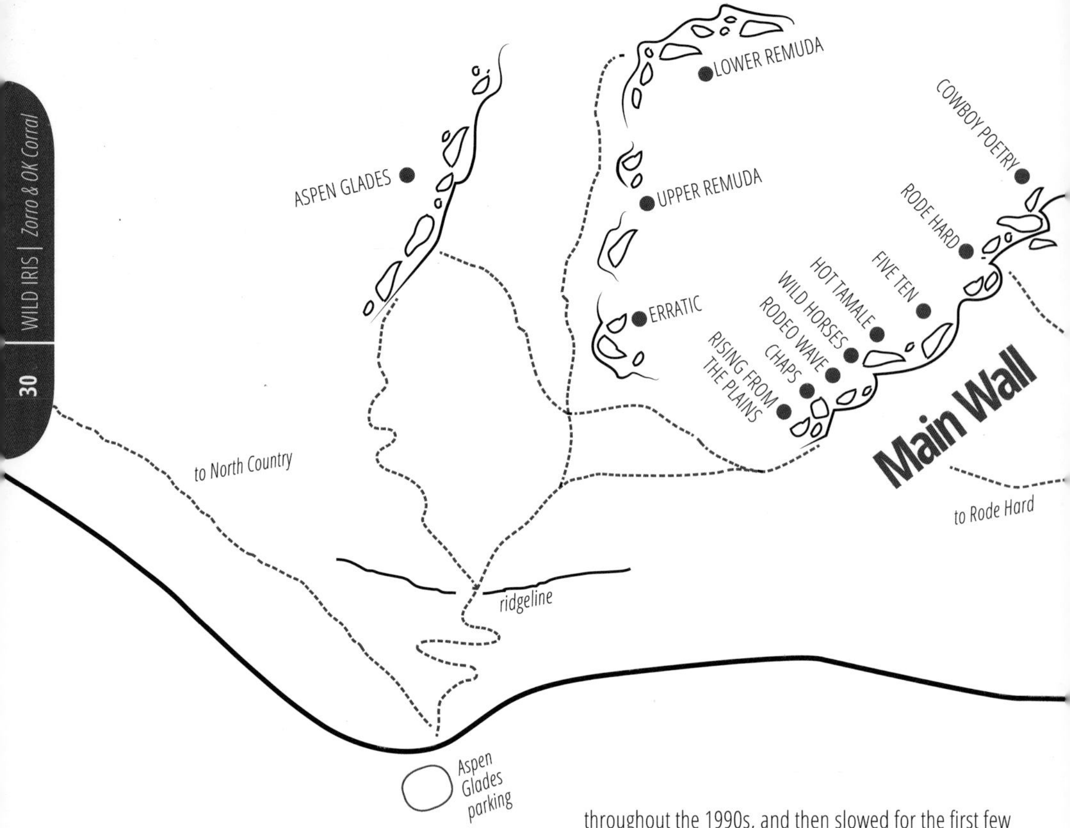

The map labels:

LOWER REMUDA

COWBOY POETRY

ASPEN GLADES

UPPER REMUDA

RODE HARD

HOT TAMALE
WILD HORSES
FIVE TEN
RODEO WAVE
CHAPS
RISING FROM THE PLAINS

ERRATIC

Main Wall

to North Country

to Rode Hard

ridgeline

Aspen Glades parking

*previous: Lindsey Stevens on Tomahawk Slam
photo Kyle Duba*

WILD IRIS

The Wild Iris area is one of the most beautiful climbing areas in America. Bone-white stone rising on a windswept ridge has yielded some of the fiercest short climbs anywhere. This area, set on the southeast flank of the Wind River Mountains has been a magnet for climbers seeking to push their limits for more than twenty years. The Wild Iris, more than any other area, defines Lander climbing.

Although there had been climbers exploring this area for a few years, Todd Skinner put this area on the map when he moved to nearby Atlantic City and declared it the crag he had searched the world for. Soon after, Todd, his wife Amy, Jacob Valdez, Heidi Badaracco, Paul Piana, and a handful of others turned it into one of the most famous sport crags in the country.

Development of new routes happened at a fierce pace throughout the 1990s, and then slowed for the first few years of this century. Since about 2010, however, the new route fever has started again. Over the past 4-5 years, we've seen 20 or more new routes go in each season at various crags. In 2013 Sam Lightner started rebolting the classics in earnest, and produced some great new climbs along with fixing the old ones.

For this guide, we have divided the entire Wild Iris into three major areas: The OK Corral (Including the OK Corral and Zorro walls), The Main Wall (featuring everything from Rising from the Plains to the Cowboy Poetry Wall), and The Aspen Glade (which includes The Aspen Glade Wall, Gun Street, the walls of The Remuda, and the Erratic.) Some areas, such as the Longbranch and Lonesome Dove have not been included due to their remoteness or scarcity of established routes.

Directions: To reach the Wild Iris Area, drive east out of Lander on Main Street. After about 24 miles (near milepost 53), take a right on the dirt Limestone Mountain Road, which is marked by both a brown Forest Service sign and a small green street sign. This this good dirt road for 1.3 miles to a fork. The left fork leads to The Aspen Glade parking area, 2.0 miles up the road. To reach parking for the Main Wall and the OK Corrall take

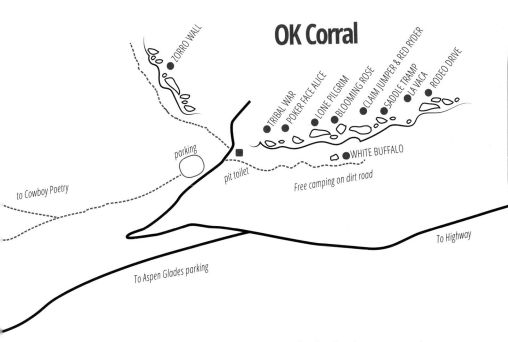

OK Corral

ZORRO WALL

TRIBAL WAR
POKER FACE ALICE
LONE PILGRIM
BLOOMING ROSE
CLAIM JUMPER & RED RYDER
SADDLE TRAMP
LA VACA
RODEO DRIVE

parking

pit toilet

WHITE BUFFALO

to Cowboy Poetry

Free camping on dirt road

To Highway

To Aspen Glades parking

the right fork, switchback up the hill, and park on the left as you crest the ridge (.08 miles past the fork). The Main Wall is to the northwest, and is clearly visable from the parking lot.

ZORRO & OK Corral

The OK Corral is the most accessible and most popular of the high country cliffs in the Lander area. This crag is stacked with moderate routes, and features shady belays, short climbs and a variety of routes for most ability levels.

The cliffs of the OK Corral have received sporadic attention from first ascentionists for years, and now boast almost as many climbs as the Main Wall. The OK Corral is approached by any of several trails leading through the woods from the rough road that passes along in front of the cliff. This road can be found just uphill from the main Wild Iris parking lot, and heads right just before you reach the pit toilet. Due to congestion on this road, it is recommended that climbers park at the Main Wall parking lot and walk the 4-6 minutes it takes to get to the majority of routes. There are several trails through these woods – look for them instead of making new ones.

The first seventeen routes described are at the Zorro section of the wall, a westfacing cliff to the north of the main wall parking lot. These routes get afternoon sun. (If you are looking toward the outhouse from the main parking area, this wall is downhill to your left.) The trail can be found by walking up the main road past the outhouse about 200 feet, looking for where it splits off downhill in a group of small trees.

CLASSICS

Annie Get your Drill (p.41)
Greenhorns in Velvet (p.41)
Wind River Muzzle Loders (p.46)

Red Ryder (p.41)
Doob Loob (p.42)

Zorro (p.33)
Tribal War (p.34)
Red as a Blooming Rose (p.39)

Drinking Dry Clouds (p.47)
Diamonds and Rain (p.42)
John Wayne (p.47)

Calamity Jane (p.36)
Hang Em'High (p.38)

29
25
32
18
3
0

 3PM-Night

 5m-10m

ZORRO **WALL**

| 12AM-PM | 10m | Vertical |

3 **3** **7** **4** **0** **0**

The first seventeen routes described are at the Zorro section of the wall, a westfacing cliff to the north of the main wall parking lot. These routes get afternoon sun. (If you are looking toward the outhouse from the main parking area, this wall is downhill to your left.) The trail can be found by walking up the main road past the outhouse about 200 feet, looking for where it splits off downhill in a group of small trees.

Routes are listed from left to right.

●1 ☐ The Hangman 10d ★
About 50 feet left of the tunnel, this is a fun route. 40' *FA Unknown, 1990's*

○2 ☐ Chico 8
This is the next route right of the Hangman, on a short slab just past the tunnel. 40' *FA Unknown, 1993*

○3 ☐ Chapito 7
Walk through the small tunnel to a short slab on the right. This is the right of two routes with chain hangers. 40' *FA Unknown, 1993*

●4 ☐ Esmeralda 11b ★★
Just after passing through the small tunnel, this is the first climb on the right. Follow bouldery moves up an overhanging section of wall. *FA Alan Pirie, 2012*

●5 ☐ The Guns I'll Never Own 11c ★
This climb is the left line on the steep block just right of the tunnel. 35' *FA Rick Thompson, 2000*

●6 ☐ Ewenanimity 11b ★
This climb is on the leaning block just right of the tunnel, as well. Fun, steep, juggy. 30' *FA Rick Thompson, 2000*

The following routes are located up the gully above the tunnel, to the left of the clean wall where Zorro is.

● 7 ☐ Friend or Faux 11c ★

Leftmost of the high routes, this is the best of the three. 50′ *FA Rick Thompson, 2000*

● 8 ☐ El Toro 12b

This is a tricky route through the high bulge. This is the center of the three existing climbs on the high tier. 60′ *FA Unknown, 1993*

● 9 ☐ Salsa for the Sole 12a

This is the rightmost route on the high wall. Start up the center of a clean face, and through the high bulge above. 60′ *FA Rick Thompson, 2000*

● 10 ☐ Poposer Cowboy 12a ★★

A lesstraveled cousin to Zorro, but a good climb nonetheless. Ain't over 'til it's over. 75′ *FA Rick Thompson, 2000*

● 11 ☐ Zorro 11c ★★★

Sustained difficulty up a beautiful face. This was the first route established at Wild Iris. This climb was bolted by Richard Collins in 1987 or 1988, and included a couple of threads as pro.75′ *FA Jacob Valdez, 1990*

● 12 ☐ Gaucho 11a ★★

A low crux leads to challenging and sustained pulling above. One of the steeper and more popular routes at Wild Iris. 60′ *FA Steve Scott, 1991*

● 13 ☐ Cirque de Suave 10b ★

This route begins in the corner, then moves out left and up a nice prow. 70′ *FA Rick Thompson, 2001*

○ 14 ☐ Huggys Pullup 8 ★

Easier climb on face right of Cirque du Suave. 40′ *FA Rick Thompson, 2001*

● 15 ☐ Wet Wipe aWhet 10b

Face and slab left of Burly Binkie. 45′ *FA Rick Thompson, 2002*

● 16 ☐ Burly Binkie 12b

Just above where the trail comes to the wall, this climb is burly from the getgo. 45′ *FA Rick Thompson, 2000*

● 17 ☐ One Trick Sheep 11a

This climb is up and right of where the trail meets the wall. 60′ *FA Rick Thompson, 2000*

TRIBAL **WAR**

10AM-PM   5m   Vertical

0 3 5 2 0 0

The first four routes climb the vertical wall with a large bulge at the top. This feature is visible from the main parking lot, and is easily reached by staying left on the trails as you enter the woods. This feature is just right of the end of the quarried section of cliff.

Routes are listed from left to right.

●**1 ☐ Rope a Star 10c ★**
Climb the first five bolts of Rope the Moon, then move left and finish up the steep wall above.
FA Jeremy Rowan, 2017

●**2 ☐ Rope the Moon 10c ★**
Follow a rounded prow to a fun and short headwall.
FA Jeremy Rowan, 2014

●**3 ☐ Western Front 11d**
A lesspopular parallel to Tribal War. Begins in a crack feature. 65' *FA Tim Roberts, 1994*

●**4 ☐ Tribal War 11b ★★★**
A really good route with a great headwall. This follows the line up the clean slab, then through the high bulge's right side. You'll have to work to get there, though. 65'
FA Pat Perrin, 1991

●**5 ☐ Stirrup Trouble 12a**
Tricky, thin route on the wall facing Tribal War. 45'
FA Unknown, 1992

●**6 ☐ Unkindness of Ravens 11a ★★**
This climb takes the blunt arete right of Stirrup Trouble. Atypical movement makes for a really fun climb. 40'
FA Sam Lightner, 2013

●**7 ☐ Stone Ranger 12b ★**
Good movement. This route takes a vertical wall through a bulge at 25 feet up. 50' *FA Leif Gasch, 2006*

●**8 ☐ Deputized 11c ★★**
This is a very good route that seems to have been overlooked over for far too long. *FA Jeremy Rowen, 2014*

●**9 ☐ Cowgirls in Chaparajos 11a★**
Face with good movement left of Urban Cowboys. Climb the puzzling face to the obvious flake feature. Strategically work that feature to the small ledge and finish up with a few jugs. *FA Jeremy Rowan 2016*

●**10 ☐ Urban Cowboys 10c ★★**
This climb was the first 5.10 on the left end of the wall. A good route, it is even better since 2016 when it was extended up the cool bulge above the original anchors. 40' *FA Eric Horst, 1992*

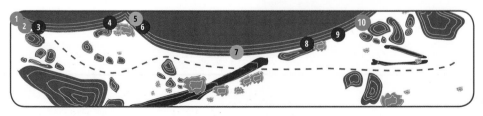

photo Kyle Duba

TRIBAL WAR 11b

Daniel Mock

POKER FACE **ALICE**

| 10AM-PM | 🚶 5m | ■ Vertical | ◧ Roof |

 5  **0 2 2 1 0**

The following routes are 25 yards east of Urban Cowboys and start on top of a series of big slabs. The Poker Face Alice roof is hard to miss. Approach by hugging the wall 50 feet right of Urban Cowboys, and sneaking through a small corridor.

Routes are listed from left to right.

○1 ☐ Prairie Rain 7
The face around the corner left of One-Eyed Jack.
FA Jeremy Rowan 2015

○2 ☐ OneEyed Jack 7 ★★
Starts above jumbled blocks. Good climbing on short wall. 30' *FA Pete Delannoy, 1992*

○3 ☐ Outlaws on the Run 6 ★★
On wall right of OneEyed Jack, really good. 35'
FA Pete Delannoy, 1992

●4 ☐ PokerFace Alice 12b ★★
Climb 5.8 wall to a rest, then left and out roof. Obviously a little burly. 50' *FA Pete Delannoy, 1992*

●5 ☐ Calamity Jane 13b ★
Breaks through the largest part of the PokerFace Alice roof. Decent pockets and punchy moves. 50'
FA Matt Lund, 1997

These climbs start off a small pillar down and right of the Poker Face Alice roof. Both routes are fun.

○6 ☐ Three Charlies Left 6
Slab route with 5 bolts. 30' *FA Unknown, 2000's*

○7 ☐ Three Charlies Right 6
Another slab route near the edge of the ledge, joins the previous route midway. 30' *FA Unknown 2000's*

The following 3 routes are in a small alcove down and east of the Poker Face Alice Roof.

●8 ☐ High Plains Drifter 11b ★
The left route on the left wall of the small alcove. Starts on jugs and ledges, moving slightly right into hard moves on clean rock. 3 bolts. *FA Pete Delannoy, 1992*

●9 ☐ Every Gun Sings Its Own Song 11c ★
Just right of High Plains Drifter and left of a big cleft in the rock. Confounding and tricky moves lead to an easier finish. 4 bolts. *FA Pete Delannoy, 1992*

●10 ☐ Don't Bring Your Guns to Town 12c ★★
Cool black wall with crimps and big moves. 45'
FA John Hennings, 2006

photo Kyle Duba

POKER FACE ALICE 12b

Justin Loyka

LONE **PILGRIM**

| 10AM-PM | 5m | Vertical | Steep |

These routes are about 100 yards east of the previous climbs where the trees thin out a bit in front of the wall. This wall is easily identified by the very clean slab of Lone Pilgrim.

Routes are listed from left to right.

●1 ☐ Battle for a Wounded Knee 11a ★★

Starts on ledges and moves past a big bush. After the vertical section, it moves up and left through a concave roof to a very strenuous finish. 40' *FA Pete Delannoy, 1992*

●2 ☐ Only the Good Die Young 11c ★

Climb a seam feature to small bulge on the left margin of the slab. 50' *FA Pete Delannoy, 1992*

●3 ☐ Lone Pilgrim 11d ★

Clean slab with devious moves, gets steeper high. 50'
FA Pete Delannoy, 1992

●4 ☐ Under the Gun 12a ★

Good climbing up flakes and pockets to anchor well below obvious, high, large roof. *FA Geoff Sluyter, 2006*

●5 ☐ + Under the Gun 13b ★

Continue up the slab then out 10' roof. 70'

●6 ☐ Heroes and Ghosts 12b ★

Bouldery and technical route, a stick clip is useful for the opening moves. Ends at a ledge below the big roof.
FA Vance White, 2007

●7 ☐ Hang 'Em High 10d★

This route climbs a dihedral to a set of anchors. then out the right side of the high roof. *FA Geoff Sluyter 2007*

●8 + ☐ Hang 'Em High 13d ★

then out the right side of the high roof.
FA Geoff Sluyter 2007

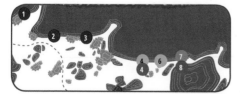

●9 ☐ Drugstore Cowboy 11c

Climb a rounded arête to the right of the roof wall. 40'
FA Pete Delannoy, 1992

The next two climbs are about 75 yards from Drugstore Cowboy, and begin in a hidden small alcove / chimney. They are not visible from the trail.

○10 ☐ Medicine Show 7 ★

Easy slab starting in a hidden chimney feature.
FA Unknown, 1996

●11 ☐ + Medicine Show 12a

Roof extension. *FA Unknown, 1996*

●12 ☐ Spaghetti Western 10d

A steeper route in the slot facing Medicine Show. 40'
FA Pete Delannoy, 1991

BLOOMING **ROSE**

| 10AM-PM | 5m | Vertical |

The following climbs are all very close together on the Red as a Blooming Rose Wall. Roues 2-5 face generally west, routes 6-12 face south. These climbs are located just west (left) of where the crag trail climbs steeply to a high point before dropping back down to Claim Jumper.

Routes are listed from left to right.

○1 ☐ Iron Horse With a Twisted Heart 9 ★

A nice slab climb on the wall west of Red As A Blooming Rose. 35' *FA Pete Delannoy, 1992*

●2 ☐ Give My Love To Rose 12b ★
This line takes small pockets right of a crack/gully, and left of the well traveled Red As A Blooming Rose.
FA John Hennings, 2006

●3 ☐ Red as a Blooming Rose 11a ★★
Thin start leads to big hold climbing at the top. 40'
FA Pete Delannoy, 1992

●4 ☐ Roll in the Hay 11a ★
Technical climbing to corner system then up ledges above. 45' *FA Pat Thompson, 1997*

●5 ☐ Stacked Deck 10b ★★
Starts on big jugs, getting tricky higher. 45'
FA Pete Delannoy, 1992

●6 ☐ Matilda's Last Waltz 10d
Awkward climbing up a prow, left of a bushy crack. 45'
FA Pete Delannoy, 1992

●7 ☐ Cowboys are my Only Weakness 11a
This climb starts on ledges, then up a rounded prow. 40'
FA Cindy Tolle, 1992

●8 ☐ Aces and Eights 10b ★
Starts above a gnarled tree, up seams and underclings.
50' *FA Pete Delannoy, 1992*

●9 ☐ Never Sit With Your Back to the Door 10b ★★
Tricky long moves up to a small ledge. 45'
FA Pete Delannoy, 1992

●10 ☐ Brown Dirt Cowgirl 10a ★★
Nice wall just left of the double corner. 40'
FA Pat Thompson, 1997

○11 ☐ Phat Phinger Phrenzy 8 ★
Climb up a strange corner feature. Fun. 50'
FA Pat Thompson, 1997

●12 ☐ Dogfight at the OK Corral 11d ★
Another rounded and tricky prow climb. 45'
FA Pete Delannoy, 1992

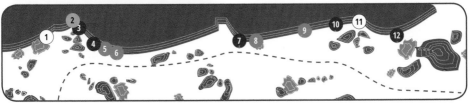

CLAIM JUMPER 10c Erin Harvey

CLAIM **JUMPER**

10AM-PM | 5m | Vertical

These six climbs are just over the small hill east of Dogfight.

Routes are listed from left to right.

○1 □ **Utah Carol 6** ★★
This route was misnamed as "Chubs 4U" in the previous edition thanks to the highly accurate and useful Mountain Project. *FA Nathan and Cheri Smith 2010*

●2 □ **Claim Jumper 10c** ★★
Rightleaning lieback seam to juggy headwall. 45'
FA Jim Stegall, 1996

○3 □ **Annie Get Your Drill 9** ★
Follow a crack feature on the prow then up face holds above. 6 bolts 40' *FA Jim Stegall, 1996*

●4 □ **Miner's DeeLight 11d** ★
Bouldery low moves to a nice rest then some more challenge. 5 bolts 40' *FA Diedre Burton, 1996*

○5 □ **Greenhorns in Velvet 8** ★
A very popular route up a nice clean slab. 40'
FA Pete Delannoy, 1991

○6 □ **Lever Action 5**
Starts on a blunt arete right of Greenhorns in Velvet.
FA Dave Quinn 2017

SADDLE **TRAMP**

10AM-PM | 5m | Vertical | Slight

The two Winchester routes are on a nice long wall behind a large pine tree about 100 feet right of Greenhorns in Velvet.

Routes are listed from left to right.

●1 □ **Winchester Pump 11b** ★★
Climb center of slab, then up bulging wall on good moves. 60' *FA Dave Doll, 1997*

●2 □ **Red Ryder 10a** ★★★
Follows a flake up the right slide of slab, then up nice headwall. 60' *FA Mike Lilygren, 1998*

○3 □ **Jabba the Hut 8**
Up a small buttress about 50 feet right of Red Ryder. Follow bolts through bulges and ledges to a high long chain anchor. 50' *FA Brian Silker, 2005*

DIAMONDS & **RAIN**

| 10AM-PM | 5m | Vertical |

2 1 0 3 0 0

The following three climbs are on a nice wall behind a group of large trees. These are just west of the obvious tiny "Pronghorn Pinnacle".

Routes are listed from left to right.

● 1 □ Doob Loob 10b ★★
This fine route follows a crack then moves left onto a face. Hard exit. *FA Ben Sears, 2014*

● 2 □ Clean Slate 12d
The very clean and blank face left of Diamonds and Rain. 40' *Equipped Ben Sears FA Vance White 2015*

● 3 □ Diamonds and Rain 12a ★★
Clean, vertical white face with cold shut anchors. 40'
FA Eric Horst, 1992

After Red Ryder, the trail meanders away from the cliff, and the routes are spaced out about 100 feet apart. The trail comes back close to the cliff at the overhanging Saddle Tramp.

● 4 □ 30 Seconds on Fremont Street 11b ★
Bouldery climbing up a short clean wall. This route is about 75 yards east of Jabba the Hut. 35'
FA Scott VanOrman, 1999

● 5 □ Back in the Saddle 10c
Somewhat tricky route up the westfacing wall just left of Saddled Dreams. 35' *FA Pete Delannoy, 1992*

● 6 □ Saddled Dreams 11d ★★
Start on Saddle Tramp, moving up and left through a small roof. Devious and fun. *FA Jeremy Rowan, 2009*

● 7 □ The Saddle Tramp 12a
Up bulge on undercuts and thin pockets. 40'
FA Pete Delannoy, 1992

● 8 □ Whips, Chaps, and Chains 11d ★★
Rightward trending route up pockets and edges through the bulge. 40' *FA Pete Delannoy, 1992*

4 ☐ When the Man Comes Around 12d ★★

Bouldery short route about 30 feet right of Diamonds and Rain. 35' *FA John Hennings, 2006*

5 ☐ Bull of the West 8 ★

Short route with 4 bolts to anchor below small tree. 40' *FA Duane Ackerman, 1999*

6 ☐ Guns of Diablo 8

Adjacent short route. 40' *FA Duane Ackerman, 1999*

LA **VACA**

☀	🚶	▮
10AM-PM	5m	Vertical

(7) (2) (0) (0) (0) (0)

The following three climbs are on a nice wall behind a group of large trees. These are just west of the obvious tiny "Pronghorn Pinnacle".

Routes are listed from left to right.

1 ☐ Sugarfoot 10c

Powerful little route that starts behind a big flake. *FA Duane Ackerman, 1999*

2 ☐ Slave 8

Face behind flake. 35' *FA Unknown, 1990's*

3 ☐ R is for Redneck 7

Slab climb that starts just right of flake, and left of a big crack. 35' *FA Unknown, 1990's*

4 ☐ La Vaca Peligrosa 8 ★★

Nice climb right of large crack. 40' *FA Damien Potts, 1999*

The following three climbs are on a nice wall behind a group of large trees. These are just west of the obvious tiny "Pronghorn Pinnacle".

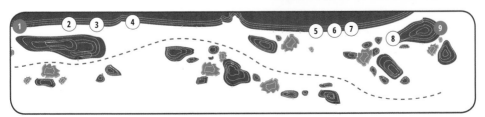

○5 □ **Britchen Strap 9** ★★
Nice route with a thin start. 45' *FA Duane Ackerman, 1999*

○6 □ **Licorice Stick 8** ★★
Again, a hard start to easier rock above. 45'
FA Duane Ackerman, 1999

○7 □ **Saddle Up 9** ★
Hardest of the three. 45' *FA Unknown, 1990's*

Two routes climb the very small pinnacle that sits in front of the cliff about 25 yards east of Saddle Up.

○8 □ **Pronghorn Pinnacle 8**
The west face, 3 bolts. 20' *FA Damien Potts, 2000*

●9 □ **Nouveau Western 10a**
This climb takes an arête on the east side of the pinnacle. 25' *FA Rick Thompson, 2000*

PETE **DELANNOY**

Pete Delannoy has been climbing in Wyoming since 1969. Having been "Sent off" to a wilderness camp as a young man (he admittedly was "no good at anything, bad at school, and short tempered") he found a strong passion for the mountains. Over the years, he worked as a wilderness instructor and mountain guide, and did his first climbing in the Lander area in Sinks Canyon around 1976.

After completing his Ph.D in chemisty in 1990, Pete moved to Salt Lake City to start post-doctoral work. That fall, he headed to Wild Iris after hearing the stories from his close friends Paul Piana and Todd Skinner. Upon

reaching the crag, hea headed not to the Main Wall, but through the trees to an untouched OK Corral. "Why the OK Corral you ask? Where else could you have your own cliff, the ability shape the flavor of the entire wall. (Later I was drawn to Spearfish Canyon, SD, because I could have my own canyon). I was like a pig in shit."

Pete spent three summer developing the OK Corral, routes at the Main Wall and Aspen Glade, and routes at less traveled areas. Pete's favorite routes in the area are Poker Face Alice (a 5.12b roof at the OK Corral), and Last Man Standing. Last Man Standing was a route Pete equipped, cleaned, and was ready to redpoint when visiting climber Eric Scully knowingly stole the first ascent during Pete's rest day.

These days, cave diving has taken over as Pete's main passion, with climbing taking a back seat. However, Wyoming always tends to draw him back. We can all hope he returns, with drill in hand, to establish more great climbs at Wild Iris.

LAST MAN STANDING 12d　　Tony Stark

RODEO **DRIVE**

10AM-PM | 10m | Vertical

4 6 5 2 0 0

This area is stacked with good routes. This once quiet area is now the busiest at the OK Corral. Approach via the cragside trail or by following the dirt road in front of the crag to near its end and then taking a well-marked trail that meets the wall near Rooster Cogburn.

Routes are listed from left to right.

○1 □ **Toast With a Great Deal of Butter 9** ★
This is a clean slabby route similar to The Hanging Tree. 45' *FA Brandon Walkinshaw, 2013*

○2 □ **The Hanging Tree 9** ★
Slab climb 50 feet right of Pronghorn Pinnacle, behind a few large pines. 45' *FA Unknown, 2000's*

○3 □ **Wind River Muzzle Loaders 9** ★★
This is a really nice climb just 10 feet right of The Hanging Tree. *FA Brandon Walkinshaw, 2011*

○4 □ **Ticks for Chicks 8** ★★
Dark slab left of chimney feature, faces SE. 4B 40'
FA Unknown, 2006

●5 □ **Ride Me Cowgirl 10b** ★★
Follows nice pockets on wall right of prow to a hard to read finish. *FA Jeremy Rowan, 2008*

●6 □ **Dirty Sally 10d** ★★
This is a cool climb with atypical movement. Finishes on a nice little headwall. 50' *FA Jeremy Rowan, 2009*

●7 □ **The Man From Laramie 10c** ★
This route climbs a rounded prow feature past several horizontals, ending at anchors below a blocky bulge. 50'
FA Unknown, 2000's

●8 □ **Rooster Cogburn 11d** ★★
This is a good climb up a clean prow with many moves that could spit you off. 50' *FA Cody Harris, 2011*

●9 □**The Duke 11a** ★★
Flakes and cracks right of Rooster Cogburn 50'
FA Rob Phares, 2014

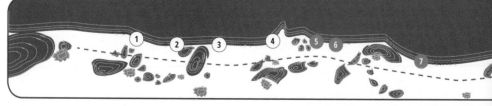

●10☐ **Western Grip 10b** ★

Right of Rooster Cogburn, this climb takes a flake and crack system to a cruxy move at the anchors. Layback the big crack until it's possible to commit to the left face. 4 bolts, 30' *FA Sophia Kim, 2012*

●11 ☐ **Rio Bravo 10a** ★

This is the leftmost route on this section of wall, just right of a big crack/corner. Climb up easy moves to a slabby top out. Fun. 40' *FA Unknown, 2013*

●12 ☐ **Imagine What I Could Do To Your Face 10b** ★★

This route starts just right of the previous climb. Take nice moves on generally good pockets up this clean less than vertical wall. 5 bolts, 40' *FA Ben Elzay, 2013*

●13 ☐ **Rodeo Drive 11d** ★

Climb grey slab in the center of the wall. A low crux leads to easy pulls above. Warmup those fingers! 4 bolts 40' *FA Unknown, 1992*

●14 ☐ **Wrong End of a Gun 11c** ★★

This is the prow route just right of Rodeo Drive. For sure one of the best routes at the OK Corral, stick clip the first bolt, then boulder through a low crux to nice, easier moves above. 5 bolts, 40' *FA Brian Dunnohew, 2012*

●15 ☐ **The Solace of Bolted Faces 11d** ★★

Climb slab with seams just left of a crack with big bushes in it. 45' *FA John Hennings, 2004*

●16 ☐ **John Wayne 12d** ★★

This is on the next section of wall right of Solace, taking a righttrending technical line through very clean rock. 55' *FA Anthony Chertudi, 2009*

●17 ☐ **Drinking Dry Clouds 12c** ★★

A powerful route up a pretty little bulge at the very right end of the cliff band. 35' *FA John Hennings, 2006*

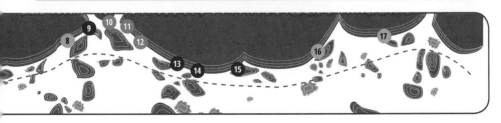

photo: Joey Scarr

MAIN WALL

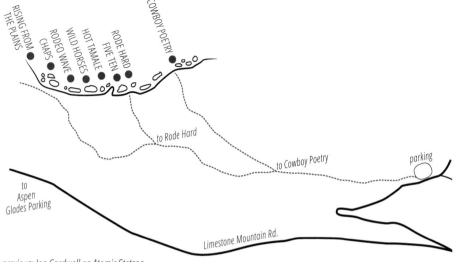

RISING FROM THE PLAINS
CHAPS
RODEO WAVE
WILD HORSES
HOT TAMALE
FIVE TEN
RODE HARD
COWBOY POETRY

to Rode Hard

to Cowboy Poetry

parking

to Aspen Glades Parking

Limestone Mountain Rd.

previous: Jon Cardwell on Atomic Stetson
photo: Joey Scarr

MAIN WALL

This is the cliff where it all began. These days, it's not the most popular crag, nor the one with the greatest concentration of routes, but it's the one that put Lander on the map. The routes are short and powerful, the stone wonderful to climb on, and each section of the cliff has a unique character. Wether you are looking for steep bulges, roofs, or technical faces, you'll find great routes in abundance.

Climbing at the Main Wall is best in the fall, but can be great all summer long. Trees provide sufficient shade, and the cool breezes coming off the Wind Rivers to the west can keep the temperatures nice, even when it is scorching hot in Lander. There are occasional afternoon thunderstorms in July and August. Avoid trying to beat these storms back to the parking lot - the exposed ridge between the crag and the parking is dangerous in a thunderstorm. It's best to just wait a few minutes and hike out once the weather clears.

Directions: To reach the Wild Iris Area, drive east out of Lander on Main Street. After about 24 miles (near milepost 53), take a right on the dirt Limestone Mountain Road, which is marked by both a brown Forest Service sign and a small green street sign. Take this good dirt road for 1.3 miles to a fork. The left fork leads to The Aspen Glade parking area, 2.0 miles up the road. To reach parking for the Main Wall and the OK Corral, take

the right fork, switchback up the hill, and park on the left as you crest the ridge (0.8 miles past the fork). The Main Wall is to the northwest, and is clearly visible from the parking lot.

Approach: The OK Corral sits east of the parking lot, uphill from the pit toilet. The cliff can be accessed via several trails that lead through the woods from the 4WD road that leads to the right of the pit toilet. Although climbers park along this road to access the cliff, it is best to reserve these spaces for those that are camping.

CLASSICS

 9
10-Night

 29
 27
 27
 21
 0

 15m-20m

Windy City (p.60)
Wind River Rose (p.60)

Easy Ridin' (p.65)
Take Your Hat Off (p.67)

The Prospect (p.58)
Nine Horse Johnson(p.65)
Cowboy Poetry (p.67)

Wind and Rattlesnakes (p.65)
Hot Tamale Baby (p.58)
Charro (p.60)

Boy (p.67)
Cow Reggae (p.55)
Last Man Standing (p.51)
Whip and Spur (p.51)
Rodeo Free Europe (p.55)

RISING FROM THE
PLAINS

| 10AM-PM | 20m | Steep |

Routes are listed from left to right.

● **1** ☐ **Rising From The Plains 12a** ★★
This is the leftmost (west) route on the Wild Iris Main Wall. Climb a vertical white wall to a grey streak that goes through a short bulge. 40' *FA Leif Gasch, 2004*

● **2** ☐ **Cowboy Killer 12b** ★★
This climb take a vertical wall with good pockets to a small bulge. A difficult move puts you on top. 40' *FA Leif Gasch, 2004*

● **3** ☐ **LG Route**
This is a unfinished route. 40' *Equipped Leif Gasch*

● **4** ☐ **A Slug of the Old What-For 13d** ★
This route begins up Adi-Goddang-Yos, then tracks left across the belly of the big bulge. 40' *FA BJ TIlden, 2007*

● **5** ☐ **Adi-Goddang-Yos 13c**
Begin in a right-facing corner, then up and right through a very steep bulge to a baffling crux. 40'
FA Paul Piana, 1991

● **6** ☐ ✎ **Half Cocked 14a** ★
Start on You Ain't Bill Hickok, then move left to finish Adi-Goddang-Yos. *FA BJ Tilden, 2011*

● **7** ☐ ✎ **Whip and Spur 14b** ★★
This hybrid starts on Hickok and then traverse all the way left onto A Slug of the Old What For. 50' *FA BJ Tilden, 2010*

● **8** ☐ **You Ain't Bill Hickok 14a** ★
Straight out the big belly. 45' *FA BJ Tilden, 2004*

● **9** ☐ **Last Man Standing 13a** ★★
Climb up the steep belly (using the first bolt of Hickok) to nice climbing on an overhanging wall. Some "aggressive cleaning" by an unknown party in the summer of 2013 has unfortunately made this climb slightly easier. 45'
FA Pete Delannoy, 1999

● **10** ☐ **County Ten Purring Champ 10a** ★★
This nice climb is on the very left margin of the wall, right where the trail breaks into the woods before reaching the Bill Hickok bulge. A boulder problem start leads to clean and easier climbing. *FA Eric Horst, 2017*

CHAPS

10AM-PM | 20m | Vertical

1 | 0 | 1 | 4 | 2 | 0

Routes are listed from left to right.

●1 ☐ **Pocket Derringer 11a**
Harder start through low bulge leads to long moves up slab. 50' *FA Pete Delannoy, 1992*

●2 ☐ **Crazy Horst 12b**
Six feet right of Pocket Derringer, follow a grey streak. 50'
FA Eric Horst, 1992

●3 ☐ **The Rustler's Cache 12b ★★**
Very powerful moves lead to bigger moves on bigger holds. *FA Lightners 2015*

●4 ☐ **The Lord Loves a Hangin' 13a**
Behind a big tree, climb up a seam feature. 50'
FA Chris Oates, 1993

●5 ☐ **Chaps 12c**
Follows a black streak past 4 bolts. 45'
FA Porter Jarrard, 1991

●6 ☐ **Horsewhipped and Hogtied 13a ★★**
Climb left and up a seam to very a crimpy crux. 50'
FA Chris Oates, 1993

●7 ☐ **Tres Hombres 12d**
Slightly overhanging on slightly terrible holds. Anchor near a small pine. 5 bolts 40' *FA Leif Gasch, 2005*

○8 ☐ **Western Sidestep 8 ★**
A strange corner climb on the right side of the wall.
FA Lightners 2015

BOB MARLEY 12a · Mandy Fabel

Other Rodeo Wave Links

∞ Atomic Ground 13d
∞ Atomic Logic 13d
∞ Genetic Logic 14c
∞ Drifting Upside Down 14c
∞ High Ground 14b
∞ Rodeo Free Stetson 14b if you do the
Stetson crux.14a if you go the high way.
∞ Cow Reggae sit start 13c
∞ Bobcat Logic from Ground sit start 12d

RODEO WAVE

10AM-PM   20m   Steep

0 | 0 | 0 | 3 | 13 | 0

Routes are listed from left to right.

● 1 ☐ **The Ranch 13a** ★

This is a steep line tucked way back between slab and wave. The strange position discourages attempts, but it's actually pretty cool. 35' *FA JD LeBlanc, 1992*

● 2 ☐ **Ground From Upside Down 13a (V6)** ★★

This climb takes jugs and pockets left of Bobcat Logic. There are no bolts - you just boulder it, stepping off onto the slab behind you if necessary. A spotter is comforting on the exit moves. 50' *FA BJ Tilden, 2010*

● 3 ☐ ✂ **Single Cell 13b** ★★

Starts off the slab on a jug at head height. Does a three bolt traverse into The Ranch.

● 4 ☐ ✂ **Mitosis 14a** ★★

Low in the grade. Starts on the Ground From Upside Down and finishes on Single Cell. There is a crux getting into Single Cell that involves a tiny right hand two finger pocket and a painful pinky lock for the left.

● 5 ☐ ✂ **Meiosis 14b** ★★

Starts on Atomic Stetson and finishes on Single Cell. This link requires the use of two ropes and one or two belayers, climbing the first half of Atomic Stetson on one rope and then transitioning to the second rope at the big jug below Bobcat Logic.

● 6 ☐ ✂ **Mutation 14d** ★★★

The mega link up. Starts on Rodeo Free Europe and finishes on The Ranch, climbing the entire wall from right to left via 80 moves. Requires the same rope transition as Meiosis. 80' *FA BJ Tilden 2016*

● 7 ☐ **Bobcat Logic 12c** ★★★

Climb up big holds on the leftmost bolt line off the slab. Most climbers clip the first bolt of Cow Reggae to keep the rope out of the way. 35' *FA Heidi Badaracco, 1992*

● 8 ☐ **Bob Marley 12a** ★

Climb three bolts up Bobcat Logic, then move right to finish Cow Reggae. 35' *FA Leif Gasch 2008*

● 9 ☐ **Cow Reggae 13b** ★★

A popular and fun route, the straight up line just right of Bobcat Logic. 35' *FA Frank Dusl, 1992*

● 10 ☐ ✂ **Babalouie 12c** ★★

Another hybrid, takes the first 2 bolts of Cow Reggae, then moves right to finish the final 2 of Atomic Stetson. 4 bolts 35' *FA Dan Michael, 1990*

● 11 ☐ **Atomic Stetson 13c** ★★

This is the third straight up line from the left, and is the lowest start on the slab to the left. 40' *FA Paul Piana, 1992*

● 12 ☐ ✂ **Atomic Cow 13d** ★★★

Starts as Atomic Stetson, then traverses left onto Cow Reggae where Babalouie goes right. 45' *FA Paul Piana, 1995*

● 13 ☐ **Rodeo Free Europe 14a** ★★

This route goes up the longest part of the wave. The hardest of the straight up lines, look for a boulder problem start to a big flake jug at bolt 2. 50' *FA Jason Campbell, 1998*

● 14 ☐ ✂ **Genetic Drifter 14c** ★★

Starts on Rodeo Free Europe, drifts left on Atomic Stetson, then finishes Cow Reggae. 55' *FA Jason Campbell, 1998*

● 15 ☐ ✂ **High Way 14b** ★

This variation to Genetic Drifter climbs one bolt higher on Rodeo Free Europe, then moves left across Atomic Stetson, finishing on Cow Reggae. *FA Unknown*

● 16 ☐ **Rodeo Active 13d** ★

The rightmost line on the wall. A very hard move (now even harder since a hold broke) leads to relatively easy climbing above. 45' *FA Andy Skiba, 1997*

Matt Harrison **TWO KINDS OF JUSTICE** 12b

WILD **HORSES**

10AM-PM | **20m** | **Vertical**

0 5 5 4 1 0

Routes are listed from left to right.

● **1** ☐ **6 Impossible Things Before Breakfast 12c**
A hard jump start leads to good climbing up the wall
above. This is the first route right of the big ledge/block
that sits below the Rodeo Wave. 45'
FA Kyle Vassilopoulos, 2014

● **2** ☐ **NFR 13c** ★
This is the leftmost of the steep lines on the Wild Horses
wall. *FA BJ Tilden, 2011*

● **3** ☐ **Two Kinds of Justice 12b** ★★★
Begins behind a large blocky formation. Popular, with
long and bouldery moves all the way. 40'
FA Porter Jarrard, 1991

● **4** ☐ **Gored By Inosine 12d** ★
A pretty wall with very long moves. Look for a big hueco
to identify this climb. 40' *FA Todd Skinner, 1994*

● **5** ☐ **In Todd We Trust 11d** ★
Just right of Gored by Inosine. This climb takes the crack
/ dihedral, with a hard exit. The name is Vance White's
nod to his friend Todd Skinner. 45' *FA Vance White, 2009*

● **6** ☐ **Limestone Cowboy 12a** ★
Behind the big pine, climbs up nice rock, but is hard to
read. 45' *FA Joe Desimone, 1991*

● **7** ☐ **Hip Boot Romance 10d** ★★
This fun climb has an awkward start, but is really neat
above. 45' *FA Steve Scott, 1991*

● **8** ☐ **Star Spangled Rodeo 10c** ★★
Mantle onto bulge between Hip Boot Romance and
Pronghorn Tramp, then continue on good holds. 50'
FA Sam Lightner, 2013

● **9** ☐ **Pronghorn Tramp 10b** ★★
Start on good holds 10 feet left of Pronghorn Love,
joining that route at the top. A recent and great addition
to the Main Wall. 50' *FA Sam Lightner, 2013*

● **10** ☐ **Pronghorn Love 11d**
Awkward moves on a clean wall lead to join Pronghorn
Tramp at the top. 50' *FA Steve Scott, 1991*

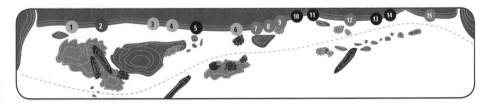

HOT **TAMALE**

 10AM-PM 20m Vertical | Slight

4 3 4 6 0 0

Routes are listed from left to right.

○1 □ Big Jake Arete 8 ★
Follows a long dark arete/prow 15 feet right of the major gully, ending near the top of the cliff. 65'
FA Sam Lightner, 2013

●2 □ Big Whiskey 11c ★
Boulder through a low bulge to a rail, then right and through another bulge to very easy ground. 60'
FA Sam Lightner, 2013

●3 □ In God's Country 12b ★
Climb a clean wall to a horizontal, then through a sequential and non obvious set of moves up the bulge.
45' *FA Eric Horst, 1992*

●4 □ Ruby Shooter 12b ★★
Popular route with great movement. 55'
FA Heidi Badaracco, 1992

●5 □ Hot Tamale Baby 12a ★★★
Also popular, also great movement. Begins in a little left-facing corner leading up to rounded prow. Wanders a bit at the top. 60' *FA Heidi Badaracco, 1991*

●6 □ Hey, Mr. Vaquero 12c ★★★
Follows a grey streak. Breaks through the left side of the low bulge on long moves, then up a tricky headwall. 70'
FA Todd Skinner, 1992

●7 □ Mexican Rodeo 12d★
The hardest of the bulges followed by the hardest headwall. There is a large pocket right at bolt one. 70'
FA Paul Piana, 1991

●11 □ The Prospect 11a ★★
Starts in a left-facing corner, then up big pockets moving left through a bulge. 50' *FA Unknown, 1990*

●12 □ The Devil Wears Spurs 10d ★★
Famous and popular, this route is getting slick! Start on big pockets near the base of a "double" pine tree. 50'
FA Carol Gogas, 1991

●13 □ Posse on My Tail 11d ★
Bouldery climbing leads to a tricky lower-angled wall above. 50' *FA Jacob Valdez, 1990*

●14 □ Wild Horses 11b
Start near small corner/chimney, then up nice pockets in the upper wall. 50' *FA Jacob Valdez, 1990*

●15 □ Jackalope and Boomslang 10a
Climbs the low-angle wall right of the main Wild Horses wall, and just left of the bottom of the gully. 45'
FA Glenda Lanais, 1991

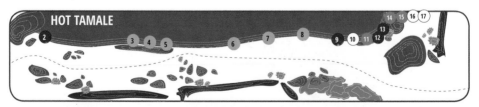

HOT TAMALE

HOT TAMALE BABY 12a   Harriet Ridley

●8 ☐ Charro 12b ★★★

Big moves on big holds, then up tricky slab and past a small roof. Look for underclings to identify the start. 75'
FA Heidi Badaracco, 1993

●9 ☐ Caballero Del Norte 11d ★

Fun hard start to thin moves high. 50' *FA Chris Oates, 1993*

○10 ☐ Windy City 8 ★★

Follow a corner/crack system, then climb right to anchors at the top. 50' *FA Jeff Leafgreen, 2000*

●11 ☐ Popo Agie Pocket Pool 10a ★

This route is left of a big dead tree right next to the wall. Good climbing up to share anchors with Windy City. 50'
FA Rick Thompson, 1999

●12 ☐ Distant Early Warning 11a ★

The face left of Osita. *FA Lightners 2015*

●13 ☐ Osita 11d

A Thin crux leads to easier ground above. A bit of a Wild Iris rite of passage. *FA Judy Barnes 1993*

●14 ☐ Digital Stimulation 10c

Big pockets into a tricky seam. Faces east and starts off a small ledge. 40' *FA Jeff Leafgreen, 2000*

●15 ☐ The Shootist 10a ★

Good pockets up a clean wall. This is the left route on the right wall of the big corner. 40' *FA Steve Scott, 1992*

○16 ☐ Wind River Rose 9 ★★

Nice slab climbing up a rounded prow, just right of The Shootist. 45' *FA Steve Scott, 1991*

○17 ☐ Jake and the Neverland Cowboys 6 ★★

This climb takes low angled rock past some great huecos just right of Wind River Rose. *FA Bechtel family 2015*

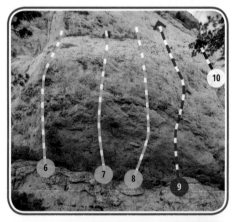

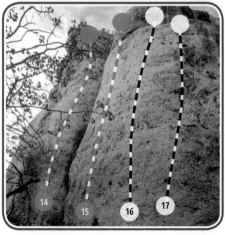

FIVE **TEN**

| 10AM-PM | 15m | Vertical |

4 **9** **4** **0** **0** **0**

The Five Ten Wall is about five minutes downhill (east) of Wind River Rose. The first three routes are left of the main Five Ten Wall, and start off a small set of ledges. The main part of the wall is easily identified by the Stonehenge Rocks sitting in front of the cliff, and the fact that most of the climbs look about 5.10.

Routes are listed from left to right.

●1 ☐ Ryobi Jr. 10b ★
Starts on the ledge system left of the Five Ten Wall. This is the face left of the tree. 40' *FA Pat Perrin, 1991*

●2 ☐ Ryobi Rustler 10d
From ledge system, climb right of the tree up an orange streak. 40' *FA Patt Perrin, 1991*

●3 ☐ Ryobi Wrangler 11a ★
Climb off the right side of ledge system, up a black streak. 40' *FA Pat Perrin, 1991*

●4 ☐ Ryobi Ranger 10a ★★
The leftmost route on the Five Ten Wall itself. Climbs up to big pockets, then through some reachy moves before easing up at the top. 50' *FA Pat Perrin, 1991*

●5 ☐ Indian Country 10b ★★
Most climbers start on the small ledge to the right, then move up and left to good pockets. A really nice route. 50' *FA Jacob Valdez, 1991*

●6 ☐ + Big Country 11c ★★
An extension above Indian Country. *FA Lightners 2015*

○7 ☐ Dynamitic 7 ★
Climb up the small left-facing corner about 10' left of the large "Stonehenge" rock that sits in front of the wall. 45' *FA Rick Thompson, 2000*

●8 ☐ Sacagawea 10b
Starts behind left side of "Stonehenge" rock. Thin hard moves. 45' *FA Elaine Chandler, 1990*

●9 ☐ Pistol Pete 10d
Starts behind right side of "Stonehenge" rock. Thin hard moves. 45' *FA Pete Delannoy, 1992*

●10 ☐ Wild Horses Keep Dragging Me Away 10c ★
Another hard slabby face. Named after Shep Vail's very short rodeo career. 45' *FA Shep Vail, 1994*

○11 ☐ You Picked a Fine Climb to Lead Me, Lucille 9★
Long moves on relatively good holds up a black streaked section of the wall. Named after Garold's wife, Lucille. Garold and Lucille are Amy Skinner's parents, and were frequent visitors to the crag in the early days. *FA Garold Whisler 1992*

●12 ☐ Latex Cowboy 10b ★★
10' left of the bushy crack. Steeper climbing on good pockets. *FA Unknown, 1990's*

○13 ☐ Good Hearted Woman 9 ★★
A nice route somehow long overlooked on the main 5.10 wall. Another example of redundant route naming, sharing the name with Vance White's 2013 route at the Pup. *FA Lightners 2015*

●14 ☐ T and T 10c ★
Clean white wall 15' left of the chockstone chimney. *FA Rick Thompson, 2000*

●15 ☐ Pistols and Gri Gris 11a
These routes are 50-60' right of the main Five Ten Wall. Hard moves low to lower-angle wall above. 45' *FA Eric Horst, 1992*

● 16 ☐ War Paint 11c

Very bouldery low moves to easier climbing above.
Shares anchors with Pistols and GriGris. 45′
FA Heidi Badaracco, 1990

○ 17 ☐ Dances With Wolves and Wind in His Hair 7 TR

These short toprope routes are up the gully right of War
Paint on a 20′ clean wall. *FA Shane Petro, 1991*

AMY **SKINNER**

Amy began climbing with her dad, Garold, in the
early 1980s around Las Vegas, Nevada. She climbed
throughout the west for years and worked part-time as a
wildland firefighter, until she met Todd Skinner in 1988.
She and Todd began dating and traveled together for a
couple of seasons before settling in Custer, South Dakota,
to climb in the Black Hills.

No sooner had they set up home-base there than the
word of limestone on the southern flank of the Wind
Rivers came their way. Todd went to take a look and

never went back to South Dakota. She packed up the
house and moved to Atlantic City in the summer of 1990,
and together with a handful of friends began developing
their dream crag. Later, they moved down to Lander for
the less-harsh winters and paved streets.

Amy and Todd opened Wild Iris Mountain Sports along
with John Howell to support their climbing habit and
to employ future climbing partners. Amy managed the
store, and the joke was that Todd didn't even have a key.
She has mentored dozens of young climbers over the 25+
years she has run the Wild Iris.

Amy was an active first ascentionist for years. Later, she
balanced climbing with running the store and raising her
three kids. After a few years' hiatus, Amy is back on the
rock and can be found behind the counter at Wild Iris
most days. She is best known for her ultra-classic route
Wind and Rattlesnakes (12a) at Wild Iris.

RODE**HARD**

10AM-PM	15m	Vertical	Roof

0 5 5 5 3 0

Routes are listed from left to right.

●1 ☐ **Jones on the Jukebox 13d** ★★
This unique climb was bolted by Todd Skinner during a heavy weather day at the crag. It sat unclimbed for 20 years until BJ Tilden did the first ascent in 2011. Step off a boulder, climb thin pockets up the roof/prow to where it leans against the adjacent wall. 40 feet.
FA BJ TIlden, 2011

●2 ☐ **Ewe on My Mind 11d** ★
Technical route that ends at the Jones on the Jukebox anchors. *FA Sam Lightner, 2014*

●3 ☐ **Full Circle 13a** ★★
This route shares the start of Copenhagen Angel, then moves left and out the biggest part of the roof.
FA Matt Wendling, 2008

●4 ☐ **Copenhagen Angel 13b** ★
Up a white wall to climb through the roof. Face up to roof is 5.11. 60' *FA Todd Skinner, 1990*

●5 ☐ **Phony Express 12b** ★
Starts the same as Rode Hard, but moves left on good pockets once you are through to roof. 60'
FA Paul Piana, 1991

11 ☐ Easy Ridin' 10d ★★★
Great climbing up flakes to small bulge and up fun wall.
55' *FA Diedre Burton, 1996*

12 ☐ Belle Star 11a ★
This is the leftmost route on the Buckskin Billy wall, about
15 feet right of Easy Ridin'. A tricky start leads to clean
and fun climbing above. 50'
FA Jeremy Rowan, 2012

13 ☐ Arizona Cowgirl 11c ★★
Thin moves to easier wall above. 50'
FA Diedre Burton, 1996

14 ☐ Cowboy Joe 10c ★
A bulge low leads to easier climbing high. 50' *FA Jeff
Leafgreen, 1999*

15 ☐ Buckskin Billy 10a ★
Tricky through the bulge, then great moves up to anchor.
45' *FA Shane Petro, 1992*

16 ☐ Hired Guns 11d
Around right of the Buckskin Billy slab, this route is a thin
and tricky pursuit. 4 bolts 40' *FA Pat Perrin, 1991*

17 ☐ 3:10 to Yuma 10b ★
Climb the short clean wall 100 feet right of Hired Guns.
40' *FA Unknown*

18 ☐ Merwin Hulbert 10d ★
The crack/flake that joins 3:10 to Yuma. Merwin
Hulbert was a famed firearms manufacturer in the
1800s. FA Unknown

6 ☐ Rode Hard and Put Up Wet 12c ★★
Climb a clean slab starting on left side of flake/crack,
heading toward a "hueco" in the roof. Devious sequence
through center of roof. This was the first route at the
Main Wall. 55' *FA Todd Skinner, 1990*

7 ☐ Nine Horse Johnson 11d ★★
Up the flake to a vertical wall with good pockets. Out the
roof on jugs / stems. 55' *FA Steve Bechtel, 2006*

8 ☐ Windy West 12b ★★
This nice climb shares the first half of Wind and Rattlesnakes, then breaks left and follows big moves up the
arete. 50' *FA Jeremy Rowan, 2011*

9 ☐ Wind and Rattlesnakes 12a ★★★
Up the nice prow, great continuous climbing on good
holds. 50' *FA Amy Skinner, 1990*

10 ☐ Tomahawk Slam 12a ★
Crack/jug climbing to a stinger move, then easier to top.
50' *FA Heidi Badaracco, 1990*

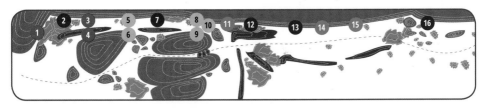

Andy Wickstrom

RODE HARD & PUT UP WET 12c

photo Zach Snavley

COWBOY **POETRY**

10AM-PM	15m	Vertical

0 6 8 4 2 0

Routes are listed from left to right.

● **1** ☐ **The Devil Wears Latex 10c** ★★
This short route is left of the main Cowboy Poetry wall, and features good pockets and fun moves. 45'
FA Unknown, 2000

● **2** ☐ **Even Cowgirls Get The Blues 11a**
Up a bulgy wall, but sneaks through the bulges on right side. 60' *FA Laurie Medina, 1990*

● **3** ☐ **Testosterone Alfresco 10d** ★
Shares the start of Sleeping Thunder, moving left after 25'. Up prow and over a small bulge. 55'
FA Rick Thompson, 2000

● **4** ☐ **Sleeping Thunder 12a** ★
Good climbing up vertical wall to a crux high, usually marked by a bail biner. 65' *FA Paul Piana, 1993*

● **5** ☐ **Cowboy Poetry 11b** ★★★
Up slab to scoop, then tricky long moves to anchor at horizonta. 50' *FA Paul Piana, 1990*

● **6** ☐ + **Cowboy Poetry 12b** ★
From horizontal clip bolt up and to the right,, then fight through bulges to upper anchor. 30' *FA Paul Piana, 1990*

● **7** ☐ **Take Your Hat Off 10b** ★★★
Hard start to jug climbing, ending at an anchor below bulge. 50' *FA Heidi Badaracco, 1993*

● **8** ☐ + **Boy 13a** ★
Continue up the headwall above Take Your Hat Off. 35'
FA Heidi Badaracco, 1996

● **9** ☐ **Buffalo Soldier 10b** ★
Edgy climbing starting on flake. 45' *FA Pat Perrin, 1991*

● **10** ☐ + **Charlie Drew That Spinnin' Bull 12c** ★
Continues through bulges above Buffalo Soldier.
FA John Hennings, 2006

● **11** ☐ **Cowboys Don't Shoot Straight 11a** ★★
Up black streak and up obvious cracks in the upper bulge. 50' *FA Amy Skinner, 1990*

● **12** ☐ **Ambush in the Night 11a** ★
Tricky thin moves just left of small pine against the wall.
45' *FA Pat Perrin, 1991*

● **13** ☐ + **Riata Man 13a** ★
Up bulging wall with obvious big pockets above Ambush in the Night. 40' *FA Paul Piana, 1991*

● **14** ☐ **Princess and the Playmate 10c** ★★
First route right of small pine, low bulge to slab. 50'
FA Pat Perrin, 1991

● **15** ☐ **Cherokee With a Crewcut 11a** ★
Climb up seam and through steep wall above with black streak. 50' *FA Garold Whisler, 1991*

● **16** ☐ **Slapping Leather 11c**
This is the face right of the seam. 60' *FA John Gogas, 1991*

● **17** ☐ **Concrete Cowboys 10c**
Wanders up and left, then back right to anchor. 45'
FA Joe Desimone, 1991

Charlie Manganiello

TAKE YOUR HAT OFF 10b

● 18 ☐ **Honed on the Range 11c** ★★
Tricky route up a clean wall. 50' *FA Patt Perrin, 1991*

● 19 ☐ **Hand-Tooled Saddle 11c**
On wall 100' right of Honed on the Range, up seams in a steep wall. *FA Unknown, 1993*

● 20 ☐ **Bucky Goldstein 12b**
Thin face right of Hand-Tooled Saddle. This is a pretty good route and would be very popular if clean.
FA Steve Scott, 1991

PAUL **PIANA**

Paul Piana spent fifteen years in Lander with the singular mission of establishing routes on the dolomite. A Wyoming native, Paul spent large amounts of time climbing all across the state, but traveled widely as a motivational speaker and professional climber. Starting in 1990, though, he traveled less, and began helping create the wonderful area we now climb in.

At almost every crag, you'll find the cleanest and best lines were probably established by Paul. Throughout this book, you'll see his name listed as first ascentionist. An equal number of routes were bolted and cleaned by Paul and first redpointed by another. He cleared trails, discovered new areas, and was pivotal in the establishment of the Climbers' Festival.

A great all-arounder, Piana has impeccable technique and was as comfortable on 5.13 slabs as he was climbing on the Rodeo Wave. More than any other climber, Paul took these crags from good to great.

When a famed female climber moved to Lander in the mid 1990s Paul asked her when she was going to start doing new routes. She said, "I don't have time to do new routes." Paul replied, "That's funny...I don't have time not to."

photo: Adam Pawlikiewicz

REMUDA & ASPEN GLADES

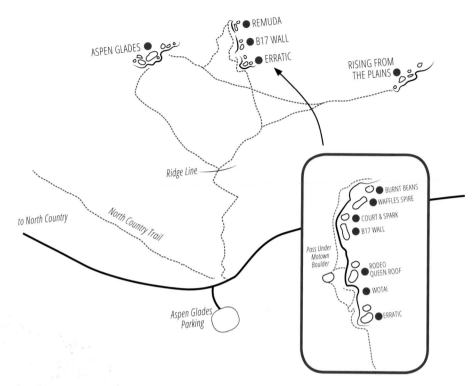

ASPEN GLADES
REMUDA
B17 WALL
ERRATIC
RISING FROM
THE PLAINS

Ridge Line

to North Country
North Country Trail

Pass Under
Motown
Boulder

BURNT BEANS
WAFFLES SPIRE
COURT & SPARK
B17 WALL
RODEO
QUEEN ROOF
WOTAI
ERRATIC

Aspen Glades
Parking

previous: Kris McCoey on Spurs Equal Velocity
Photo: Adam Pawlikiewicz

ASPEN GLADES

The back side of Wild Iris is home to some of the best climbs anywhere. The valley behind the Main Wall includes the cliffs of the Aspen Glade, The Remuda, and the Erratic, as well as assorted other cliffs. The Aspen Glade wall features some of the cleanest stone at Wild Iris. This wall faces southeast and is pleasant late into the fall. For summer climbing, the walls of the Remuda and Erratic offer shade most of the day. Be warned, though, that the routes on these walls tend to be very difficult – this is not a beginner's crag.

Directions: To Reach the Wild Iris Area, drive east out of town on Main Street. After approximately 25 miles, take a right on the dirt Limestone Mountain Road (this sign tends to get stolen a lot, so look for a stop sign and cattle guard, which tend to be stolen less frequently). Take this road for 1.3 miles to a fork. To reach the Main Wall parking and the OK corral, take the right fork, switchback up the hill, and park on the left as you crest the ridge. To get to the Aspen Glade, stay left at the fork. Take this road about 2 miles until you begin to enter a wooded area. Look for parking on the left, near a less-traveled dirt road.

Approach: From this parking area, walk back up Limestone Mountain Road about 50 yards, and take a trail through the woods to the left (north). The hike takes you out of the woods and switchbacks to the crest of the ridge. From here, you can see the cliffs. At this point you can take a trail north/left that leads you to the left end of the Aspen Glade Wall, or bear right / east to the other crags. If you go right, you will walk roughly east. Walk roughly east on a trail that is occasionally a two track. About a quarter mile after cresting the hill, the trail splits, with the right fork heading toward the Main Wall, and the left fork dropping into the valley ahead. The trail descends and eventually reaches a 4way intersection near some large dead t rees. To approach the Aspen Glade, go left at this intersection. This should be really obvious, as there is a big cliff to your left with an aspen glade in front of it. As you near the cliff, you'll branch left on a lessworn trail. To reach the Remuda, also go

photo Kyle Duba

ASPEN**GLADES**

| 10AM-PM | 20m | Vertical | Roof |

  0 9 13 13 3 0

This wall can be approached via a faint trail that comes in along the cliff from the west near Ambuscado, or by following the trail in from the 4way intersection at the dead trees. If this approach is used, you reach the cliff at Don't Paint Your Wagon.

left, but bear right at the bottom of the hill, staying on the eroded trail that heads down into the woods before reaching the Aspen Glade wall (see map). The Erratic is reached by going straight at the intersection. You really can't miss it. Going right leads you uphill and to the very west end (Rising From the Plains) of the Main Wall. You an also reach the Remuda via the newly restored cliffside trail. To do this, approach as for the Erratic, but follow a good trail that drops into the woods from the Erratic area near Big Medicine. The trail descends through the bouldering area called Motown, then passes sparsely developed cliffs until rejoining the Remuda trail near Court and Spark.

Routes are listed from left to right.

●1 ☐ **Ambuscado 11d** ★★
Follows very steep line on the back of the huge, leaning detached slab. 100' left of Spurs wall. 35'
FA Steve Bechtel, 2005

●2 ☐ **Night Flying Woman 11a** ★★
Starts right of a of bushy gully with a couple of thin moves, then up great rock on good holds. 40'
FA Ellen Bechtel, 2005

●3 ☐ **Buffalo Skull 11d** ★
Good climbing up a bulging wall. Trends right and breaks a little roof at the top. 70' *FA Joe Desimone, 1991*

●4 ☐ **Straight Outta Hudson 12c** ★★
Bouldery through the left side of a big roof at bottom, up an easier slab, then through the biggest part of the upper roof. 70' *FA Steve Bechtel, 2005*

●5 ☐ **Spurs Equal Velocity 12a** ★★
Climb through right side of the low roof (5.11), then up the slab to a 6' roof. 70' *FA Heidi Badaracco, 1992*

●6 ☐ **All He's Got 11c** ★★
A super route. Take the face just right of Spurs Equal Velocity up a small corner to solid climbing up a vertical wall. Rest, then punch it through the roof using the big hueco, moving left to an anchor above. 70'
FA Sam Lightner, 2013

●7 ☐ **All He's Ever Gonna Have 10a** ★★★
Another great climb, this route goes up vertical and less than-vertical rock past great holds. 65'
FA Lightners, 2013

CLASSICS

 4

All He's Ever Gonna Have(p.73)
Lonesome Cowboy (p.74)
Wotai (p.85)

Night Flying Woman (p.73)
Little Buckaroo(p.74)
Lonely Are The Brave (p.74)

Butch Pocket & The Sundance Pump (p.75)
American Beauty(p.76)
Burnt Beans and Coffee (p.81)

Cowboy King(p.76)
Throwin The Houlihan (p.83)

17
36
29
10
3

10-7PM

15m-20m

● 8 ☐ Mutt Ridin' Monkey 10d ★★
Nice climbing up a long face. 65' *FA Tom Addison, 1992*

● 9 ☐ Californios 11b ★★
Continuous moves up a vertical to slightly overhanging wall, starting in a small corner/crack feature. 65 '
FA Tom Addison, 1992

● 10 ☐ Snowblind 12b ★
This climb is the first you'll encounter as you drop into the gulley right of Californios. A bouldery stat leads to easier moves high.
FA Rachel Stewart and Shadow Ayala 2017

● 11 ☐ Whore's Gold 12a ★★
On the shorter section of cliff between the "Spurs" wall and "Gun Street" there are four nice climbs. This is the leftmost line, a slightly overhanging and powerful line protected by 4 bolts. 45' *FA Sam Lightner, 2013*

● 12 ☐ Drink and Wickedness 13a ★★
This steeper climb starts in a small bulge and heads up through a face with some seams. 45'
FA Sam and Liz Lightner, 2014

● 13 ☐ Hillbilly Hoedown 12a ★
This steeper climb starts in a small bulge and heads up through a face with some seams. 45'
FA Joe Desimone, 1991

● 14 ☐ Trixie 11b ★★
This climb had a stinger start to nice moves up a crack feature. A tricky top out ends the route. 10 feet right of Hillbilly Hoedown. *FA Liz Lightner, 2013*

● 15 ☐ Prime Bovine Arête 11c
On the buttress halfway between Spurs and Gun Street, up a hourglass prow. 50' *FA Joe Desimone, 1991*

● 16 ☐ Lonesome Cowboy 10c ★
Good climbing, but really short. 30' *FA Pete Delannoy, 1992*

● 17 ☐ Miss Yvonne Rode the Horse 11b ★
Steep wall with good holds to clip anchors. 30'
FA Steve Bechtel, 2004

● 18 ☐ Young Guns 10d ★★
Really nice climbing on big holds up a black and gold wall left of Little Buckaroo. 30 feet. *FA Vance White, 2010*

● 19 ☐ Little Buckaroo 11b ★★★
Really fun climbing on big moves to clip anchors. On westfacing wall. 30' *FA Heidi Badaracco, 1992*

● 20 ☐ Bovine Intervention 10d ★
Just right of Little Buckaroo pillar, long moves up vertical wall to short crux. 50' *FA Steve Bechtel, 2006*

● 21 ☐ Lonely are the Brave 11a ★★
Up steep wall with good holds to crux finish. 45'
FA Tony Jewell, 1991

● 22 ☐ Don't Paint Your Wagon 12a ★★
Good pockets and good moves. Tricky. 45'
FA Craig Reason, 1991

● 23 ☐ Branded 12a ★
Up center of wall, follows flakes and small pockets. 5B
45' *FA Ray Ringle, 1991*

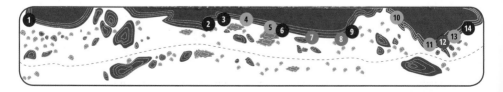

●**24** ☐ **Butch Pocket & the Sundance Pump 12a** ★★★

Nice moves on big holds up seam feature to an attention-getting crux. 50' *FA Pete Delannoy, 1992*

●**25** ☐ **Gun Street Girl 12b** ★★★

Good climbing up sinker pockets to a high crux. 50' *FA Heidi Badaracco, 1992*

●**26** ☐ **Sweet Tart of the Rodeo 10d**

Powerful moves up short overhanging face to lower angle top. 45' *FA Tricia Stetson, 1997*

●**27** ☐ **Dirt Bag 11d** ★

Begins atop orangelichened flake. Ascend thru bulges, trending left. Strangeposition, but good moves. 50' *FA John Warning, 1996*

●**28** ☐ **Sweating Bullets 10a**

Up left side of slabby wall. 45' *FA Mike Strassman, 1992*

●**29** ☐ **Sweaty Balls 10b** ★★

This is the center slab route. A thin start leads to good movement. *FA Steph Bolton, 2016*

● 30 ☐ Sweaty Bully 10b ★★

Good climbing up steep rock to slab. 50'
FA Rick Thompson, 2000

● 31 ☐ Whiskey Toast 12a ★

Hard long moves. A bit sporty toward the top. 50'
FA Jacob Valdez, 1991

● 32 ☐ Fist Full of Quickdraws 11d ★★

Good moves on nice rock. The best of the three routes on this wall. 50' *FA Sam Lightner, 1991*

● 33 ☐ The Quick and the Dead 11d ★

Tricky climbing on sloping pockets. Good route. 50'
FA Tony Jewell, 1991

● 34 ☐ Bronc Twister 13b ★★

Up dancy slab to twotiered roof. 5.12+ through first roof, move left, then the business. 75' *FA Todd Skinner, 1992*

● 35 ☐ Cowboy King 13b ★★★

Shares start with Bronc Twister. After first roof crux, breaks right where Bronc Twister breaks left. Good pockets, but hard moves. 75' *FA Scott Milton, 1999*

● 36 ☐ American Beauty 12b ★★★

a hard move low leads to easier slab rambling, then up to long roof moves. 75' *FA Heidi Badaracco, 1998*

● 37 ☐ Jolly Rancher 12c ★

Very tricky low face to easier climbing at top. 70'
FA Paul Piana, 1999

● 38 ☐ Choke Cherry Eyes 12a ★★★

Continuous fun moves up a vertical wall then through bulge at top. 70' *FA Paul Piana, 1999*

photo Chris Beauchamp

Harriet Ridley **AMERICAN BEAUTY** 12b

THE **REMUDA**

| NONE | 25m | Vertical | Slight |

(4) (1) (12) (10) (1) (3)

The B17 Wall & Remuda are best reached by heading north (downhill toward the Aspen Glade Wall) from the 4way intersection at the dead trees. Keep right where the path splits, heading downhill into the trees keeping right of the drainage. Follow this trail (sometimes a bit hard to follow) for 10-12 minutes (further than you think you should go...) until it reaches the beautiful clean walls that make up the Remuda. The trail reaches the wall near Court and Spark. There are several new routes right of Court and Spark along trail toward Erratic. From Court and Spark, move uphill (west) about 100 yards to find the climbs in a small alcove near some large steps in the trail. This is called the B17 Wall.

B17 WALL

B17 WALL

6 METEETSEE PETE ●

to Erratic

5 RELUCTANT DRAGON ●

4 DUCES WILD ●

3 SHADY LADY ●

2 CELESTIAL SIREN ●

1 DUCHESS OF FUBAR ●

to Court & Spark

REMUDA

B17 WALL

Routes are listed from left to right.

●1 ☐ **Duchess of FUBAR 11d ★**
Follow a crack halfway up the wall and then finish on delicate moves. FA Sam Lightner, Lindsey Stevens, 2016

● 2 ☐ **The Celestial Siren 12a ★★**
Cool climbing through a bulge right of Duchess of FUBAR.
FA Sam Lightner, Mike Lilygren, 2016

●3 ☐ **Shady Lady 11a ★**
A crack leads to a long vertical wall to a slab.
FA Liz and Sam Lightner, 2016

●4 ☐ **Duces Wild 11b ★**
This climb starts in a bulge then exits onto a slab. This is just left / east of the large steps in the trail.
FA Sam and Liz Lightner, 2016

○5 ☐ **Reluctant Dragon 9**
A crux start leads to easy climbing above.
FA Rydell Stottlemyer and Sam Lightner, 2017

○6 ☐ **Meteetsee-Pete 5 ★★**
A nice, low-angled prow. This is a good route for younger or less experienced leaders. FA Matisse Weaver, 2016

REMUDA

Routes are listed from right to left

●7 ☐ **SL Route (Open Project)**
Unfinished route. Right of Dun Roamin' Estimated around 12b. Equipped Sam Lightner

●8 ☐ **Dun Roamin' 11d ★★**
This fine climb starts with some thin moves, then follows a crack feature past good pockets to a bulging lieback finish. FA Jeremy Rowan, 2017

●9 ☐ **Court and Spark 12b ★★★**
Good moves through thin face, then up a nice prow. Ends on ledge. 60' FA Heidi Badaracco, 1994

●10 ☐ **Buck a Move 13a ★**
Good climbing up the clean face left of Court and Spark. 45' FA Heidi Badaracco, 1993

●11 ☐ **The Devil's Herd 11d**
Shares start with Ghost Rider, then moves right at upper wall. 55' FA Unknown, 1990's

●12 ☐ **Ghost Rider 11d ★**
Start with a hard move, then to easy climbing up a prow. Rest, then tackle the hard wall above. Popular but not classic. An alternate start was bolted to the right of the original. This was done in hopes of avoiding the unpleasant start of Ghost Rider. This start is harder than it looks and isn't that fun. 55' FA Mike Dahlberg, 1991

photo Noam Argov

GHOST RIDER 11d   Kyle Vassilopoulos

●13 □ **Hey Boo-Boo 12b ★★**

Climb a not-very-cool slab (10c) right of Pedophie Moustache to a clean and fun headwall. *FA Sam Lightner 2016*

●14 □ **Pedophile Moustache 11c**

Starts right of Crooked Darlin', but climbs straight up, crossing that route and ending slightly left. 40'
FA Jeff Wendt, 2002

●15 □ **Crooked Darlin' 11a**

Diagonalling line. A bit contrived, but easier than other route on the wall. 45' *FA Heidi Badaracco, 1994*

●16 □ **Closed Project**

This climb takes the leftmost line on the wall, past big pockets to a thin section near the top. Anchors only.

The following routes are on a small detached spire that sits between Crooked Darlin' and the Burnt Beans area.

○17 □ **Bear Necessities 6R**

Follows the east ridge of the spire from the south face (between main wall and spire). Climb to the ridge on relatively exposed moves, reach over the arete with a long sling and clip the anchor of The String, then on to a ledge and another bolt. Do a 5.6 move then easier ground to the summit. Use the anchors for Bearly There to belay. Sharp. Could be a few loose flakes. *FA Sam Lightner, 2016*

○18 □ **Chicken and Waffles 8**

Start this route on the back side of Waffles Spire.
FA Sam Lightner, 2016

●19 □ **Bear Down 11c ★**

Fourth route from the left on the north side of the spire, the rightmost on the wall as of this writing.
FA Sam Lightner and Mike Lilygren, 2016

●20 □ **Bearly There 11b ★★**

Third route from the left on the spire, just right of the tree growing behind a flake.
FA Mike Lilygren and Sam Lightner, 2016

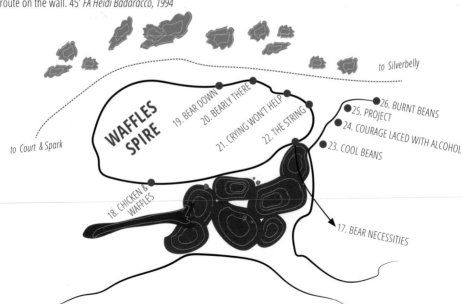

●21 ☐ Cryin' Won't Help 11b ★★
Second route from the left on the spire. Nice, thin climbing. *FA Sam Lightner, 2016*

●22 ☐ The String 11a
The leftmost route on the spire, takes a prow/arete feature on the right side of the gully. *FA Sam Lightner, 2016*

●23 ☐ Cool Beans 12a ★
This climb starts in the gully between the two walls. It takes slabby moves up to a large chockstone, which is welcome but breaks up the climbing. Hard moves lead up and left from the chockstone.
FA Katariina Rahikainen and Ben Sears, 2017

●24 ☐ Courage Laced With Alcohol 12b ★★
Fine climbing up a less-than-vertical wall, working between large pockets on otherwise thin terrain. A final crux guards the anchors. *FA Ben Sears, 2017*

●25 ☐ SB Route (Closed Project)
The clean face right of Burnt Beans and Coffee.
Equipped Steve Bechtel, 2016

●26 ☐ Burnt Beans and Coffee 12c ★★★
Long pulls between big pockets, with a tough crux at the end. 60' *FA Paul Piana, 1996*

●27 ☐ Silverbelly 12d ★★★
Up center of beautiful white wall, long moves on little pockets. 55' *FA Paul Piana, 1996*

●28 ☐ Britch Adjustment 10c ★★
This climb takes the crack feature left of Silverbelly.
FA Luke Lubchenco, 2017

●29 ☐ Coyote Vacuum 12b
On the very left side of the Silverbelly wall, start in under-clings, then tricky moves to the top.40'
FA Heidi Badaracco, 1996

Beyond Coyote Vacuum are several cool boulders and short walls leading down the valley through the trees. Although most of these seem too short for routes, about 10 minutes down hill through the boulders, you'll reach one last tall block. There are two routes on this block, and room for a few more. Both routes face Northeast, or down valley from the approach.

●30 ☐ John Wayne Never Wore Lycra 12a ★
This climb takes the right line on the wall and follows a prow feature. *FA Paul Piana 1992*

●31 ☐ The Rapping Duke 12a ★★
This climb takes the left line on the wall.
FA Paul Piana 1992

photo Kyle Duba

BURNT BEANS 12c — Sara Rottenberger

photo Kyle Duba

MOONSHINE 14d BJ Tilden

THE **ERRATIC**

| NONE | 20m | Vertical | Slight |

The first six routes are on the Erratic itself, the remainder are another 150 yards downhill and east on a nice buttress.

Routes are listed from right to left

● **1** ☐ **Throwin' the Houlihan 14a ★★★**
Step off boulder then up long moves on small pockets. The direct start boulder problem has been climbed, raising the route difficulty slightly. 50' *FA Todd Skinner, 1991*

● **2** ☐ **Moonshine 14d ★★**
BJ Tilden's longtime project, this route was finally climbed in 2012. Start in the seam feature, then move up and right on continuous thin and long moves. 50'
FA BJ Tilden, 2012

● **3** ☐ **Ghost Moon 13d ★**
Starts first 2 bolts of Moonshine, then left to finish on Heart Full of Ghosts. 50' *FA Leif Gasch, 2005*

● **4** ☐ **Heart Full of Ghosts 14a ★**
Takes the line just left of the prow on monos and long moves. 50' *FA Todd Skinner, 1997*

● **5** ☐ **When I Was a Young Girl, I Had Me a Cowboy 13a ★★**
Up the center of the steep left wall of the Erratic with many possible sequences. 45' *FA Amy Skinner, 1995*

● **6** ☐ **County Ten Gunslinger 12c ★**
A shorter, bouldery line on the very left side of the Erratic. Established in the summer of 2013 by Jonathan Siegrist between efforts at repeating Moonshine. 40'
FA Jonathan Siegrist, 2013

Kat Butler **WHEN I WAS A YOUNG GIRL** 13a

●13 ☐ Pocket Hero 10a ★★
This climb starts in a seam on a grey slab, then moves up a nice clean wall with big pockets. *FA Lisa Horst, 2014*

●14 ☐ Pale Face Magic 10d ★
Climb up a right facing corner then out right and up a tricky face above. 55' *FA Steve Scott, 1992*

●15 ☐ Swallow the Gravy 10d ★
is a vertical face with several horizontals, approximately 15 feet left of Pale Face Magic.
FA Sam and Liz LIghtner, 2014

●16 ☐ I'm a Lead Farmer, Motha' F*&^er 11b ★★
Steep rock trending right. starts behind a pine tree and climbs up and left to a flake feature.
FA Sam and Liz Lightner, 2014

●17 ☐ Medicine Man 11c ★★
Down around corner from Pale Face Magic, climb up the dihedral, then out a bulging wall to right. 50'
FA Steve Scott, 1991

●18 ☐ Alpen Thunder 11d ★★
Straight up version of Medicine Man.
FA Sam Lightner, 2014

●19 ☐ Hold My Beer... Watch This 11d
A bit of a party trick. Arete, to big roof, to arete. The taller you are, the harder it is.
FA Mandy Fabel, Sam Lightner, 2014

The following routes are about 150 feet left of Hold My Beer..., but are best approached by descending through the trees via the trail to the Remuda, then exiting right near the Motown bouldering area. The cliff base is talus and is difficult for small children and dogs.

●20 ☐ Queen of England 10d ★
This route climbs the very right side of the Rodeo Queen wall. Starts on a slabby, rounded prow, then passes several bulges. The climb was finished just after UK's "Brexit" vote. *FA Brian Fabel 2016*

●7 ☐ Wutang 11b ★
Just right of Wotai, has a slab crux low to cool moves above. Tricky. 45' *FA Unknown, 1990's*

●8 ☐ Wotai 10d ★★★
Start in crack, then move right onto a nice face with a small roof at the anchors. 45' *FA Melissa Quigley, 1992*

●9 ☐ Full Retard 11d
Just left of Wotai and up the right side of the arete through the roof. *FA Sam Lightner, Mike Lilygren, 2014*

●10 ☐ Whoa Nelly 11b ★
This climb is around left of Wotai, facing east. Up flakes and thin moves left of the prow. 45' *FA Jeff Wendt, 2002*

●11 ☐ Medicine Trail Relay 10b ★
This climb takes the right side of the east-facing slab 40 feet left of Whoa Nelly. *FA Taylor Spiegelberg 2017*

●12 ☐ Big Medicine 10b
Grey slab with thin moves, faces west on the next section of cliff left of Wotai. 55' *FA Steve Scott, 1991*

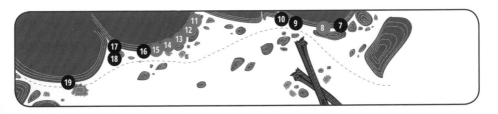

21 ☐ Booty Sweat 12b ★

This climb takes the long face right of Fat Bottom Girls. The climb is worth doing just to visit the world beefiest anchor. *FA Lightners, 2014*

22 ☐ Fat Bottom Girls 12d ★

A boulder problem leads to nice big holds up a clean face, then to a rest below the bulge. Pass the bulge on big moves (12b) and save some for the tricky top-out. *FA Jesse Brown, 2013*

23 ☐ ✎ Rodeo Queen 12b ★★

This climb follows the crack feature start of Out To Pasture past 4 bolts, then steps right to finish on Fat Bottom Girls. *FA Jesse Brown, 2013*

24 ☐ Out To Pasture 14b ★★

Climb the nice crack feature to a little bulge, then up to a good rest. From here, punch the center line through the roof aiming for a solitary pocket over the lip. BJ named this climb in honor of his retirement from new routing at Wild Iris. *FA BJ Tilden, 2017*

25 ☐ Queen of Hearts 12a ★★

Follows a seam feature up the face to a long move, and then out a relatively easy roof above. *FA Jesse Brown, 2013*

26 ☐ Blood Orange 12a ★

Thin climbing up a nice wall leads to an easier section before the roof. This is the leftmost route on this sector at this point and can be identified by large amounts of orange lichen on the rock. *FA Shadow Ayala, 2017*

photo Chris Beauchamp

QUEEN OF ENGLAND 10d

Jon Cardwell

DAVE **DOLL**

Although climbing in Lander "started" in the early 1990s, Dave Doll moved here to climb in 1975. Climbing with his wife Sara and various friends, Dave repeated many of the early Sinks Canyon climbs, as well as a large number of alpine routes in the Wind Rivers. He climbed a lot in the first few years in Lander, but as partners left Dave climbed less and less. In 1994, his interests were rekindled with the opening of Lander's first rock gym, The Gravity Club.

Dave became fast friends with Paul Piana, the gym's owner, and started climbing limestone with Paul and his wife Heidi.

In 1997, Doc decided to get on board with bolting limestone routes, and established Stud Alert, at Sinks Main Wall. He went on to add dozens of classics in the area, taking time to carefully pick out great lines whenever he could, always looking for routes that would "speak" to him. Climbing with Piana, Todd Skinner, Kirk Billings, and others, Dave has put in great lines at almost every crag in the area. After Paul moved away and Todd died, Dave stepped away from new routes for a few years. Starting in 2013, though, Doc was back at it, bolting and sending some of his hardest routes ever. "I've still got six to ten unclimbed lines to do," he confides...but he's not saying which ones they are.

The following four routes are located about halfway between Rodeo Queen and the Remuda along the cliffside trail. Although they were once rarely climbed, they have recently been rebolted and are getting good reviews.

● 27 ☐ The Ugly 11c
This climb takes a face left of an obvious seam through a small bulge. 40' *FA Jim Kanzler, 1992*

● 28 ☐ The Bad 11b
This is a clean face with good pockets. Trend left at the top. 40' *FA Jim Kanzler, 1992*

● 29 ☐ The Good 11c
Up a prow feature that gets steeper the higher you go. 40' *FA Jim Kanzler, 1992*

● 30 ☐ Angel Eyes 11b
Climb the prow between crack to the left of The Good. Angel Eyes was the nickname of "The Bad" character in The Good, The Bad, and The Ugly. 40' *FA Unknown, 2000's*

photo: Kyle Duba

NORTH COUNTRY

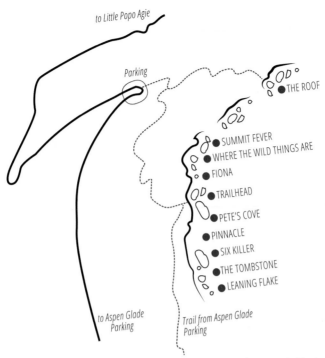

to Little Popo Agie

Parking

THE ROOF

SUMMIT FEVER
WHERE THE WILD THINGS ARE
FIONA
TRAILHEAD
PETE'S COVE
PINNACLE
SIX KILLER
THE TOMBSTONE
LEANING FLAKE

to Aspen Glade
Parking

Trail from Aspen Glade
Parking

Previous: Brian Fabel on All Manner of Wonderments
Photo: Kyle Duba

NORTH COUNTRY

The North Country sits on the northwest flank of Limestone Mountain. Although development began here in the early 1990s, the area has remained unpublished because of parking issues. The main drivers in developing this area were Kirk Billings, Todd Skinner, Dave Doll, and a few others. This area stays shady until early afternoon in the summer and is a good alternative to the Remuda for summer climbing. A note: The North Country is a small area, and if the switchback parking is full, chances are the crag will be quite crowded.

Approach: To reach the North Country, drive to Limestone Mountain Road from Lander (approximately 24 miles south on WY 28), and follow that road past the Wild Iris turnoff (bear left at the fork) and past the Aspen Glade parking area. You'll descend a west-facing hill until you reach a switchback. The parking is inside the switchback, and the trail to the crag starts on the outside of the turn. It is critical that you don't park along the road or on the outside of the switchback. If there are not spots to park at the switchback, there are more parking spots near the next switchback, about a half-mile down the road.

In summer 2018, the forest service plans to establish an approach trail from the Aspen Glade parking area. This will access the crag near the Tombstone, and will ba a slightly longer, but flat and quick approach to the crag. When this trail is established it will help address the parking issue at the switchback.

CLASSICS

Shark Wrestling (p.95)
Summit Fever (p.93)
Jack Attack (p.97)

R.U.N.N.O.F.T. (p.99)
Organized Climb (p.97)
Lying, Unconstant Succubus (p.95)

Perry the Wind (p.91)
We Thought you was a Toad(p.95)
Call Down the Thunder(p.102)

Hour of Death (p.99)
One Eyed Fiona (p.99)
Gunshow (p.91)

4

13

26

27

8

3

3pm-PM

15m-20m

THE **ROOF**

| 3pm-PM | 15m | Vertical | Roof |

0 1 2 5 1 1

This is the leftmost developed crag at the North Country. The wall's main feature is a 10-20 foot roof that is breached by 5 different routes. Most of the routes were established in the summer of 2003. This sector is best reached by splitting off the approach trail about 5 minutes from the car, and taking the long, leftward diagonal for another 10 minutes.

Routes are listed from left to right

●1 ☐ Project
Left side of roof This route might or might not ever get done. Marked by a solitary first bolt.

●2 ☐ Ten Percenter 12b ★
Up continuous 5.11 climbing then through a 10 foot roof on horizontal rails. *FA Steve Bechtel, 2003*

●3 ☐ Nothing But Sky 12d ★
Climb a vertical wall (11c) to a 12' roof.
FA Steve Bechtel, 2004

●4 ☐ Gun Show 13d ★
Takes the face just left of the corner/crack, then up through the roof to an exit crux. *FA BJ Tilden, 2012*

●5 ☐ Parry the Wind 12b ★★
If it is windy anywhere, it will be windy here. Climb up flakes along a seam, then move right and up a good prow to a rest below the roof. Move right and out the roof along the major rail system. *FA Kirk Billings, 2001*

●6 ☐ The Final Frontiero 12d ★★
Climb a difficult slab wall to a rest, then out the right side of the roof. Many climbers opt to start via Parry the Wind and move right just before the roof. *FA Todd Skinner, 2004*

●7 ☐ Planet Maybel 11d ★
The first route right of the roof. Tricky climbing on good pockets. *FA Steve Bechtel, 2003*

●8 ☐ Beta Can-Can 12a
Second route from the left on the wall right of the roof. Also tricky. *FA Steve Bechtel, 2003*

●9 ☐ The Egress 11d
Good climbing to a strange crux. *FA Steve Bechtel, 2003*

●10 ☐ Calistan 10d ★
This is the best route on the wall right of the roof.
FA Steve Bechtel, 2003

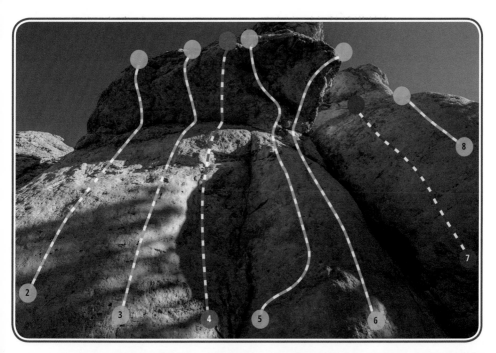

photo Kyle Duba

PARRY THE WIND 12c Travis Their

SUMMIT **FEVER**

3pm-PM | 15m | Vertical

(1)(2)(5)(4)(0)(0)

This is the leftmost end of the main area. It is about a five minute walk right of the roof.

Routes are listed from left to right

●**1** ☐ **Grizzly Bear Underwear 12d**
Difficult slab climbing up the middle of the face, right where the trail descends away from the cliff toward The Roof area. *FA Mike Anderson, 2013*

●**2** ☐ **All Loved Up 12a** ★
A thin crux leads to nice moves between good pockets above. *FA Steve Bechtel, 2010*

●**3** ☐ **Syrene Song 11b** ★★
Superb climbing through the low bulge, then up a nice wall to top. *FA Paul Piana, 2002*

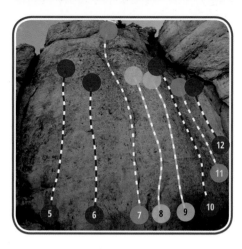

○**4** ☐ **Summit Fever 9** ★★
A popular face that ends near the "summit" prow.
FA Dave Doll, 2000

●**5** ☐ **Hoosier Sooner 11c**
This climb is the leftmost on the less-than-vertical wall between Summit Fever and the bulging roof of All Manner of Wonderments. Start near a tree stump.
FA John Hennings, 2004

●**6** ☐ **Hoosier Right 11d** ★
Climb the face right of the tree stump.
FA John Hennings, 2005

●**7** ☐ **Tree Hugger 10d** ★
This climb takes the crack feature up the center of the face, climbing past two small pines. 80'
FA Long-Haired Jim, 2005

●**8** ☐ **The Raptor Sanction 12a**
A steep start leads to thin moves up high. 60'
FA John Hennings, 2004

●**9** ☐ **The Lawn Dart 12c** ★
Clean climbing on thin pockets. 60' *FA John Hennings, 2004*

●**10** ☐ **Fireballs of the Eucharist 11b** ★
This is the last long route on the wall. 60'
FA Jamie Axelrod, 2002

●**11** ☐ **The Lillies of the Goddamned Field 10d** ★
A shorter slab route with cool pockets.
FA Todd Skinner, 2005

●**12** ☐ **Mr. MooDoo 11d**
A technical prow/face just left of the big corner/chimney.
FA Mr. MooDoo, 2004

WHERE THE **WILD** THINGS ARE

| 3pm-PM | 15m | Vertical | Slight |

0 **1** **3** **1** **1** **0**

Routes are listed from left to right

●**1** ☐ **All Manner of Wonderments 11d** ★★
Superb climbing up an arête then through bulges to an anchor above the horizontal. *FA Paul Piana, 2004*

●**2** ☐ **Span of Constant Sorrow 14a** ★
Climb a right-facing arete (actually the left side of the "Wild Things" crack) then through a 5.12 bulge. Move up and left then through a hard bulge, then through the bigger, less-featured bulge guarding the anchors. The name says it all. *FA Zack Rudy, 2013*

●**3** ☐ **Angry Birds 12a** ★
Shares the start with Span of Constant Sorrow, then moves right and up into a small corner.
FA Todd Skinner, 2004

●**4** ☐ **Where the Wild Things Are 10b** ★★
Climb a hand/fist crack starting in a small dihedral.
FA Kirk Billings, 1999

●**5** ☐ **Devils in Baggy Pants 11b** ★
This is the center of the long, clean face right of the crack.
FA Kirk Billings, 2000

●**6** ☐ **Remember the Captain 11c** ★
A bit squeezed, this is a sustained route just right of the prow. *FA Dave Doll, 2013*

FIONA **WALL**

| 3pm-PM | 15m | Vertical |

1 **1** **3** **5** **1** **0**

This is the clean, just-past-vertical wall around the corner from Where the Wild Things Are. These are high-quality routes and are very popular.

Routes are listed from left to right

●**1** ☐ **Man of Constant Sorrow 11d** ★
The prow route, starts with shallow monos, then finished up a cool rib at the top. *FA Todd Skinner, 2002*

●**2** ☐ **We Thought You Was A Toad 12b** ★★
Starts at two "mouth-shaped" jugs, then up and left on sustained terrain. *FA Todd Skinner, 2002*

●**3** ☐ **Ramblin' Bob 12d** ★★
A harder version of We Thought You Was a Toad, big moves on thin pockets. *FA Todd Skinner, 2002*

●**4** ☐ **One-Eyed Fiona 13a** ★★
The first route established on this wall, this is a technical and demanding climb up the center of the wall.
FA Kirk Billings, 2002

●**5** ☐ **Wicked Felina 12a** ★★
This climb starts on thin pockets just left of the Succubus corner. A low crux leads to sustained good pocket climbing. Stepping right for the first couple of bolts is possible and drops the grade to 11d. *FA Paul Piana, 2002*

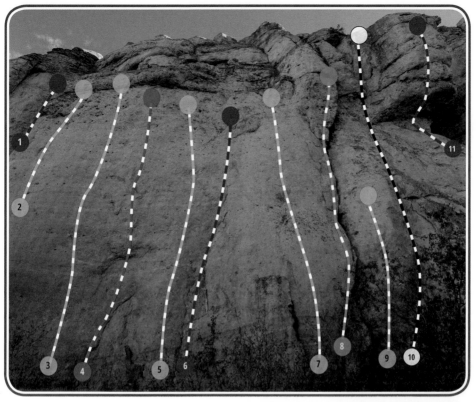

●6 ☐ Lying, Unconstant Succubus 11a ★★
This nice climb takes a corner/crack system to a pocketed headwall. *FA Paul Piana, 2003*

●7 ☐ Soggy Bottom 12a
This is the clean, low-angled face to the left of the wide Pappy O'Daniel crack. *FA Paul Piana, 2002*

●8 ☐ Pappy O'Daniel 10b ★
Climb along, and sometimes in, a wide crack, then exit up an overhanging prow to the left at the top.
FA Steve Bechtel, 2008

●9 ☐ Do Not Seek the Treasure 12d
Very hard moves on a rounded wall. *FA Todd Skinner, 2004*

○10 ☐ Shark Wrestling 9 ★
Climb up a crack system that has a "shark fin" flake near the start, then up a dihedral at top. *FA Dave Doll, 2002*

●11 ☐ Sack Full of Hammers 11c ★★
Move up a low angle arête (5.7) to rings, then through a square-cut roof and up a vertical headwall.
FA Paul Piana, 2002

photo Kyle Duba

MAN OF CONSTANT SORROW 11d Ryan Morris-Brady

TRAILHEAD **WALL**

| 3pm-PM | 15m | Vertical |

(1) (4) (4) (2) (0) (0)

This is the wall where the trail from the switchback parking area meets the cliff.

Routes are listed from left to right

● **1** ☐ **I Don't Want Fop, God Dammit 11c** ★★
The left route on the face, this climb features long moves between generally good pockets. *FA Paul Piana, 2002*

● **2** ☐ **Dapper Dan Man 12b** ★★
Start in underclings and flakes, then move left and up. *FA Paul Piana, 2002*

● **3** ☐ **Organized Climb 11d** ★★
Starts same as Dapper Dan Man, then moves right at bolt 3. *FA John Hennings, 2005*

● **4** ☐ **The Knife Fighter 12a** ★
Starts up the crack then straight up where crack goes right. Little pockets. *FA Kirk Billings, 2001*

● **5** ☐ **Domestic Disturbance 10a** ★★
Climb the right-facing crack then undercling up and right to anchors. *FA Mike Lilygren, 2002*

● **6** ☐ **Lots of Respectable People Have Been Hit by Trains 11d**
Up the low-angle prow right of Domestic Disturbance. *FA Todd Skinner, 2003*

● **7** ☐ **Anybody Care Fer a Gopher? 10b**
Up a chimney, then a rounded prow. *FA Dave Doll, 2003*

● **8** ☐ **Jack Attack 10b** ★★
This route takes the left side of the clean slab. *FA Brandon Walkinshaw, 2011*

● **9** ☐ **Kill it, Skin it, Wear it 10a** ★★
This is the center clean slab. *FA Ben Elzay, 2011*

○ **10** ☐ **Unknown 9** ★
The right slab route. *FA Brandon Walkinshaw, 2012*

● **11** ☐ **The Dumbest Smart Person I Know 11b**
100' right of the previous climbs. Up asteeper, short wall on big moves. *FA John Hennings, 2004*

PETE'S **COVE**

3pm-PM	15m	Vertical

0 2 3 4 0 0

Routes are listed from left to right

●1 ☐ **Coatimundi Left 10c ★★**
Great route, just right of the corner. *John Hennings, 2004*

●2 ☐ **Coatimundi Center 10b ★★**
Super climbing on big holds...after the first move.
FA John Hennings, 2004

●3 ☐ **Coatimundi Right 11b ★★**
A hard slab move start leads through a bulge on long
pulls. *FA John Hennings, 2004*

●4 ☐ **Hogwallop 11a ★**
Follow a crack feature with 5 bolts. *FA Steve Bechtel, 2011*

●5 ☐ **This Here's Pete 11d ★★**
This overhanging clean wall was the first one at the North
Country. *FA Pete Delannoy, 1992*

●6 ☐ **Cow Killer 12c**
This is the leftmost climb on the large trophy-shaped wall
left of the pinnacle. *FA Paul Piana, 2004*

●7 ☐ **Mixaphorically Speaking 12b ★★**
Super climbing up a flake and crack feature to a steep
headwall with exit crux. *FA Paul Piana, 2004*

●8 ☐ **Singin' Into a Can 12b ★**
Follow the face left of an orange-lichened crack, then
work up a double bulge above. *FA Paul Piana, 2004*

●9 ☐ **Odyssey and Oracle 12b ★★**
Splits right off Singin' into a Can at half height.
FA Steve Bechtel, 2014

PINNACLE **AREA**

3pm-PM	15m	Vertical

0 2 4 1 0 0

Routes are listed from left to right

●1 ☐ **Triumph of the Subjective 11b ★★**
This climb takes a corner to a bulge, then up the wall
above right of the pinnacle. *FA Todd Skinner, 2003*

●2 ☐ **We're in a Tight Spot 10c ★**
The left of two routes in the gap between the pinnacle
and the main wall. *FA Todd Skinner, 2004*

●3 ☐ **Damn, We're in a Tight Spot 10c** ★
The right route. *FA Todd Skinner, 2004*

●4 ☐ **Banished From Woolsworth 11b** ★★
Arête on the left side of the small pinnacle.
FA Todd Skinner, 2004

●5 ☐ **Beat Up By a Bible Salesman 12c**
This is the clean, gently overhanging face right of Banished From Woolsworth. *FA Todd Skinner, 2004*

●6 ☐ **R-U-N-N-O-F-T 11c** ★★
A slightly overhanging wall with monos and edge.
FA Todd Skinner, 2004

●7 ☐ **Bonafide 11b** ★
The west-facing low-angled route on the pinnacle.
FA Amy Skinner, 2004

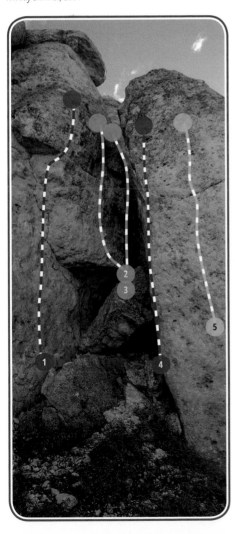

SIX KILLER

| 3pm-PM | 15m | Vertical |

(0) (0) (0) (4) (2) (0)

This is a clean section of wall 100 yards right of the pinnacle. These clean routes have not seen much action, mostly because they are isolated from the main climbing areas.

Routes are listed from left to right

●1 ☐ **Sixkiller 12a** ★
This climb is on the lower-angled left margin of the wall.
FA Todd Skinner, 2003

●2 ☐ **Day of Rage 12a**
The first of the longer routes. *FA Todd Skinner 2003*

●3 ☐ **Eight Hours to Die 12d** ★
FA Todd Skinner, 2004

●4 ☐ **Hour of Death 13a** ★
FA Todd Skinner, 2004

●5 ☐ **Blood for Blood 13a**
FA Todd Skinner, 2004

●6 ☐ **Dead Man Walking 12b** ★
This takes the right arete on the wall.
FA Todd Skinner, 2003

photo Ben Crawford

WE THOUGHT YOU WAS A TOAD 12b

Max Owens

THE **TOMBSTONE**

| 3pm-PM | 15m | Vertical |

0 0 2 2 1 2

The Tombstone is about 5 minutes further south/right from the Sixkiller Wall. It is a tall, clean piece of stone with a terrifying "tombstone" sitting on the ledge atop Call Down the Thunder. Most of the route names here come from the movie "Tombstone."

Routes are listed from left to right

●1 ☐ **Skin That Smokewagon 11d** ★★
This climb takes a nice clean wall with good pockets.
FA Paul Piana, 2003

●2 ☐ **I'm Your Huckleberry 12c** ★★
A bouldery start leads to a bouldery midsection followed by a bouldery exit. *FA Paul Piana, 2003*

●3 ☐ **You're No Daisy 13b** ★
A Piana project, this clean and awkward route was sent about 10 years after Paul equipped it.
FA Mike Anderson, 2013

●4 ☐ **Project**
The bolt line right of You're No Daisy

●5 ☐ **Project**
the line left of Call Down The Thunder

●6 ☐ **Call Down The Thunder 11d** ★★
Climb a corner to a nice wall above, then to an anchor below the bulge. *FA Todd Skinner, 2004*

●7 ☐ + **Call Down The Thunder 12c** ★★
Press on through the bulge above, then up the Tombstone proper. Unmatched for position
FA Todd Skinner, 2004

LEANING **FLAKE**

3pm-PM | 15m | Vertical | Slight

1 | 0 | 2 | 1 | 2 | 0

This area is up and right of the Tombstone.

Routes are listed from left to right

● **1 ☐ Don't Forsake Me 11b**
Climb a blank white face. Still a bit sharp.
FA John Hennings, 2005

● **2 ☐ + Don't Forsake Me 12a**
Climb out the slightly harder double bulge. Still a bit sharp. *FA John Hennings, 2005*

● **3 ☐ Norm is a Good Man 11c**
Not a great climb. *FA John Hennings, 2005*

● **4 ☐ Abby Normal 13a**
The face right of Norm Is A Good Man.
FA Mike Anderson, 2013

● **5 ☐ Non-Partisan Anti-Chinese League 13b**
A superhard bulge leads to clean climbing above.
FA Todd Skinner 2004

○ **5 ☐ The Far Country 9**
This is the short, clean face 50 feet right of Non-Partisan Anti-Chinese League. *FA John Hennings, 2005*

TODD **SKINNER**

Todd Skinner is a man that needs little introduction. Often seen as the father of modern climbing in Lander, Todd was a major player in the growth of difficult rock climbing worldwide throughout the 1980s and 1990s. One of the first full-time climbers, he traveled the world looking for the ultimate "home base" from which to launch expeditions. His criteria included powerful climbing and unexplored rock... and Lander fit the bill perfectly. Starting in 1990, Todd and his wife Amy moved to Lander and began exploration of the local crags.

Todd extablished the first climb at the Wild Iris Main Wall, and went on to extablish more climbs in the area than any other person.

Hugely focused on building a strong community of climbers, Todd helped to start Wild Iris Mountain Sports and establish the International Climbers' Festival. He was constantly inviting climbers to stay in his home and was alawys the first to loan gear, books and even vehicles to others in the name of exploration.

Although Todd is best known as a pioneer in exploring the big walls of the world, he was a talented and driven rock climber who was almost perfectly adapted to the fingery and powerful climbing at the Wild Iris. Todd's legacy in Lander climbing lives on in other climbers' willingness to lend a hand, to try just that little bit harder, and to alawys walk around the next corner to see if even more climbing awaits.

LITTLE POPO AGIE

photo: Caroline Treadway

FREAK MOUNTAIN

STRAWBERRY ROAN

SWEAT LODGE

YOUNG MOUNT

Sweat Lodge, Ghost Town and Roan Parking

to North Country and highway

Previous: Tom Rangitsch on Romulus
Photo: Caroline Treadway

LITTLE POPOAGIE

Little Popo Agie is the next major river system south of Sinks Canyon, which holds the Middle Fork of the Popo Agie. The river drains out of the high Maxon Basin, and drops a few thousand feet over about five miles of rugged canyon. This beautiful and dolomite-filled canyon is not new on climbers' radar; in fact one of the first lines ever bolted in the area was The Strawberry Roan in 1990. Over the years, the canyon and surrounding area have received sporadic development, but the difficult access and the wide availability of other great climbing kept the area's visitors to a minimum.

Of the several areas described in this chapter, Wolf Point is both the hardest to access and the best known. Guarded by an hour's drive and a hike of close to the same duration, the cliff is one of the most futuristic in America. The rest of the canyon features more great climbing and easier access.

The sparsely developed Freak Mountain Wall and Strawberry Roan area will leave most climbers jawdropped at the potential. The Sweatlodge, with its brilliantly unlikely geometry will keep climbers in the cool shade every day until the end of time. On the north side of Young Mountain, across the canyon from the Wolf Point wall,

WOLF POINT

Little Popo Agie River

PO SHADY SIDE

Wolf Point, Shady Side Parking

OST TOWN

creek crossing

cattle guard

are the Ghost Town and the several sectors of the Little Po South Side wall. These north-facing crags include The Pup, Ben's Block, The Den, and more. These north-facing crags each feature just a handful of established climbs, but have potential to hold hundreds of routes each.

There is no arguing that climbing in the Little Popo Agie area is adventure sport climbing. You'll find hard approaches, very few tick marks, and rough roads to the crags. You'll also escape the crowds and touch some of the finest stone Lander has to offer.

CLASSICS

⎯

Young as the Morning(p.134)
Blood Moon(p.145)
Year of the Wolf (p.149)

━

Wild as you Want to Be (p.157)
Dominant Species(p.157)
Mystique (p.136)

━

Bark at the Moon (p.157)
Starscream(p.136)
Ghost in the Machine (p.118)

━

Strawberry Roan (p.113)
Ghost Dance (p.)124
Silver Bullet (p.137)

8

18

30

41

45

34

10-Night

15m-20m

Rattlers

photo: Adam Amick

STRAWBERRY ROAN

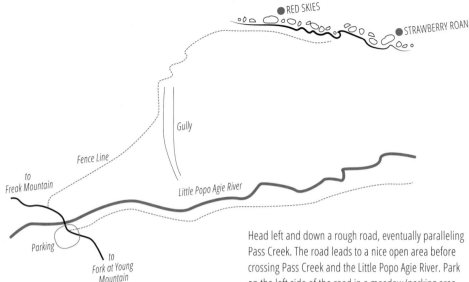

Previous: Leif Gasch on Strawberry Roan
Photo: Adam Amick

STRAWBERRY ROAN

This is the southernmost extension of Little Popo Agie Canyon, on the lower flanks of Freak Mountain's west side. The wall is easily identified from across Pass Creek Valley both because of its clean, steep walls and its red color. The first route bolted here is the famed Strawberry Roan, a long arete climb on the right margin of the wall. This crag sports only a few routes, but promises good potential. The season is difficult, though - access is limited in winter and spring, and the crag tends to be very hot in summer months.

Directions: To access it via Pass Creek, drive to Limestone Mountain Road from Lander (approximately 24 miles south on WY 28), and follow that road past the Wild Iris turnoff (bear left at the fork) and down into the Pass Creek valley. You'll descend some switchbacks, and go past a left hand turn into the Pass Creek cabins, a group of private summer homes. After winding down a hill, and past some gentle curves, you'll hit a fork in the road near the base of Young Mountain. If you were to go right, you'd head for Wolf Point and Wolf Pup.

Head left and down a rough road, eventually paralleling Pass Creek. The road leads to a nice open area before crossing Pass Creek and the Little Popo Agie River. Park on the left side of the road in a meadow/parking area before crossing Pass Creek.

Approach: From the parking area, cross the shallow Pass Creek, then walk another 100 yards to the Little Popo Agie River. This can be very high and swift early season, so use caution before mid-July. Wade the river where the 4WD road crossed, then break right from the road on the other side. Follow a fence line toward the cliff, then break right near a prominent gully, following faint trails to the wall above.

We have provided the information on this crag primarily because of the massive potential it represents. In the next few years there could be well over 100 good routes in this sector, and the wall goes on for more than a mile down river from the last established line. Along with Wolf Point, this wall represents the future of Lander development.

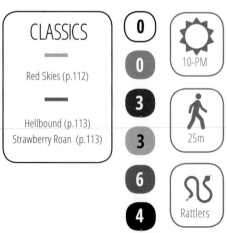

CLASSICS

―	
Red Skies (p.112)	
―	
Hellbound (p.113)	
Strawberry Roan (p.113)	

0
0
3
3
6
4

10-PM

25m

Rattlers

photo Ben Herndon

Inge Perkins · **STRAWBERRY ROAN** 13d

STRAWBERRY ROAN

10am-PM

25m

Slight

  3 6 4

Routes are listed from left to right

●1 □ **KP Route**

This climb is on the lefthand side of the crag about 100 feet right of the end of the cliff. Starting on some ledges, it takes a seam with a squarecut roof to the left of it at half height. As of this writing there are three bolts, a blank section, and then three more bolts to the anchor. 70' *Equipped Kyle Phillips*

●2 □ **Red Skies 12b ★★**

Around 250 feet right of the previous climb there is a large flake / slot against the wall that you can walk behind. About 30 feet right of this there is a small "Stonehenge" arch at the base of the wall. This climb takes the sweeping steep line above the arch, just right of a left-facing corner 70'. *FA Kyle Williams, 2006*

●3 □ **Red Dwarf 11c ★**

This climb is right of Red Skies and follows a streaked wall starting on thin flakes.. 60' *FA Rob Phares, 2015*

●4 □ **Inge's Route 13a**

This route still needs to be cleaned and properly bolted, but was redpointed in 2015. *FA Inge Perkins, 2015*

●5 □ **Pancho Villa 12b ★★**

This is the nice steep sweep of rock on the right end of the "Red Wall," about 125 yards left of the Strawberry Roan. *FA Rob Phares, 2015*

●6 □ **The Kybosh 14a ★★**

A hard boulder problem at the third bolt leads to moderated climbing in the middle and a mid 5.13 finish. *FA BJ Tilden, 2015*

●7 ☐ All the Pretty Horses (Closed Project)

Pretty line to the right of "The Kybosh" estimated to be 13d . *Equipped Tom Rangitsch*

●8 ☐ Hellbound 14a ★★★

One of the best in the area for the grade. 12+ climbing leads to the headwall. The top features powerful, technical, and unrelenting movement on great stone.
FA BJ Tilden, 2016

●9 ☐ No Country for Old Men 14a ★★

Starts on Blood Meridian and breaks left just below the headwall. Harder crux than Hellbound but less sustained. *FA BJ Tilden 2017*

●10 ☐ Blood Meridian 13d ★★

Climbs the groove just left of Strawberry Roan.
FA BJ Tilden, 2015

●11 ☐ The Strawberry Roan 13d ★★

One of the first routes bolted in the area, this climb received little attention for almost 20 years. The route takes the long right-facing arete on the right margin of the wall. *FA Leif Gasch, 2013*

●12 ☐ AS Route

This Unfinished line has anchors and a couple of bolts on the wall right of the Strawberry Roan.
Equipped Aaron Steele

●13 ☐ Red Heat 11d ★

This climb takes the left side of the left face on the "Red Prow", the next major feature down canyon from the Roan, about 150 yards 80'.
FA Scott Carson and (Salt Lake) Dave Anderson, 1994

●14 ☐ DC Route (Open Project)

This project takes the pink streak. *Equipped Dylan Connole*

●15 ☐ Criminal Mind 12b ★★

The next section of wall is a really clean slab with a waterfall running down it. This climb takes the face just left of the waterfall. Somewhat sporty at the top.60'
FA Dylan Connole, 2014

●16 ☐ Blue Diamond 11b ★

This climb takes the nice face just right of the waterfall, finishing below the overhang.60' *FA Dylan Connole, 2014*

photo: Ben Herndon

GHOST TOWN

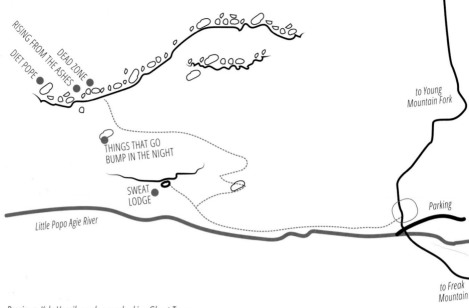

STRAWBERRY ROAN ●

Previous: Kyle Vassilopoulos overlooking Ghost Town
Photo: Ben Herndon

GHOST TOWN

Directions: To access the Ghost Town, drive to Limestone Mountain Road from Lander (approximately 24 miles south on WY 28), and follow that road past the Wild Iris turnoff (bear left at the fork) and down into the Pass Creek valley. You'll descend some switchbacks, and go past a left hand turn into the Pass Creek cabins, a group of private summer homes. After winding down a hill and past some gentle curves, you'll hit a fork in the road near the base of Young Mountain. If you were to go right, you'd head for Wolf Point and Wolf Pup.

Head left and down a rough road, eventually paralleling Pass Creek. The road leads to a nice open area before crossing Pass Creek and the Little Popo Agie River. Park on the left side of the road in a meadow area before crossing Pass Creek.

Approach: From the parking, cross the road and find a path near the small "Pass Creek" sign. Take this path down along the river for 5-10 minutes, moving down near the river in a meadow, then past a small marshy area onto a sidehill. Once on the sidehill, the trail is fairly well marked and easy to follow as it climbs toward the cliffband ahead. A couple of minutes up this part of the trail will afford you the first view of the Sweat Lodge entrance.

Just before reaching the cliffband right of the Sweat-lodge, you can switchback up an open meadow. You'll eventually end up on a nice, open bench. Follow this on downriver another 10-15 minutes, until the cliffband begins to turn the corner of the canyon. Just after the cliff turns to the north, you'll reach the first of the established routes, near a large slot/cave that blows cool air most of the summer.

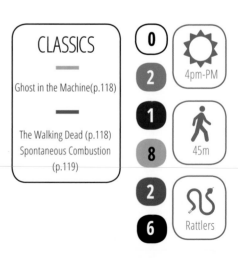

CLASSICS

—
Ghost in the Machine (p.118)

▬
The Walking Dead (p.118)
Spontaneous Combustion (p.119)

0		4pm-PM
2		
1		45m
8		
2		Rattlers
6		

EX MACHINA 10c

photo Ben Herndon

Inge Perkins

GHOST **TOWN**

| 10am-PM | 45m | Slight |

0 2 1 8 2 6

The first route described is on the freestanding boulder below the main crag.

Routes are listed from left to right

● 1 ☐ **Things That Go Bump in the Night (Closed)**
Equipped by Tom Rangitsch

DEAD ZONE

● 2 ☐ **Ex Machina 10c**
A "weird" route on the right margin of the wall. Shares anchors with Ghost in the Machine. *FA Todd Skinner, 2003*

● 3 ☐ **Ghost in the Machine 12c ★★★**
The arete feature. *FA Todd Skinner, 2003*

● 4 ☐ **Dead Man's Party 12b ★★**
The next route left of Ghost in the Machine.
FA Tom Rangistch, 2015

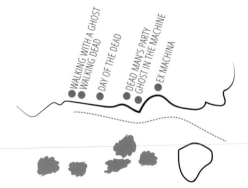

● 5 ☐ **Day of the Dead (Closed Project)**
Difficult direct start to the Walking Dead.
Equipped Todd Skinner

● 6 ☐ 🔗 **The Walking Dead 13c ★★★**
Link from Walking With a Ghost to Day of the Dead. Comes in from the left traversing after bolt 4 to get to the fourth bolt on the next route, has one bolt in the traverse. *FA BJ Tilden, 2015*

● 7 ☐ **Walking with a Ghost 12b ★**
Equipped by Kirk Billings, follows a crack.
FA Alex Honnold, 2014

RISING FROM THE ASHES

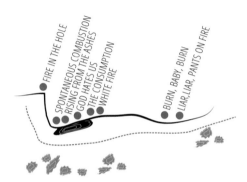

● 8 ☐ **Liar, Liar, Pants on Fire 11c ★**
Was supposed to be a warm-up. It is not. A tricky intro leads to sequential moves up high. *FA Tom Rangistch, 2017*

● 9 ☐ **Burn, Baby, Burn 12a ★★**
This climb has a low crux, then fun pockets up high.
FA Tom Rangitsch, 2017

● 10 ☐ **White Fire (Closed Project)**
Equipped Tom Rangitsch

● 11 ☐ **The Consumption (Closed Project)**
The tall line right of Skinner's God Hates Us.
Equipped Tom Rangistch

● 12 ☐ **God Hates Us (Open Project)**
On his first recon of this wall, Todd Skinner turned the corner and saw the long, clean overhang and quipped, "God hates us." This was in reference to Todd's preference of short, powerful routes, versus this route's long, continuous overhanging nature. *Equipped Todd Skinner 2003*

● **13** ☐ **Rising From the Ashes (Closed Project)**
Rising From the Ashes Has been wet the last few seasons.
Equipped Tom Rangitsch

● **14** ☐ **Spontaneous Combustion 13d** ★★★
The Awesome arete line. *FA Tom Rangitsch, 2016*

● **15** ☐ **Fire in the Hole 12d** ★
A bit of the new route sandiness, but a good climb.
FA Tom Rangitsch, 2016

DIET POPE

● **16** ☐ **Todd's 12a** ★★ This climb takes a line of
pockets on the right side of a clean, vertical wall. 50'
FA Todd Skinner, 2002

● **17** ☐ **Diet Pope 12c** ★
This climb takes the grey streak right of Buffalo Pillow.
Climb on sculpted holds, through a small overhang. 60'
FA Steve Bechtel, 2003

● **18** ☐ **Buffalo Pillow 12a** ★★
Climb a vertical wall to a horizontal break at about 20
feet, then up nice pockets on the gently overhanging wall
above. 60' *FA Steve Bechtel, 2002*

● **19** ☐ **Hellbent for Heather 10b** ★★
This climb takes huecos and big pockets up a nice wall
just right of a large gully. 40' *FA Kirk Billings, 2003*

TOM **RANGISTCH**

Somehow, Tom Rangitsch went from young buck to old guard. A native of Kemmerer, Wyoming, Tom has been climbing in Lander since the early 1990s. What started out as weekend trips from Laramie during college turned into summers in Lander, to full time residence after completing medical school.

An excellent all-around climber, Tom has continued to progress through the grades throughout his 20+ years climbing. From an early age, though, Tom felt the need to contribute to the climbing in the area. His first full summer in Lander was 1994, when Baldwin Creek's main wall was first being developed. It was there he bolted his first-ever route, Beelzebubba.

Over the next several years, Tom was in and out of Lander and made repeats of myriad classics as well as adding new routes of his own at many areas. To date, he has equipped more than fifty routes in the area.

After Tom's good friend Todd Skinner died in 2006, Tom thought a lot about what he wanted out of the sport and decided that Todd's dedication to exploration and pushing his limits were great qualities to emulate. He began exploring in earnest and opened dozens of new routes in addition to discovering whole new crags. Areas such as The Sanctuary in Sinks Canyon, The Sweat Lodge in LIttle Popo Agie Canyon, and Masada in the Sweetwater ROcks might still be largely undiscovered if not for Tom's pioneering spirit.

Tom's proudest contribution to new routes is his line Romulus (13c) at Wolf Point, which is saying a lot... Tom has many three star classics to his name. His favorite Lander area route is Pretty Hate Machine, at Sinks, because "It was really hard for me and took a long time to do. I learned a lot about tenacity and not giving up and trying really hard to accomplish something that at first felt impossible."

These days, TOm still works hard at opening new routes. His latest drive is getting others excited to revisit the Ghost Town wall, which suffered damage from a fire soon after development began there. Tom thinks this will be Lander's best summer area. He lives in lander with his wife Teresa and sons Taran and Pablo.

SWEAT LODGE

photo Kyle Duba **TRAIL OF TEARS** Tom Rangistch

Previous: Kris Hampton on Ghost Dance
Photo: Becca Skinner

SWEAT LODGE

The Sweat Lodge is one of the most unique cragging experiences you'll have. For years, climbers walked by the opening to this cave/flake crag in search of crags without ever looking inside. In 2009, Tom Rangitsch decided to have a look. What he found was a wildly overhanging crag with 50-70 foot long routes that never, ever see the sun. The crag is formed by a huge flake of rock that has fallen against the main cliff, forming the ultimate weather and sun shelter.

Directions: To access the crag, drive to Limestone Mountain Road from Lander (approximately 24 miles south on WY 28), and follow that road past the Wild Iris turnoff (bear left at the fork) and down into the Pass Creek valley. You'll descend some switchbacks, and go past a left hand turn into the Pass Creek cabins, a group of private summer homes. After winding down a hill and past some gentle curves, you'll hit a fork in the road near the base of Young Mountain. If you were to go right, you'd head for Wolf Point and Wolf Pup.

Approach: Head left and down a rough road, eventually paralleling Pass Creek. The road leads to a nice open area before crossing Pass Creek and the Little Popo Agie River. Park on the left side of the road in a meadow area before crossing Pass Creek.

From the parking, cross the road and find a path near the small "Pass Creek" sign. Take this path down along the river for 5-10 minutes, moving down near the river in a meadow, then past a small marshy area onto a sidehill. Once on the sidehill, the trail is fairly well marked and easy to follow as it climbs toward the cliffband ahead. A couple of minutes up this part of the trail will afford you the first view of the Sweat Lodge entrance. Follow the trail up to the cave, and then scramble inside to access the routes.

Because of the steep and loose nature of the entrance to this area, it's probably not a good choice for small children or dogs.

CLASSICS

—	**0**
Skinwalker (p.124)	**2**
Peace Pipe (p.127)	**5**
Whiskey Drunk (p.124)	**5**
—	
Plastic Shaman (p.124)	**9**
Ghost Dance (p.124)	**1**

4pm-PM

45m

Rattlers

SWEAT **LODGE**

10am-PM	30m	Slight

0 2 5 5 9 1

Routes are listed counter clockwise

●1 ☐ **Sundance 10b** ★
This climb starts in the gully below the entrance scramble to the main cave. Take a vertical face to anchors just below the start of Skinwalker. You can easily combine the two pitches, though there is no change in grade. 40'
FA Luke Bertelsen, 2014

●2 ☐ **Skinwalker 11d** ★★
This climb steps off the blocks just above the cave's entrance, and moves left along a small ledge / shelf. Clip the first bolt of Whiskey Drunk. After about 10 feet of traversing, move up the very steep arete above. Move left and up the vertical wall above to finish. 50'
FA Tom Rangitsch, 2012

●3 ☐ **Whiskey Drunk 12c** ★★★
This climb starts on the left margin of the wall, following big holds to a steep crack / lieback feature. Finish behind the big leaning block. 70' *FA Matt Wendling, 2010*

●4 ☐ **Manifest Destiny 12d** ★
This is the second straight up line from the left. Bouldery climbing through a small bulge to the lip of the overhang. Then a no hands rest, followed by a 12a move up the next bulge. 65' *FA Matt Wendling, 2010*

●5 ☐ **White Devil 13d** ★★
This climb is the third line from the left. Goes straight up to the lip of the bulge and then to a no hands stance. Do another boulder problem, then rest, and then finish with a third crux. 55' FA *BJ Tilden, 2013*

●6 ☐ **Ghost Dance 13c** ★★★
Same start as White Devil, but goes right through the steepest part of the bulge, hits the yellow sandy arete, then one more hard move to get back to the left set of anchors at the ledge. *FA Matt Wendling, 2010*

●7 ☐ **Training Wheels 13b** ★★
Starts on the steep undercut, then follows a very blunt arete on liebacks. Gets to a good shake, then joins Ghost Dance for the finish up the sandy arete.
FA Tom Rangitsch, 2010

●8 ☐ **Medicine Wheel 14a** ★★
This climb shares the same start as Training Wheel but go straight up after the good shake. Reaching right at the crux drops the grade to 13d. Move left at the top to share anchors with the previous two routes. 60'
FA Zack Rudy, 2013

●9 ☐ **Plastic Shaman 14a** ★★★
 Starts by a big hueco on the steep rock.Move up and left to a crappy rest at the big horizontal pocket band, then through an interesting sequence to get to the lip.
FA BJ Tilden, 2010

●10 ☐ **Fire Water (Impossiple Project)**
This is rightmost line of bolts on the steep side of the wall, leading to an anchor in the apex of the cave. "Maybe impossible" says BJ Tilden, who bolted it.

●11 **Trail of Tears 12c** ★★
 Shares the first 4 bolts of Fire Water, then traverses right to a crazy stemming exit out the cave. 50'
FA Tom Rangitsch, 2014

●12 ☐ ✎ **Fire Shaman 13d ★★**
Traverses the pocket band to link the bottom of Fire Water into Plastic Shaman. *FA BJ Tilden, 2010*

●13 ☐ ✎ **White Destiny 13a ★★**
Links White Devil into Manifest Density.
FA Matt Wendling, 2010

●14 ☐ ✎ **Medicine Shaman 13d ★**
Medicine Wheel into Plastic Shaman.
FA Kyle Vassilopoulos, 2014

●15 ☐ ✎ **Plastic Wheels 13c ★**
Plastic Shaman start into the Training Wheel finish.
FA Chris Marley, 2013

●16 ☐ **Smallpox 11c**
This climb takes a short overhanging section to share anchors with Fire Water. 40' *FA Jesse Brown, 2010*

●17 ☐ **Cry Hollow 11b**
This climb trends left to join Smallpox at the top. 40'
FA Jesse Brown, 2010

●18 ☐ **Rocky Mountain Surprise 10a ★**
This climb takes the crack feature. 45' *FA Vance White, 2010*

●19 ☐ **Big Chief, Little Hat 12a ★**
This is a techy and fun route, but not a good warm-up for the steep stuff. 40' *FA Jesse Brown, 2010*

WHISKEY DRUNK 12c

photo Kyle Duba

Viviana Gomez

●20 □ **Peace Pipe 11a** ★★
This climb starts just left of the dihedral. Big moves on good holds make this the standard warm-up. 40'
FA BJ Tilden, 2010

●21 □ **Indian Giver 11d** ★
This climb takes the next crack right of the dihedral crack, then up onto the big chockstone above.
FA Jesse Brown, 2010

●22 □ **Sweating Bullets 12b** ★★
 Like several other routes in the Lander area, this route shares its name with another climb. This is the slab route on the outside of the cave on the south wall. Technical and good climbing, this is obviously not your typical Sweat Lodge route. 65' *FA Fritz Mercer, 2011*

LITTLE **SHADY**

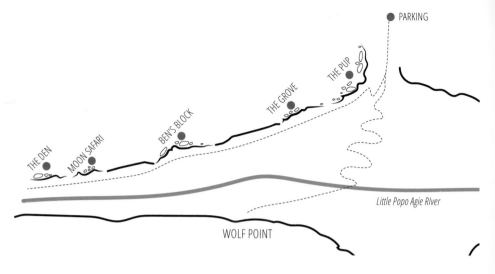

PARKING

THE PUP

THE GROVE

BEN'S BLOCK

MOON SAFARI

THE DEN

Little Popo Agie River

WOLF POINT

Previous: Darren Flack on Silver Bullet
Photo:Kyle Duba

LITTLE SHADY

Little Shady is the north facing crag that sits across the canyon from the Wolf Point Cliff. Unlike many crags in Lander this cliff catches shade until mid afternoon. The shady side has seen a lot of development in the last three years, and is now a full crag featuring a handful of moderate classics. The rock is a little frail due to the Pass Creek fire that ripped though the canyon in 2003, but the rock cleans up nicely. It features mostly vertical and slightly overhanging climbing.

Directions from Lander: Drive south on WY 28 approximately 24 miles to Limestone Mountain Road. Follow this road past the Wild Iris turnoff (bear left at the fork) and down into the Pass Creek valley. You'll descend some switchbacks, and go past a left hand turn into the Pass Creek cabins, a group of private summer homes. After winding down a hill and past some gentle curves, you'll hit a fork in the road near the base of Young Mountain. Bear right (east) and go around the flank of Young Mountain, first ascending, then descending into the next valley. Stay on the main road, crossing a small creek and then following forest service signs. PLEASE stay on designated roads due to marshy road conditions in the spring. After the road passes though the marsh section, you'll pass close to a group of trees on the left. Bear left

at a fork in the road here, skirting the trees until reaching a small parking area and campsite in the trees.

Approach: From the parking area, drop down toward the drainage, looking for a climbers' path that winds through the trees. You'll descend through aspen and some standing dead trees for about 5 minutes, right after crossing the drainage you will see are large cairn, and a faint trail that breaks right. Follow this trail all the way up to the Pup. Keep following this trail around the NW facing corner to an obvious trail that will take you all the way down to the Den.

CLASSICS

Old as the Sea (p.134)
Whoopee (p.131)

Heisenberg (p.136)
Blood Moon (p.145)
Vomit Comet (p.139)

Puppy Love (p.132)
New Kids on Ben's Block (p.136)
Mystique (p.136)

Fight Like a Brave (p.131)
Star Scream (p.136)
Stories Across the Sky (p.142)

Silver Bullet (p.137)
Celestial Mechanics (p.139)

8
10
15
13
5
13

3PM-Night

15m-35m

Rattlers

Rockfall

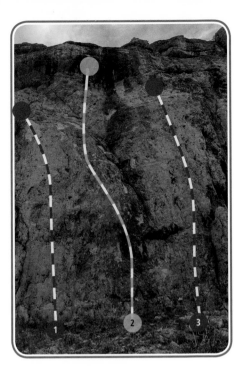

●3 ☐ Slither 11c ★

Climb a clean wall to anchors below the bulge. An extension (Slithering 5.11d) adds slightly to the difficulty.
FA Jeremy Rowan, 2013

○4 ☐ Elzay Route 8 ★

This climb is on the right side of the grey slabby wall. Climb the slab right of the major flake to anchors below an overhang. 45' *FA Ben Elzay, 2012*

○5 ☐ Whoopee 6 ★★

This climb takes the right side of the 2-piece large flake. 40' *FA Vance White, 2012*

●6 ☐ Yipee 10b ★

This climb starts in the small cleft left of the flake. Climb up nice pockets to the top of the slab. 55'
FA Brandon Walkinshaw, 2012

● 7 ☐ Fight Like a Brave 12c ★★

About 25 yards left of Yipee, there is a vertical wall with a huge overhang above. This climb takes easy terrain to the overhang, then traverses the rail system. A difficult route to clean the draws from. 90' *FA Vance White, 2013*

● 8 ☐ Lone Wolf 13a ★

This route takes the long black water streak 50 feet left of Fight Like A Brave. 100' *FA Vance White, 2014*

● 9 ☐ Cub Corner 10b ★

This climb is a left-facing corner with a crack in it. 50'
FA Vance White, 2013

THE **PUP**

3PM-Night | 10m | Rattlers | Vertical

(2) (4) (6) (2) (1) (0)

This is the first wall on your right as you enter the canyon. There is a trail that breaks to the right marked by a huge cairn. If you follow this trail up the hillside there will be a faint fork with a trail to the right that will lead up to routes 1-3, or if you continue left It will meet up with the wall at routes 7-13.

Routes are listed from right to left

●1 ☐ Jer Bear 11d ★

Starts off a "pillar" flake right where the approach trail meets the wall. Climb the clean wall skirting the upper wave on the right. 70' *FA Jeremy Rowan, 2013*

●2 ☐ Wolf Pack 12c

Just left of Jer Bear, starts near a left-trending flake system. Climb a vertical wall to a high crux bulge. 70'
FA Vance White, 2013

●10 ☐ ✛ Cub Cake 11c

This is the long extension of Cub Corner. Pulling the rope can be problematic. *FA Griffin Heydt, 2013*

●11 ☐ Puppy Love 11c ★★

Down the wall a bit from Cub Corner is a cool little buttress with two prominent aretes about 20 feet apart. The right one is slightly harder. 50' *FA Rob Phares, 2014*

●12 ☐ Puppy Chow 11b ★

This is the left arete. 50' *FA Vance White, 2014*

●13 ☐ Good Timin' Man 10d

Past the aretes, the trail drops down below a black slab. This route follows the right side of the slab. Above the vegetated ledge, move up and left along a flake. Higher, you'll move back right to finish. 70' *FA Vance White, 2013*

● 14 ☐ Good Hearted Woman 10b

About 20 feet left of Good Timin' Man. Follow the slab that ends left of the obvious high crack. 70'
FA Vance White, 2013

●15 ☐ Teardrops and Laughter 11b ★

Follow slab moves up to a "headwall" left of a crack.
FA Vance White, 2013

photo Kyle Duba

FIGHT LIKE A BRAVE 12c Vance White

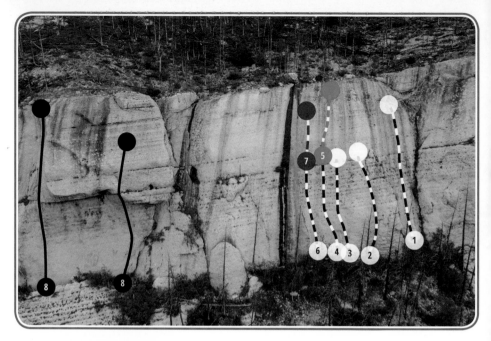

THE GROVE

| 3PM-Night | 15m | Rattlers | Vertical |

5 1 1 0 0 2

This crag is located right after the first fork in the trail. Take a right and follow the wall up to a large clean slab area. This wall is easy to spot due to the water streak that is almost always running.

Routes are listed from right to left.

○1 ☐ Who Dun It 9
This climb is the right-most route on the wall. It follows ovbious large pockets all the way to the top of the cliffband 75' *FA Ben Sears, 2017*

○2 ☐ Splintered Sunlight 7 ★★
Climb up just the the left of the "pillar" using side pulls, pockets, and jams. 60' *FA Ben Sears, 2017*

○3 ☐ North of Nowhere 9 ★
This climb takes the clean face just left of Splintered Sunlight. When rapping into bolt this climb somehow the knot tying Ben's Bosch to his harness came loose and the drill plumbited 50 feet onto the scree below. Luckily it was unharmed. 60' *FA Ben Sears, 2017*

○4 ☐ Old as the Sea 7 ★★
This route climbs up the shallow scoop to a very enjoyable jug filled head wall. 80' *FA Ben Sears, 2017*

●5 ☐ + Old as the Sea 10b ★
This is the airy 4B extention up clean rock. If you like slabs this is for you! 80' *FA Ben Sears, 2017*

○6 ☐ Young as the Morning 8 ★★
This climb follows a seam up to a very juggy pocket band. 75' *FA Ben Sears, 2017*

●7 ☐ + Young as the Morning 11d
This is the exciting/scary 2B extention that goes up through very small holds on the pretty slab above. 75' *FA Ben Sears, 2017*

●8 ☐ Carnage (Closed Project)
This route climbs through the wave-like feature on the egg shaped roof. Follow decent pockets up ever steepening terrain to an exciting move at the lip. This route is estimated to be around 12d. 60' *Equipped Ben Sears 2017*

●9 ☐ Vicious Vixen (Closed Project)
This unfinished route climbs up just left of the roof to a beautiful gold and grey headwall. When finished this route will be about 11c. 75' *Equipped Zack Rudy, 2016*

photo Kyle Duba

STARSCREAM 12a Alana Benson

BENS **BLOCK**

3PM-Night   20m   Rattlers   Vertical

0 2 5 5 2 2

Keep following the obvious trail for a few hundred yards until you see a large water streak. Routes 1-3 are accessed through a faint trail up before the large rock leaning against the wall and routes 4-7 are reached by a trail leading up to a small cave.

Routes are listed from right to left.

●1 ☐ New Kids on Ben's Block 11b ★★
Climb up through a sequential pocket crux and finish on easier terrain to the anchors. This is the right-most route on the wall. 65' *FA Tony Stark, 2016*

●2 ☐ Heisinberg 10c ★★
This climb starts off the small block leaning aginst the wall. Follow pockets and crimps up to an exciting finish. This is a great warmup for the area. 65' *FA Kyle Duba, 2016*

●3 ☐ Black Widow 11c
Climb just right of the leaning block up a consistent face to the anchors at 70'. *FA Ben Sears, 2016*

●4 ☐ Mystique 11d ★★
This climb starts under the leaning rock. It has a very thought provoking beginning with just enough holds, and is followed by a engaging headwall . 85'
FA Ben Sears, 2016

●5 ☐ Star Scream 12a ★★★
This climb follows the ovbious water streak up immaculate stone. It is one of the best 12a's in Lander! 100'
FA Ben Sears, 2016

● 6 ☐ King Pin (Open Project)
This climb starts just left of the water streak. It features a powerful opening into a reachy crux. It then climbs up clean stone to the top of the cliff. It is estimated to be around 13a. 95' *Equipped Ben Sears, 2016*

●7 ☐ Wreck it Ralph 11b
The climb starts up the right facing dihedral and climbs up the pretty grey stone above.70' *FA Ben Sears, 2016*

Keep hiking left about 200 yards to reach routes 8-16

●8 ☐ Explosive Vegetation 10c
Like its name, this route has relentless vegetation growing from the pods in the crack. When this route is weeded it is a great warmup for the area.
FA Ben Sears, 2016

●9 ☐ Plains Walker 11d ★
This climb features tricky pocket moves up a clean white face. 75' *FA Ben Sears, 2016*

10 ☐ Force of Nature 12b ★★

This route climbs up a seam to a ovbious large pocket. It is then followed by a gorgeous headwall. Make sure you are ready for some delicate moves at the top! 100'
FA Ben Sears, 2016

11 ☐ Psychic Venom 12a ★

This climb starts on a flake leaning aginst the wall. Climb up on tricky pockets to the top of the slab. 75'
FA Ben Sears, 2016

12 ☐ Howl from Beyond 12b ★

This climb follows the smaller of the two aretes in the area. It features relativly easy pocket climbing and has a stinger crux at the end. 75' *FA Ben Sears, 2016*

13 ☐ Golden Child 12b

This route follows good pockets up to a faint gold streak on the head wall. 75' *FA Vance White, 2016*

14 ☐ The Nature of It 13b ★★

This is the beautiful clean face that goes up to the right of the arete. It features delicate pockets and crimps. 110'
FA Inge Perkins, 2017

15 ☐ Silver Bullet 13a ★★★

This is the "king line" Tony ventured out here in 2015 to bolt this beast making it the first line to be put up down canyon from the Pup. Climb up into a exposed, picturesque relentless arete. 100' *FA Tony Stark 2016*

16 ☐ TS Route (Open Project)

Beautiful and Blank streaked wall. 55'
Equipped Tony Stark, 2016

photo Kyle Duba

MYSTIQUE 11d — Ana Junker

photo Kyle Duba

Tom Rangitsch **SILVER BULLET** 13a

● **2** ☐ **Vomit Comet 10d** ★★
This route climbs through multiple one and two finger pockets up to a fun headwall. 60' *FA Luke Lubchenco, 2016*

These routes are located about 50 yds to the climbers left.

● **3** ☐ **The Fifth Element (Open Project)**
This is a closed project that climbs up through pockets and crimps. This route goes around 13b. 60'
Equipped Tony Stark, 2016

● **4** ☐ **Star Dust 13a** ★
This route is identified by a faint grey streak. Climb through some technical pockets up to a large leftward lunge. 60' *FA Tony Stark, 2016*

● **5** ☐ **Celestial Mechanics 13b** ★★
Start off a large block and climb through a relentless v7 boulder problem on one and two finger pockets. 60'
FA Tony Stark, 2017

photo Kyle Duba **SNOT ROCKET** 10d — Luke Lubchenco

MOON **SAFARI**

 3PM-Night | 30m | Rattlers | Vertical

① ② ② ④ ② ②

Keep following the trail down about another 5-10 minitues from Bens Block until you reach routes 1 & 2. Routes 3-12 are located on the huge wall with a ramp going from the left to the right of it.

Routes are listed from right to left.

● **1** ☐ **Snot Rocket**
Unfinished route. Estimated around 11a. 80'
Equipped Ben Sears, 2016

Ben Sears **MOON SAFARI** 12c

photo Kyle Duba

6 ☐ Cats Under the Stars 11d ★
This route is located above a large rock. Climb up past a slab ramp into a very enjoyable jug-filled headwall. It is followed by a technical crux guarding the anchors. Lots of exposure! 105' *FA Ben Sears, 2016*

7 ☐ Stories Across the Sky 12b ★★
Climb up past the slab ramp into varied climbing using two finger pockets, crimps, and slopers. 80'
FA Ben Sears, 2016

8 ☐ Oasis in Space 12a ★
This climb starts at the left-most part of the ramp. It climbs up a series of bulges with good rests in between. It has an airy finish. 80' *FA Ben Sears, 2016*

9 ☐ Moon Safari 12c ★★★
This route is located just right of a huge flake leaning against the wall. Climb up through a technical bottom section to a good rest, then up into the steeper headwall with a pleasant surprise before the anchor. 100'
FA Ben Sears, 2016

10 ☐ Ground Control 11b ★★
This climb features technical climbing on crimps, and pockets up to the first anchor at the top of the flake. It has an excellent 5B extention that continues to the top of the cliff. 100' *FA Tony Stark, 2016*

11 ☐ + Major Tom 12b ★
This is an excellent 5B extention that continues to the top of the cliff. 100' *FA Tony Stark, 2016*

12 ☐ Galactic Debauchery 10a
This route starts just up the hill from Ground Control. It climbs up the grey slab. 70' *FA Luke Lubchenco, 2016*

Hike on an unmarked trail along the wall to a steep scree field. Halfway down you will find a route on your right. This route is about halfway between Moon Safari and The Den.

13 ☐ Outer Limits 8
This fun adventure climb takes you to the top of a large pillar-like feature. 80' *FA Luke Lubchenco, 2016*

BLOOD MOON 10d Ben Sears

photo Luke Lubchenco

THE DEN

3PM-Night | 45m | Rattlers | Vertical

0 1 1 2 0 7

Ironically this was the first part of the cliff developed, yet the furthest away form the parking. Jessie Brown and Ben Sears first rapped in from the top inbetween Moon Safari and the Den in late 2014. Developing momentum started, then died off quickly apparent by all the unfinished routes.This small crag has potential for quality routes in the future.

Routes are listed from right to left.

●1 ☐ **TS Route (Closed Project)**
This is the first route you approach on this wall. It climbs up a beautiful, sustained vertical wall. Estimated to go at 12+/13-. 60′ *Equipped Tony Stark 2015*

●2 ☐ **RP Route**
This is an unfinished route. 60′ *Equipped Rob Phares, 2015*

●3 ☐ **RP Route**
This route is unfinished. 60′ *Equipped Rob Phares, 2015*

● 4 ☐ **More Spunky than Funky** 11a ★
This route begins on the ovbious crack feature and climbs through multiple crimps, laybacks and jugs. 75′
FA Justin Loyka, 2015

●5 ☐ **BS Route (Open Project)**
This is the next pretty black streak that you approach on the wall. It climbs through small holds low up to a baffling crux up high. Estimated to be mid 5.12. 60′
Equipped Ben Sears, 2015

●6 ☐ **Blood Moon** 10d ★★
This excellent route follows the large right facing dihedral. Use pinches and laybacks to gain the ledge then run it to the anchors. 50′ *FA Ben Sears, 2015*

●7 ☐ **Cinder and Smoke** 12b ★
Start just in-front of a large flake on a black streak with orange hangers. Weave up through a thin difficult low section, to a very enjoyable headwall. 70′
FA Ben Sears, 2015

●8 ☐ **VW Route** 12a ★
Walk about a hundred feet the the left and this is the first route you come to. Climb up a slightly steep wall passing a few hard moves up to the chains. 60′
FA Vance White, 2017

●9 ☐ **VW Route**
Unfinished route up overhanging terrain. 65′
Equipped Vance White, 2015

●10 ☐ **JB Route**
Unfinished route up overhanging terrain.65′
Equipped Jessie Brown, 2015

●11 ☐ **JB Route**
Unfinished route up overhanging terrain. 65′
Equipped Jessie Brown, 2015

WOLF **POINT**

photo: Ben Herndon

ZACK'S ARETE
THE SEVENTH CONTINENT
WOLF POINT CAVE
TWICE AS LOUD AS REASON
TELEPATHIC WIENER MISSLE

WOLF POINT

Little Popo Agie River

*Trail Towards
Shady Side Walls*

SHADY SIDE

Parking

CLASSICS

0

2

Wild as you Want to Be
(p.157)
Seventh Continent (p149)
Dominant Species (p.157)

7

Natural Selection (p.149)
Dr. Green Thumb (p.157)
Bark at the Moon (p.157)

12

Lycanthrope(p.153)
Twice as Loud as Reason
(p.157)
Reemed Out (p.153)

24

9

11AM-4PM

60m

Rattlers

Rockfall

*Previous: Kyle Vassilopoulos on Bark at the Moon
Photo: Ben Herndon*

WOLF POINT

To access Wolf Point (as well as Wolf Pup), drive to Limestone Mountain Road from Lander (approximately 24 miles south on WY 28), and follow that road past the Wild Iris turnoff (bear left at the fork) and down into the Pass Creek valley. You'll descend some switchbacks, and go past a left hand turn into the Pass Creek cabins, a group of private summer homes. After winding down a hill and past some gentle curves, you'll hit a fork in the road near the base of Young Mountain. Bear right (east) and go around the flank of Young Mountain, first ascending, then descending into the next valley. Stay on the main road, bearing left at any forks, eventually dropping into a nice parking area / campsite in some trees at the top of a drainage.

Approach: From the parking area, drop down toward the drainage, looking for a climbers' path that winds through the trees. You'll descend through aspen and some standing dead trees, crossing the drainage after five minutes, and walking below the Wolf Pup cliff. The trail is easier to follow as you drop into the canyon. Switchback down to the river (15-20 minutes) and cross at the bridge / fixed rope. From here, you'll switchback up the hill and eventually gain a long east-trending trail that takes you toward the huge cave / amphitheater. One final set of switchbacks (it's about 15 minutes total from the river to the cave) leads you to the wall, near the "shared start" in the middle of the cave.

WOLF **POINT**

11AM-4PM | 60m | Rattlers | Steep

 0 **2** **7** **12** **24** **9**

Routes are listed from left to right.

● **1 ☐ Zack's Arete (Closed Project)**
This is the futuristic arete that's maybe 300 yards left of
the main sector of routes. It is clearly visible above the
approach trail on your way up from the river.

● **2 ☐ TS Route (Open Project)**
Takes the Mission Critical corner, then traverses left out
the undercling flake. *Equipped Todd Skinner*

● **3 ☐ Mission Critical 11c** ★
This route was bolted by Todd Skinner in 2005, during
his one visit to the wall. Starts in a left-facing corner just
past the highest point on the hill left of the main cave.
Climb the corner past five bolts, then turn the overhang
and continue up the wall above. 100'
FA Steve Bechtel, 2012

● **4 ☐ The Sick and the Weak 11c** ★
Black wall left of reintroduction. *FA Sam Lightner, 2014*

● **5 ☐ Reintroduction 10d** ★★
This is a nice climb that takes a vertical black wall starting
at the high point on the hill. 20 feet right of Mission
Critical. 90' *FA Sam Lightner, 2013*

● **6 ☐ Natural Selection 12a** ★★
Start on flakes and ledges, moving up a slightly overhang-
ing wall with hard to read sequences. 50'
FA Jonathan Siegrist, 2013

● **7 ☐ Brotherhood of the Wolf 12c** ★
Just right of Natural Selection, this climb is a technical
and devious line up a prow feature. 50'
FA Jonathan Siegrist, 2013

● **8 ☐ Year of the Wolf 10b** ★★
This is a right-facing corner system. The first route at the
cliff, this climb was bolted in order to access the top.
Climb the big corner on liebacks and jugs to anchors at a
ledge. The route continues to the top, but you should not
go up there...it sucks. 60' FA *Steve Bechtel, 2004*

● **9 ☐ The Seventh Continent 11b** ★★★
This route starts the big "tombstone" flake, then moves
right and up the vertical wall above. It breaks a 3-foot
roof at about 60 feet up. 90' *FA Steve Bechtel, 2004*

● **10 ☐ Thinning the Herd 12c**
Vertical climbing on thin holds to a bulging wall above.
15 feet right of The Seventh Continent. *FA Zack Rudy, 2012*

● **11 ☐ Eat What You Kill 12c** ★★
Nice climbing up a vertical to overhanging wall. Engaging.
90' *FA Kyle Vassilopoulos, 2012*

photo Kyle Duba

BJ Tilden **GOD OF WAR** 14c

12 ☐ Snake Shot 13b ★

A burly ramble up the bulging wall left of the cave.
FA Jonathan Siegrist, 2013

13 ☐ The Lycanthrope 13a ★★★

A long route with many hard sections. Stays on your right
to the end. 100' FA Tom Rangitsch, 2012

14 ☐ Talk is Cheap & Money Buys Whiskey (P)

Equipped Kyle Vassolopolous

15 ☐ House of Sticks 12d ★★

A hard lower wall leads to a no hands rest on a flake
/ ledge, then up through a second bulge to anchors at
100'. FA Steve Bechtel, 2013

16 ☐ + House of Bricks 13b ★★

Continuing up the vertical and hard to read grey streak
above House of Bricks takes you to the top of the cliff for
a solid long route of 140'. FA Kyle Vassilopoulos, 2013

17 ☐ + House of Hell 13c ★★

Climb House of Sticks to the triple length perma draw,
then move right and finish on the unrelenting orange
headwall of Hell or Highwater. 140' Tilden 2014

18 ☐ Hell or Highwater 14c ★★

The line through the steep bulge right of House of Sticks.
FA BJ Tilden, 2016

19 ☐ Sheep Eye 14b ★★★

Very hard pocket moves up the steep wall left of the
"shared start" in the cave. Joins Remus at the rest, then
finishes the headwall. 100' FA BJ Tilden, 2014

---

*The next several routes all share a start in a crack feature.
There are two sets of bolts, on one the left of the crack and
one on the right. These allow two climbers to be on the routes
above at the same time. Obviously, climb the left set of bolts
if you are climbing left, the right set if you are climbing right.*

---

20 ☐ Remus 13b ★★

This climb takes the shared start, and goes straight up to
an underclling rest below a small roof. Move left, and up
the overhanging wall above, ending at an anchor at the
big band of pockets. 100' FA Tom Rangitsch, 2012

21 ☐ + Reemed Out 13c ★★★

The extension to Remus, this goes to the top of the cliff.
140' FA Jonathan Siegrist, 2013

22 ☐ Romulus 13c ★★★

Take the shared start, and follow Remus to the underclling rest. From here, move up and right, fighting through
the steep wall above to anchors at the big pocket band.
100' FA Tom Rangistch, 2013

23 ☐ + God of War 14c ★★★

This is the "king line" of the Wolf Point cave. Climb
Romulus to the 30m anchors, then continue up the black
streak above to the top of the cliff. 140' FA BJ Tilden 2017

24 ☐ Alpha Male 13d ★★★

This climb takes the shared start to the 4th bolt, then
moves up and right. After a couple more bolts, the routes
split again. Alpha Male goes left and through the big
belly, ending at the 100' mark, with anchors at the big
band of pockets. 100' FA Kyle Vassilopoulos, 2012

●25 ☐ + **Big Bad Wolf 14a** ★★★
The superb extension to Alpha Male. 140'
FA Kyle Vassilopoulos, 2014

●26 ☐ **The Beholder 13a** ★★
The first cave route, and the third route equipped at the crag. Shares the same start as Alpha Male, but continues to trend right where Alpha Male goes up. This route ends in a huge hueco. *FA BJ Tilden, 2012*

●27 ☐ + **Wolfsquatch 13c** ★★
Climb The Beholder to the hueco. Climb around the hueco to the left and continue to the top on sustained edges.

●28 ☐ + **Be Bolder 13b** ★★
Climb the Beholder to the hueco / anchor, then step right and finish on Stalk and Ambush adds a nice boulder problem. 110' *FA Kyle Vassilopoulos, 2014*

●29 ☐ **Stalk and Ambush 14c** ★★
Next line right of the shared start. Pull through a V11 boulder problem on the low bulge, then fight the pump to the upper crux. Continue to anchors that sit up and right of the large hueco. 100' *FA Jonathan Siegrist, 2013*

●30 ☐ **Okami (Closed Project)**
This line shares the start of Kill Em All, then moves left to tackle the steep wall right of Stalk and Ambush.
Equipped Kyle Vassilopoulos, 2014

●31 ☐ **Wolf it Down 14b** ★★
Starts on Okami then breaks left and finishes on Stalk and Ambush *FA BJ Tilden, 2014*

●32 ☐ **Kill Em All 14b** ★★
This climb begins about 50 feet right of the Stalk and Ambush start. Great climbing on pockets and edges
FA BJ Tilden, 2012

●33 ☐ **Spitting Venom 14c** ★
Start on Stalk and Ambush splitting left at half height.
FA Jonathan Seigrest, 2013

●34 ☐ **ZR Route (Closed Project)**
Bolts up the center of the cave *Equipped Zack Rudy, 2011*

●35 ☐ **BJ Route (Closed Project)**
Equipped BJ Tilden, 2011

●36 ☐ **BJ Route (Closed Project)**
Grey Streak. line just left of King Thing.
Equipped BJ Tilden, 2014

●37 ☐ **King Thing 14a** ★★
Sustained pocket pulling with a variety of beta
FA BJ Tilden, 2013

●38 ☐ **Gangbusters 13d** ★★
Great climbing with a perplexing and oddly difficult crux down low. *FA BJ Tilden, 2013*

●39 ☐ **TR Route (Closed Project)**
Equipped Tom Rangitsch

●40 ☐ **The Howling 11c**
This climb takes the chossy butt crack on the right margin of the cave. 80' *FA Vance White, 2011*

Sasha Digiulian **BARK AT THE MOON** 12c

photo Ben Herndon

BIG BAD WOLF 14a Kyle Vassilopoulos

●41 ☐ **Call of the Wild 12c ★★**
Shares the start of Bark at the Moon then moves left to tackle the steep grey wall. 100' *FA Tom Rangitsch, 2013*

●42 ☐ + **White Fang 13c ★★★**
Three bolt extension to Call of the Wild. probably adds a number grade. *FA Tom Rangitsch, 2018*

●43 ☐ **Bark at the Moon 12c ★★★**
The first line right of The Howling crack. Steepening wall with great movement. 100' *FA Tom Rangitsch, 2013*

●44 ☐ + **Full Moon Rising 13b ★★**
The extension to Bark at the Moon. Sustained crimping and gastons. 130' *FA Tom Rangitsch, 2013*

●45 ☐ **Fredo 12b ★**
The next line right of Bark at the Moon, look for a prow feature at bolts 3-4. Once this route gets cleaned, it will be great. "I know it was you Fredo. You broke my heart." 90'

●46 ☐ **Jah Wolf 12c ★**
Climbs the face / corner system right of Fredo for 30m. *FA Kyle Elmquist, 2015*

●47 ☐ **Dominant Species 11d ★★★**
This route takes a low-angle face to a great, steep and juggy headwall with a finishing crux. The best warm-up for the cave climbing. 90' *FA Zack Rudy, 2013*

●48 ☐ **Wild as You Want to Be 11a ★★★**
Takes the face right of Dominant Species.
FA BJ TIlden, 2014

●49 ☐ **Dr. Green Thumb 12a ★**
This climb is another 100 or so yards past Dominant Species, and takes a right-facing dihedral up to a nice bulging wall. 80' *FA Tony Stark, 2012*

●50 ☐ **99 Problems But a Jug Ain't One 11d ★★**
40 feet right of Dr. Green Thumb, this climb takes an un-likely looking line up a vertical wall, then breaks through the bulging wall above on fun moves. 80'
FA Zack Rudy, 2012

●51 ☐ **Laidback 12b ★**
This route climbs the seam feature near up the vertical wall near the left end of the big roof. The seam is the business, the bulges are 5.11. 90' *FA BJ Tilden, 2012*

●52 ☐ **Twice As Loud As Reason 13b ★★★**
One of the all-time classics, this route takes an ever-steepening wall up the outside wall of the dihedral/ roof. 80' *FA BJ Tilden, 2012*

●53 ☐ **Telepathic Wiener Missile 12c ★★**
About 50 yards beyond the roof, this climb and the next climb the lower-angled wall to the bulging wall above. Look for a large juniper tree near the base.
FA Brian Dunnohew, 2012

●54 ☐ **TL Route (Closed Project)**
Takes the wall right of Telepathic Wiener Missile.
Equipped Tim Long

FOSSIL **HILL**

photo: Kyle Duba

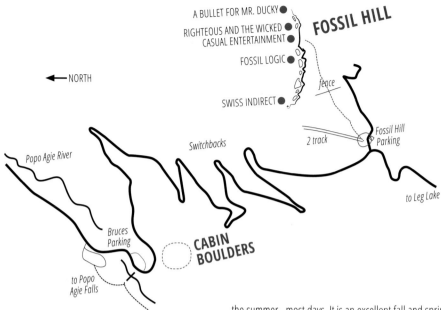

Previous: Zack Rudy on the send of Asian Orange
Photo: Kyle Duba

FOSSIL HILL

This wonderful crag sits on the high ridge south of Sinks Canyon. It is reached by driving from Lander, up Sinks Canyon past the Bruce's Parking Area (11.3 miles from downtown), and up the switchbacks until the first hill is crested (about 5 miles past Bruce's). At this point, the cliff will be visible to your left, and a left turn possible into a large parking area with a pit toilet. Park here. The climber's trail heads east of the 4WD scars on the hill above the parking lot, and is a faint footpath heading at an easy diagonal incline. Follow this trail past a barbed-wire fence, and eventually into forest below the cliff. The trail comes to the cliff at the climb "Two Ducks and an Angel".

Approach: Routes 1 to 5 might be best accessed by walking straight uphill from the parking area, as they are quite removed from the bulk of the climbs. Follow the 4WD scars toward the large prow of rock for these climbs. Fossil Hill is bighorn dolomite, but tends to have more edges than pockets. It also tends to be a little taller than most of the local cliffs. This cliff sits at a slightly higher elevation than the Sinks crags, and is slightly cooler in

the summer...most days. It is an excellent fall and spring crag; access depends on when the switchbacks are open for traffic. Typically, the road is open from Memorial Day until around Thanksgiving.

The first climbs at Fossil Hill were done in the summer of 1991 by Frank Dusl, Greg Collins, Hans Florine and friends. The first season here yielded nearly half the routes at the cliff. Over the following years, the "usual suspects" Todd Skinner, Dave Doll, Steve Bechtel, and Paul Piana added most of the remaining routes to this wonderful crag. Now boasting more than 50 climbs, this is a nice respite from the heat of Sinks Canyon and the endless pocket-pulling of Wild Iris.

CLASSICS

Two Ducks and
An Angel (p.166)
A Bullet for Mr. Ducky (p.169)

Merely Mortal(p.164)
Casual Entertainment (p.164)
Channel Zero (p.163)

Hang Fire(p.164)
Hips like Cinderella (p.164)

The Righteous
and the Wicked (p.167)

FOSSIL HILL

10AM-PM | **20m** | **Vertical**

(4) (8) (16) (22) (9) (12)

Routes are listed from left to right.

●1 ☐ Speed Goat 10c ★
This short route takes the overhanging wall on the south side of the detached block at the western prow of the cliff. 40' *FA Christian Gauderer, 2016*

●2 ☐ Fossil Reality (Closed Project)
This climb takes the prominent splitter through a horizontal roof, then up easier ground above.
Equipped Steve Bechtel

●3 ☐ The Swiss Indirect 11b ★
This route is at the prow of Fossil Hill, about 1/4 mile west of the main climbing. The climb tackles the right side of the nice west-facing arete. 70'
FA Dennis Vandenbos, 1998

●4 ☐ The Dutch Directissimo 10c ★
This climb follows the pocketed wall right of the Swiss Indirect. 70' *FA Dennis Vandenbos, 2000*

●5 ☐ Project (Closed Project)
Vertical face climb in the gully right of the Dutch Directissimo. *Equipped Ben Venter*

●6 ☐ Burly but Sensitive 12c
Start with powerful moves on sidepulls in the seam then break right to crimps and pull a long balancy move to get a pocket. FA Dylan Connole, 2014

●7 ☐ Milk Bone 13b ★★
This climb sits 250 feet left of Fossil Logic, on a short slightly overhanging wall. Follows hard pockets up a pretty orange face. 50' FA *Gary Wilmot, 1992*

●8 ☐ Project
This project is on the first big prow of the main Fossil cliffs, about 100 feet left of Fossil Logic.

●9 ☐ SB Route (Open Project)
The high bulge, anchors only. This is about 15 feet left of Fossil Logic. *Equipped Steve Bechtel*

●10 ☐ Fossil Logic 11c ★★
Start climbing up the big corner with a left-arcing crack. After about 50 feet of moderate climbing, move right and out the big wave on big holds. 70'
FA Heidi Badaracco, 2000

●11 ☐ Hell Bent for the Horizon 12d ★★
This long and unique climb takes the tall west-facing wall right of Fossil Logic. Technical face moves lead to bigger holds on a steeper wall above. 100' FA *Hans Florine, 1992*

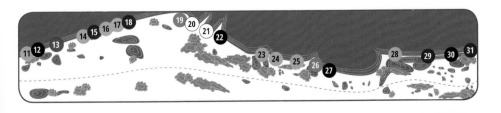

FULL NICKEL 11b   Hannah Dwyer

● **12 ☐ Sound of Silence (Open Project)**
The prow project. This route has been attempted for nearly 25 years. *Equipped Frank Dusl*

● **13 ☐ Tremors 13a ★★**
Tremors is just right of the prow. Hard long moves on crimps and monos. Named after the 90's sci-fi film. Household Chemicals, Graboids, and Hell Bent for the Horizon also were named from this film. 70'
Frank Dusl, 1992

● **14 ☐ Unforgiven 12d ★**
Continuously bouldery moves on some really thin holds. A bit sharp, but worth doing for the "mono match rest". 70' *FA Frank Dusl, 1991*

● **15 ☐ Channel Zero 11d ★★★**
This climb starts with a tricky boulder problem that is usually pretty chalked up. Above, you'll get to do enjoyable long moves up a pretty streak. 65'
FA Hassan Saab, 1992

● **16 ☐ Household Chemicals 12b**
A hard start on tricky moves leads to a beautiful upper wall. 70' *FA Andy Outis, 1992*

● **17 ☐ Graboids 12a ★**
Powerful moves low to a fun bulge above. The nice climbing through the bulge is a bit "engaging" but is not too hard. 70' *FA Hans Florine, 1992*

● **18 ☐ No Seats in Hell 11c ★★**
Continuous climbing on good moves leads to a baffling crux at the top. 70' *FA Dave Doll, 2000*

● **19 ☐ Furniture in Heaven 10a**
This is the rightmost route on this section of wall. This route is not clean, and is only climbed because it is the easiest route at this end of the cliff. 60' *FA Unknown, 2001*

○ **20 ☐ Feel The Bern 7 ★★**
This climb takes a low-angled face right of Furniture in Heaven. This route, like many others, shares its name with another, previously established, route.
FA Dave Doll, 2016

○ **21 ☐ Happy Feat 8 ★**
The route just right of Feel The Bern *FA Dave Doll, 2016*

● **22 ☐ DD Route (Closed Project)**
This climb follows low-angled rock to a 6-foot roof.
Equipped Dave Doll

● **23 ☐ Highjackers 12c ★**
This route is down and right of the Channel Zero wall. Climb up seams and liebacks to hard moves. Would be great with the removal of a couple of questionable flakes. 60' *FA Greg Collins, 2001*

● **24 ☐ From Hell to Breakfast 12b ★**
Vertical climbing up a pretty wall with hard long moves. 60' *FA Paul Piana, 2000*

● **25 ☐ Diamond Mouth 12c ★**
The right route on the wall. Baffling crux after crux up a techy wall. Good climbing. 60' *FA Paul Piana, 2000*

● **26 ☐ Show Love 10d**
Start in a left-facing corner then go right and up the face above. 65' *FA Greg Collins, 2000*

● **27 ☐ GC Route**
One bolt marks a possible line through the low bulge.
Equipped Greg Collins

● **28 ☐ King of Fools 12b ★**
Long and hard moves, follow a wall of vertical climbing on crimps to a high bulge. 80' *FA Greg Collins, 1993*

● **29 ☐ Queen of Spades 11d ★★**
This one has a crimpy start. Thin moves up a vertical wall, then strenuous above the small roof to the anchors. 80'
FA Sue Miller, 1993

● **30 ☐ TS Route**
face behind tree - partially bolted and cleaned
Equipped Todd Skinner

● **31 ☐ The Empty Quarter 11d ★**
Starts up a thin flake (the route's namesake) to good moves. A bit burly through the top bulge. 85'
FA Kirk Billings, 2000

● **32 ☐ Transitions 10b ★★**
Follow a low-angle wall right of a corner to a bulge.
FA Dave Doll, 2015

● **33 ☐ + Transitions 11c ★★**
Continue to the overhanging wall above. 80'
FA Dave Doll ,2015

● **34 ☐ Full Nickel 11b ★**
Good climbing on varied rock just right of The Empty Quarter. Look for a rough grey slab to start. 85'
FA Dave Doll, 2001

●35 ☐ Merely Mortal 11a ★★
Begin in a right-facing corner on the left side of the "roof wall", then up a vertical wall to anchors. This is a popular first pitch for climbers trying projects on the wall to the right. 80' *FA Sue Miller, 1991*

●36 ☐ Divine Providence 11d ★
This climb splits right from Merely Mortal at bolt 3, then climbs the bulge above. 70' *FA Sam Lightner ,2016*

●37 ☐ Vision of a Kiss 12b ★★
One of the best on the wall. Fight through long moves on vertical rock to a really good bulge. 80' *FA Frank Dusl, 1992*

●38 ☐ Hips Like Cinderella 12c ★★★
Do a hard low crux, a nice vertical wall, then a hard finishing bulge. The name comes from a Pixies song. 85' *FA Frank Dusl, 1993*

●39 ☐ Sauce 12c ★★★
Climb a technical vertical face to a two-tiered bulge above. This route was in terrible shape for over 20 years after the first ascent. Rebolted and cleaned, it is now excellent. 80' *FA Frank Dusl, 1992*

●40 ☐ Casual Entertainment 11c ★★★
Starts up the big pillar, then up and right on pockets to follow the prow through bulges. Great holds and exposure at the end make this a classic. 80' *FA Dave Doll, 2000*

●41 ☐ Hang Fire 12a ★★★
Sustained difficulty and pump. Look for a big hueco near bolt 3. Expect many cruxes and great climbing. 80' *FA Heidi Badaracco, 1992*

●42 ☐ Tender Prey 12a ★★
Underclings and sidepulls lead to easier climbing, then through a tricky roof. 80' *FA Steve Bechtel, 2000*

○43 ☐ The Motivator 8 ★★
Start by climbing a crack / face and then up good holds on the right margin of the big chimney. Fun, clean climbing. *FA Dave Doll, 2015*

●44 ☐ Learning To Fly 13a ★
The ultimate boulderer's route, start on the 5.11 face left of Space Needle, then climb up into a left-facing corner below the large squarecut roof. Break left and through the biggest part of the roof. *FA Steve Bechtel, 2017*

●45 ☐ Into The Black 12c ★★
Shares the same face/corner to the roof with Learning to Fly, but steps right and breaks the roof through a shorter section. Bouldery. *FA Steve Bechtel, 2016*

●46 ☐ Space Needle 11d ★★
Climb a crack in a corner past a tiny tree, then through two bulges. 70' *FA Heidi Badaracco, 2000*

photo John Wesely

THE RIGHTEOUS AND THE WICKED 13a   Elijah Luna

●47 ☐ Two Ducks and an Angel 10b ★★
This climb starts in the corner just right of Space Needle. A challenging crux takes you to a prow, which you follow to a hard-looking exit. This is a fairly popular first pitch of the day. 80' *FA Heidi Badaracco, 2000*

●48 ☐ Monster Match 13c ★★
Climb a concave bulge to an easy face above. This route, Flying Roundhouse, Legend of Norm, and Fibonacci Shimmer were all problem names in the Lucky Lane bouldering gym in Lander. 75' *FA Scott Milton, 2004*

●49 ☐ Flying Roundhouse 12d ★★
Take a face to an undercling, then right to follow a seam through the bulge, then up the headwall above. 80'
FA Steve Bechtel , 2000

●50 ☐ SB Route (Open Project)
The face with almost no holds. *Equipped Steve Bechtel*

●51 ☐ The Ol' Double Diamond 12b ★
Climb a corner with a wide crack in it to above the lip of the roof on its right, then traverse to the prow. Follow the prow on easing terrain. 70' *FA Todd Skinner, 2000*

●52 ☐ The Legend of Norm 12b ★★
Start same as Double Diamond, but traverse right around the prow to good, long moves up the vertical wall right. 70' *FA Todd Skinner, 1999*

●53 ☐ When the Cubans Hit the Floor 14a ★★
Under the roof, climb up a crack/corner to a rail through the 10 foot roof, then up hard the wall above. 60'
FA Todd Skinner, 2001

● **54 ☐ Fibonacci Shimmer (Open Project)**
Another 25 year project, featuring two 5.14 cruxes. A really pretty wall. *Equipped Steve Bechtel*

● **55 ☐ The Righteous and The Wicked / On Devil's Wings 13a ★★★**
This is the chalked-up line through the right side of the bulge. Originally done by Frank Dusl, the route traversed right just after the first crux and joined the Unnamed 13b to finish at a single bolt anchor midway up the wall. In 2001, Paul Piana added a major extension (6-7 bolts) that tackles two more cruxes and features wild moves on the beautiful upper wall. He redpointed the route on September 11th, and came home to the terrible news of what had happened that day. He thus named the extension "On Devil's Wings", a headline in reference to the attack. Most climbers simply refer to the whole route as The Righteous and The Wicked, though Paul deserves much credit for this route's classic nature. 90'
FA Frank Dusl 1992, Piana 2001 complete route

● **56 ☐ Valkyrie 13b ★★**
This route originally featured lots of loose flakes and ended at a halfway anchor. It was rebolted and extended to the top in 2017, and is now an excellent 30M line.
FA (First part) Frank Dusl, 1992 (complete route)
Steve Bechtel, 2017

SAM **LIGHTNER**

SB: When did you start climbing?
SL: Early 80's in the Tetons. Hard to say when it really took off, but it was unstoppable once Mark Newcomb and I could drive. I realized it would be the driving force in my life once I got to U of Wyo and found I wanted to go to Vedauwoo over ANYTHING available in college life.

SB: When did you first visit the Lander area to climb? Under what circumstances?
SL: I came over in 1986 on spring break and climbed Gunky. Then in 1989 (I think) was living part time with Todd and Amy (Skinner) and Jacob Valdez in Custer, SD. I was going home to Jackson for a few days when Todd got a call from Holly saying she had "found limestone that looked like the stuff he climbed in France." Todd asked me to drive south around South Pass. I saw the rock just off the road and wrote it off. Todd talked to Holly again and decided to look for himself. He found Wild Iris the next week and called me back.

SB: What inspired you to add the routes you did?
SL: I love the art of building a new route. It's exploring on a small scale, and if it turns out good you get lots of compliments from your clan. Since the first day I went climbing I have looked at the walls to the sides of what I climbed and thought "what would those moves be like... what is that hold like?" I just love the exploration aspect of it.

SB: Route you are most proud of establishing here?
SL: Probably "All He's Ever Gonna Have" or "Zozo's Dance" A lot of people get enjoyment out of those lines, and they were overlooked for years.

SB: Any favorite anecdotes of your time here?
SL: I love that our climbing areas are still wild places... I go to Wild Iris by myself to repair routes or build new ones, and I'm a little nervous every time I start hiking... we still have grizzly bears and wolves and it is a wild place. Hell, it's incredible that we hunt there in the Fall after we are finished climbing. There may not be another area like that in the world. I also love to see how popular this area has become. We didn't believe anyone would ever come here when we first started developing because it was so far from populated areas. Well, Todd might have, but I didn't. Now it is this major climbing area in America, and it has a great heritage. Being a part of the early years in something that is a success is a really satisfying feeling that I never would have imagined 30 years ago.

SB: What are your future plans?
SL: We moved back to Wyoming and to Lander for the community as much as anything else. Lander is my home for the rest of my days, if I get to keep a say in it. I want to work for the climbing community and build new routes and, if possible, hold off the pains of aging as long as possible so I can keep climbing and establishing new routes.

HANGFIRE 12a   Sean McNamara

●57 ☐ **Fly Bones 13a ★**
Just left of the big corner. This climb takes an ever-steepening wall past several cruxes. 80' *FA Paul Piana, 2001*

●58 ☐ **Enter the Dragon 12c ★★**
Techy vertical climbing just to the left of Asian Orange
FA Ben Sears, 2014

●59 ☐ **Asian Orange 13c ★★**
A beautiful orange streak on a low-angle wall. A technical masterpiece. Bolted and abandoned by Greg Collins (he called the project Asian Rut), this was redpointed by Paul Piana years later. 75' *FA Paul Piana, 2003*

●60 ☐ **Big in Japan 12a ★**
Technical face climbing with several cruxes, tackling a bulge near the top. 80' *FA Steve Bechtel, 2000*

●61 ☐ **Maybe in the Next World 12a ★**
Thin moves up a slab, then through a strenuous bulge. Similar to Big in Japan, but not quite as fun. 80'
FA Frank Dusl, 1993

●62 ☐ **There Goes My Gun 11c ★★**
Climb the crack starting near some big blocks at the base. At 55 feet, you can lower off (5.9) or continue through the tough to read finish. 75' *FA Steve Bechtel, 1999*

●63 ☐ **Dig For Fire 11d ★**
8 feet right of There Goes My Gun. Thin climbing on the lower wall leads to some nice long pulls up high.
FA Steve Bechtel, 2017

●64 ☐ **Vortec 10c**
Twenty feet right of There Goes My Gun, a thin slab leads to steeper climbing to finish. 65' *FA Jeff Leafgreen, 2000*

●65 ☐ **Boom Stick 12a ★★**
From Vortec, the trail drops away from the wall, below some large boulders. Pass 2 of these monsters, and find an east-facing 45 degree wall with big pockets. Super short, but really fun. 30' *FA Steve Bechtel, 2000*

○66 ☐ **Mariner Prime 2 ★★**
This short, well-featured slab sits just across the gully from Boom Stick. *FA Sam Bechtel (age 7) 2015*

●67 ☐ **DD Route (Closed Project)**
This climb takes the long prow feature on the wall just uphill from where the trail emerges from the boulders. *Equipped Dave Doll*

●68 ☐ **CG Route (Closed Project)**
This climb will go up the left margin of the wall where Hero or Zero is located. *Equipped Christian Gauderer*

●69 ☐ **Hero or Zero 11c ★**
Another 150 yards past Boom Stick. From Boom Stick, continue on the path east until you regain the main cliffband. The following three routes are on the tallest and cleanest section of wall. Take a steep wall to a bulge, then a vertical wall above. 80' *FA Dave Doll, 2000*

●70 ☐ **A Bullet for Mr. Ducky 10c ★★★**
20 feet right of Hero or Zero. Great climbing up to water groove. 75' *FA Dave Doll, 2000*

●71 ☐ **Don't Call Me Shorty 11d ★**
This line is another 30 feet right of Mr. Ducky. Vertical climbing on edges and small pockets. 50'
FA Dave Doll, 2000

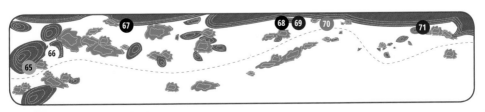

SINKS **CANYON**

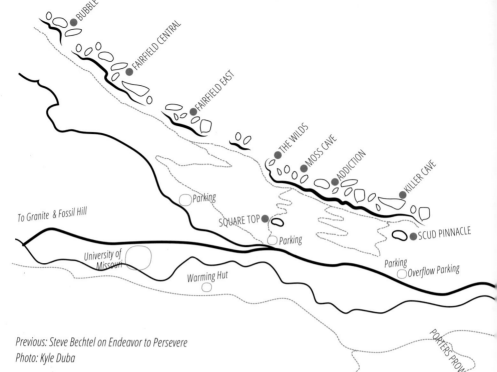

Previous: Steve Bechtel on Endeavor to Persevere
Photo: Kyle Duba

SINKS CANYON

When driving into Sinks Canyon, the first cliffs you'll see are the canyon's sandstone walls. These cliffs line the first few miles of the canyon and attracted its first climbers. The first recorded ascents date back to the 1950s when climbers used the canyon as a practice area before heading into the mountains. In the 1960s and 1970s there was much activity on these walls. During that time these cliffs were a major climbing area for the National Outdoor Leadership School.

These days, climbers visit the sandstone areas of the canyon infrequently. Although a few classics such as Gunky and the Standard Route see traffic most weekends, chances are you won't be waiting in line to get on a route. Be aware than much of the hardware on these crags is dated and should be used with extreme caution. Fixed pitons on any route were likely placed at least 30 years ago and will not hold a lead fall.

Many of the climbs described here are of nothing more than historical interest to the climbers of today. But for climbers in search of a little more adventure than the OK Corral provides, the Sandstone of Sinks Canyon is worth a look.

SANDSTONE

SANDSTONE CLASSICS

▭
Gunky (p.177)
Royal Edge (p.189)

▬
Zen the Cat(p.177)
Honeycomb(p.178)
Halk Walk (p.183)

▬
Dag Nab it (p.177)

▬
Main Street Cattle Drive(p.184)
Wee Doggies (p.180)

31

31

18

14

0

2

10AM-PM

20m

Vertical

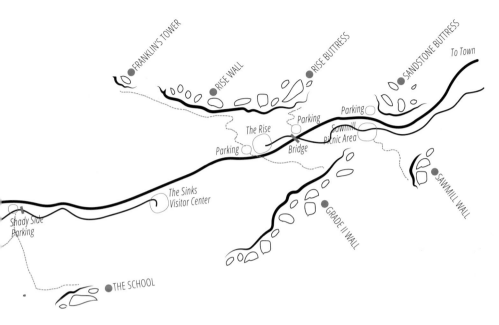

FRANKLIN'S TOWER

RISE WALL

RISE BUTTRESS

SANDSTONE BUTTRESS

To Town

Parking

Parking

The Rise

Sawmill
Picnic Area

Parking

Bridge

The Sinks
Visitor Center

Shady Side
Parking

GRADE II WALL

SAWMILL WALL

THE SCHOOL

photo Zach Snavley

SURPLUS FUSION REACTION 13a

Alex
Bridgewater

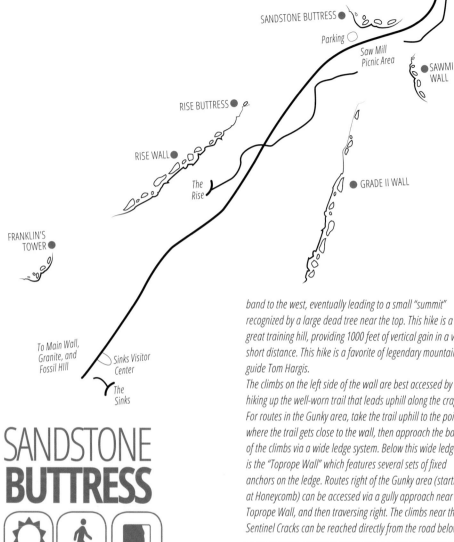

FRANKLIN'S TOWER

RISE WALL

RISE BUTTRESS

The Rise

To Main Wall, Granite, and Fossil HIll

Sinks Visitor Center

The Sinks

SANDSTONE BUTTRESS

SAWMILL WALL

Saw Mill Picnic Area

Parking

SANDSTONE BUTTRESS

To Lander

GRADE II WALL

SANDSTONE
BUTTRESS

| 10AM-PM | 2m | Vertical |

| 16 | 11 | 9 | 5 | 0 | 0 |

This is the most popular of the sandstone walls. With an easy approach and descent, good parking, and warm, south-facing exposure, this is a great crag most of the year. There are several easier routes which are appropriate for teaching, as well as hard, scary testpieces. The canyon's most popular multi-pitch route, Gunky, sits as the centerpiece of this crag. Above this buttress is a short band of limestone called the Boulder Band. This short wall holds dozens of well-traveled boulder problems and is a good place for a lonely climber to get a workout. The trail to this wall continues above the

band to the west, eventually leading to a small "summit" recognized by a large dead tree near the top. This hike is a great training hill, providing 1000 feet of vertical gain in a very short distance. This hike is a favorite of legendary mountain guide Tom Hargis.

The climbs on the left side of the wall are best accessed by hiking up the well-worn trail that leads uphill along the crag. For routes in the Gunky area, take the trail uphill to the point where the trail gets close to the wall, then approach the bases of the climbs via a wide ledge system. Below this wide ledge is the "Toprope Wall" which features several sets of fixed anchors on the ledge. Routes right of the Gunky area (starting at Honeycomb) can be accessed via a gully approach near the Toprope Wall, and then traversing right. The climbs near the Sentinel Cracks can be reached directly from the road below.

Routes are listed from left to right.

● 1 ☐ Unnamed Slab 10a ★
The leftmost climb on this wall, just right of a large juniper tree. Two bolts on a very featured face, then past a ledge and up lesser-quality climbing above. 4 bolts, 60'
FA Unknown

● 2 ☐ The Longest Yard 10d
This climb starts above a small black cave, and the base is near a round granite boulder. Do an exposed traverse into a corner, then up. After about 20 feet, escape right on big holds. Above, move left and up slabby, easier moves to the top. Small cams, wires, 60'
FA Greg Collins, 1982

GUNKY 8 Elyse Guarino

3 □ New Sensations 12d ★

First of the new breed. Starts above a little black cave, moving up and right on big holds to a thin, hard crux. Clip a tatty thread, then continue up to a ledge. Above, move up and right to a hanging flake. Small cams or wires supplement QDs. FA Greg Collins, 1989

4 □ The Maverick 12a ★

This route starts on a limestone band just right of two big junipers. Climb up to sandstone, through a small bulge, then follow bolts and drilled angles up a black streak right of some seams. FA Greg Collins, 1988

5 □ Dag Nab It 11a ★★

One of the first pure sport routes in Lander. Climb up the limestone wall and past the bushy horizontal then up a slabby wall to a right-facing overlap. 8 bolts, 70'
FA Rob Hess, 1990

6 □ Friday the 13th 10dR

This climb starts in a right-facing corner capped by a square-cut white roof. Pass the roof, then follow rounded cracks that can be a bit bushy. FA Mike Collins, 1986

7 □ Barstool Grooves 6R

Climb a widening crack up a left-facing corner to a ledge. Move right 15 feet on the ledge, then up a big, right-trending groove. Above, the route shares the final 20 feet with Gunky. Bring big gear and a broom.
FA Greg Collins, 1981

8 □ Arapiles Revisited 12b ★

A classic of sorts, used to be the "must do" route for the grade. Less popular since the swell of so many great 12b routes in the area. Crank up face, then out the big bulge on sloping, big holds. Wall above is yet to be climbed.
FA Chaz Fischer, 1989

9 □ Gunky 8 ★★★

A pretty climb, this is a two or three-pitch affair with a wide variety of climbing. Fixed anchors. Standard rack.
FA Unknown, 1969

10 □ Funky Monkey 11c

This climb takes the steep, leaning seam above No Name Crack. After the initial intimidating crux moves, the climbing eases off above. 90' FA Eric Sawyer, 1994

11 □ No Name Crack 7 ★★

This is the first crack right of Gunky, a left-facing flake to a bolted anchor at a ledge. Gear to 3 inches. 40'
FA Unknown 1960s

12 □ Standard Start 5 ★

Aother left-facing crack that gets good and wide near the top. Anchors at ledge. 40' FA Geoff Heath, 1967

13 □ Cardboard Crack 8

This is a left-facing dihedral with a nice brown patina that leads to a funky overlap. Climb up to ledge on easier moves. 45' FA Unknown

● 14 □ Ryan's Romp 11a ★

This sport route climbs up steep limestone to a sandstone slab above with a seam. Really fun climbing on this and the following three climbs. 50'
FA Tom Hargis, 2005

● 15 □ Zen the Cat 10c ★★

Up a highly bolted limestone wall to the slab above. 50'
FA Tom Hargis, 2005

● 16 □ Brady's Sandbox 10a

Follow a bolted limestone wall to a crack above. Small rack up to 2.5" 50' FA Tom Hargis, 2005

● 17 □ Lucky's Refuge 11b ★★

Again, limestone climbing leads to technical sandstone slab climbing above, up a right-facing feature. 50'
FA Tom Hargis, 2005

● 18 □ Jump For Juniper 11bR

A standard-setting route at the time of the first ascent. Climb the first pitch of the Standard Route. At the ledge, step left to a 5.9 corner crack below a roof. Climb up to a band of broken rock, then traverse left under the roof. Turn the roof at an odd slot feature, then negotiate some scary, thin moves. Continue up on less-steep and easier ground. 2 pitches. Standard rack. FA Don Peterson, 1978

19 ☐ Standard Route 5 ★

 This route starts in the major gully right of Gunky. Pitch one climbs up easy stone to nice ledges. Above, stay right of the corner / roof by climbing cracks on the face. Use cracks and corners to reach a short chimney and then exit onto a big ledge. The third pitch follows a much easier corner for about 40 feet to the top. Standard rack.
FA G Heath, R Rosenthal, and Juan Laden, 1966

20 ☐ Dare 8R

A variation to the last pitch of the Standard Route. From near the top of the chimney, step right and up a nice, but scary, slab. Small cams, wire. 40' *FA Unknown, 1980s*

21 ☐ Armadillo Exit 9R

Follows the first pitch and half of the second on Standard Route. Move right at a small stance to a left-facing, rounded crack. Can be done in either two or three pitches. *FA Unknown, 1970s*

22 ☐ DOA 9R

This is the corner just right of the Standard Route. Pitch 1 follows a corner to a ledge, then up and left on liebacks. Climb on face holds to a ledge and belay. Pitch 2 two can be done by moving left to join the Armadillo Exit, or by traversing right and finishing up the final pitch of Honeycomb. Standard rack with extra small cams.
FA Mike Collins, 1986

23 ● ☐ Honeycomb 10b ★★

Pitch one follows a corner, traverses left, then up easy terrain to a belay at a ledge. The fun pitch two climbs steep huecos, hen traverses slightly right to a crack ending at a large stance and a belay. The third pitch takes easy stone to a 5.8 exit crack. Bring a small rack and some extra medium and long slings.
FA D Peterson, C Simer, L Smith, 1976

24 ☐ Haldicheck 8 ★

Pitch one takes a sandy corner through an overhang, ending on a spacious ledge. Above, climb the right-facing corner, ending on a ledge at a bolted belay. Continue to the top via a large, flaring crack. Standard rack.
FA Joe Haladick, 1976

25 ● ☐ Group Grope 5.10cR ★

This intimidating route takes steep corners and flakes left of the Sentinel Chimney. First done in three pitches, it's possible to link pitches one and two. Lots of small pro.
FA Randy Cerf, Scott Fisher, M Allison, 1978

26 ☐ Sentinel Chimney 7 ★★

This semi-classic climbs up a squeeze to a ledge, then up a corner to a second ledge and a belay. Above, climb the chimney to another ledge and belay, or continue a bit higher to link itches 2 and 3. Above, climb ramp/cracks to top. Rap the route or walk off right. Small standard rack and several slings.
FA Randy Cerf, G Heath, B Brudigam, 1976

27 ☐ Sentinel Cracks 8 ★

This route takes left-facing corners right of the chimney. One pitch or two short ones get you to a big ledge. Traverse left to join Sentinel Chimney or rappel. Standard rack. *FA John Hauf, 1984*

28 ● ☐ Sentinel Crack Direct 11aR

A face route with three bolts. *FA Rob Hess, 1990*

29 ● ☐ Sandy But Dandy Direct 10aR

Hard-to-protect corner and crack that leads to the end of the opening traverse of Sandy But Dandy. After joining that route for a pitch, head straight up over a small roof. After you surmount the overhang (crux), finish on easier ground. *FA T Walter, J Hauf, 1986*

○30 ☐ Sandy But Dandy 8 ★
Start by traversing along a prominent, left-leaning lieback crack. At the end of the crack, head straight up another crack system in a left-facing corner, finishing at a small pod stance below an overhang. Move 20-30 feet right into a prominent right-facing corner to finish. Standard rack. *FA T Walter, M Miller, 1986*

●31 ☐ Five Year Plan 12a
Face/slab with cool movement. Clip 4 drilled angles, supplementing with thin gear, and belay at a welcome ledge. Finishes on Sandy But Dandy. *FA Eric Sawyer, 1990*

●32 ☐ Baby d'Angles 11d
A slightly easier climb than Five Year Plan, protects with small gear and drilled angles. *FA Eric Sawyer, 1989*

●33 ☐ Gravity in Chains 10d
The easiest and best of the bolted slabs on the right side of the buttress, this one ends at a nice ledge. *FA Mike Collins, 1983*

●34 ☐ Illusions of Lander 11bX
Slab with thin gear and notoriously bad bolts. Best not to fall. *FA Greg Collins, G Flam, 1982*

○35 ☐ Rick's Roof 8
This climb is located in the alcove above the previous routes. *FA Rick Horn, 1967*

This short wall sits below the main Sandstone Buttress route Honeycomb. These climbs feature fixed anchors along the top of the cliff, which is the wide ledge below the main buttress. Approach from the left as coming up directly from the road is really unpleasant bushwhacking. Code Blue and Road Test are both worthwhile climbs. Climbs are best found by locating the anchors on the ledge above. The routes are listed left-to-right.

○36 ☐ Unnamed 7TR

○37 ☐ Unnamed 8TR

●38 ☐ Lateral 10TR
FA Eric Sawyer, 1988

●39 ☐ Dorsal 10TR
FA Eric Sawyer, 1988

●40 ☐ Code Blue 11TR
FA Eric Sawyer, 1989

●41 ☐ Road Test 12aTR
FA Greg Collins, 1981

RISE **BUTTRESS**

10AM-PM	10m	Vertical

This is the next wall up canyon from the Sandstone Buttress. It features an orange-colored prow above the bridge where the road crosses the Popo Agie river just below the Rise. To reach the crag, park near the bridge and follow game trails up to the base. Climbs are described right-to-left, as one approaches from below.

Routes are listed from right to left.

●1 ☐ The Howl 10d ★
This climb is the first crack on the right side of the buttress. Follow a varying crack in a corner system. Cruise through awkward moves, then up through a rough roof move. Easier climbing leads through a second roof near the top. Standard rack. *FA Randy Cerf, Scott Fisher, 1977*

○2 ☐ Asleep at the Wheel 7
Not popular, this is the next crack left of The Howl. Follow a nice crack to a slanting ledge, then fight up wide junk to the top. Bring goggles. *FA Jim Ratz, 1984*

●3 ☐ Fear of Flying 10dR
Junky rock leads to a fun (?) hand-to-fist crack, to more junk. *FA S Fisher, Randy Cerf, 1978*

●4 ☐ D.O.E. 12b ★
Fun, rail riding sport route. Thru cool rail roof and up sandy face above. 50' *FA Greg Collins, 1986*

●5 ☐ ScAiry 11c
One of the more singular pitches in the canyon. Follow a thin crack to a rightward traverse along a horizontal/ledge.. Step out onto the rounded prow and enjoy the air below. Bring long slings. *FA Eric Sawyer, 1994*

●6 ☐ Adelita 10c ★★
Start same as ScAiry, but move left at the end of the initial crack. Finish on Green Wall. *FA Tom Bol, 1989*

○7 ☐ Green Wall 8
This is the major crack system. Looks nice, not so nice. *FA E Elison, S Gipe, 1981*

●8 ☐ Wee Doggies 12a ★★
This is a great, leaning crack in a corner. The best of the sandstone 5.12s. *FA Greg Collins, Rob Hess, L Berger, 1984*

RISE **WALL**

10AM-PM **15m** **Vertical**

5 7 1 2 0 0

The Rise Wall is the massive and intimidating wall that sits above the Rise of the Popo Agie. You can reach the wall by parking at the Rise parking area, and following faint trails uphill. These climbs aren't as popular as they used to be, so established trails are nonexistent. Higher in the canyon, to the left of the Rise Wall, is Franklin's Tower. This blond-colored open book is a nice looking chunk of rock. For climbs on Franklin's Tower and Hawk Walk, it might be best to approach from the Visitor Center parking area, as it gives you a slightly higher starting elevation.

Routes are listed from right to left.

●1 ☐ Way Roof 10b

Scramble up 4th and 5th class terrain to a stance below a high and prominent roof. This is a right-facing roof crack climb. *FA Eric Sawyer, 1981*

●2 ☐ If It's Tuesday in Wyoming 10a

This climb takes a clean left-facing corner into an adventurous groove. *FA Mike Collins, 1982*

●3 ☐ Made For Aid 12a

This thin crack climbs the center of the varnished wall. Originally aided, then toproped free. This route was led in 2011. *FA Griffin Heydt, 2011*

●4 ☐ The Buzz 10dR

The big brother of The Sting. Climb up to an obvious hanging spike, then up the thin left side of the orange pillar. Join the Sting for one pitch. From the ledge atop pitch 2, climb straight up and through the stout offwidth roof. *FA Randy Cerf, Scott Fischer, 1978*

●5 ☐ The Sting 10a ★★

The best route on this section of wall. Climb discontinuous corners to reach the left side of the obvious orange pillar, and then climb it to its top. Move into the chimney, then left out its top (crux) and climb to the big ledge above. Exit the wall by scrambling right.
FA Randy Cerf, Scott Fischer, 1977

○6 ☐ Dumb Bunnies 9

This climb takes a roof crack/groove/grovel on the right side of a prominent white roof. Not that great.
FA Greg Collins, Larry Berger, 1980

●7 ☐ Fat Back 10b

This route is on the short wall below the ramp up to The Snake. Climb a non-cool groove to a handcrack through a left-facing roof crack.
FA Greg Collins, Reave Castenholz, 1980

belay on a ledge. 130ft Pitch two is the crux, passing two bolts up the limestone band then to a sloping ledge. Follow bolts up a steep corner, exiting right and up to pods in crack, then to an easy face to spacious ledge. 110ft. Pitch three starts following 2 bolts up a varnished face past a sandy mantle. Traverse ledges left and up to another ledge, then take an easy crack to the summit and rap anchor. 80 ft. Rap the route with a single 70m making sure to stay to climbers left on the final rap. 11 draws, gear to 2.5" *FA Griffin Heydt, Matt Wendling, 2012*

○10 □ Freak Factor 9
This climb starts just right of The Dungeon, taking a clean offwidth crack that parallels The Dungeon and joins it at the belay. Share pitch two's chimney with that route, then move right at the chockstone for pitch three, a character-building ramble to the top of the wall. *FA Rick Horn, John Horn, 1967*

○11 □ The Dungeon 8
This climb takes the big corner system in the middle of the Rise Wall. It starts just left of a prominent overhang-ing prow. Follow left-facing flakes in a grey-white corner to a bolted belay at a ledge below the chimney. Pitch two climbs this big chimney to a belay at a stance below a big-ass chockstone. Move left and up a thinner crack above. *FA Rick Horn, John Horn, 1966*

○12 □ Leaning Pillar 7
This small pillar has two climbs on either side of it, both 5.7. This is about halfway between Hawk Walk and the Dungeon.Rap from the top. 60'

●13 □ Eagle Dance 11a
This is a variation to the start of The Eagle. This is a left-leaning layback with some fixed gear. *FA Greg Collins, 1984*

●14 □ The Eagle 10c ★
Climb up limestone for about 10 feet, then make hard moves to a right-leaning crack. Take this into the left-leaning crack above. Once established in this crack, the climbing eases up. Climb to a ledge, then up easier rock to a second ledge. Follow the easy (5.7) crack above to the top of the wall. Standard rack. *FA Don Peterson, Scott Fisher, Randy Cerf ,1978*

●15 □ Hawk Walk 10d ★★
Pitch one takes a cool left-facing flake to a nice ledge (5.7). Above, work left and up through overhanging terrain to an easier crack above. The crux can be avoided by joining pitch 2 of the Eagle. *FA Geoff Heath, Randy Cerf, 1984*

○8 □ The Snake 8
To reach this route hike up grass ramps and ledges 50-70 yards left of The Sting. Scramble up a low-angle slab into a prominent left-facing corner (5.7) and climb it to a ledge. Traverse left on this ledge about 60 feet and then take another corner to the top. *FA, Jef Woods, 1977*

●9 □ Revival 12a ★
A short-lived revival, but a couple of new routes went up on the sandstone in 2012. This three pitch line is on the nice buttress right of Freak Factor. Pitch one: fingers in varnished crack with one bolt to 4 bolts up face, past a small ledge to easy cracks which are followed to a bolted

FRANKLIN'S
TOWER

10AM-PM | 15m | Vertical

1 | 1 | 0 | 0 | 0 | 0

Routes are listed from right to left.

●1 ☐ Franklin's Tower 10bR
This is the big, light-colored corner. Climb wide cracks
and ledges (5.10) to a belay stance. Above, the climbing
is in a thinner and easier crack.
FA Greg Collins, George Flam, 1981

○2 ☐ Zombie Dance 7 ★
This climb takes varied corners and ledges left of the
main corner. *FA Chaz Fisher, Phil Powers, 1987*

SAW **MILL**

10AM-PM | 10m | Vertical

2 | 2 | 5 | 4 | 0 | 2

*The Sawmill Wall boasts a high concentration of hard routes,
and the best sandstone in the canyon. In the late 1980s, this
crag was the scene of all the hard climbing action in the area.
With the rise in popularity of climbing on the steeper, more
solid dolomite stone, this wall has fallen out of popularity.*

*Sawmill is the first cliff you pass on the way into Sinks
Canyon. It's located on the left side of the road, across the
Popo Agie river, just upstream from the last house (a geodesic
dome). Do not approach this wall via the driveway to this
house. Rather, park at the Sawmill picnic ground or the
Sandstone Buttress parking area, and cross the river. Once
on the other side, you'll walk downstream, cross the shallow
Sawmill Creek, and reach this west-facing wall.*

Routes are listed from left to right.

●1 ☐ Born To Be A Cowboy 12b ★
This climb is a thin left-facing corner that starts right
where the electric fence is bolted to the cliff (this will
make sense when you see it). Tech stem and tips lieback-
ing. Be suspicious of the 20+ year-old pin placements!
Zero-type cams are useful. *FA Greg Collins, 1988*

●2 ☐GC Route (Open Project)
This climbs a cool clean face to a smooth groove. Looks
wild! *Equipped Greg Collins*

●3 ☐ Good, Bad, and Ugly 10c ★
Follow the thin seams and edges right of the big dihe-
dral. Small cams and nuts supplement bolts.
FA Greg Collins, 1987

●4 ☐ Main Street Cattle Drive 12a ★★
A classic of sorts, this climb takes the line of edges and
seams just right of the center of the clean face.
FA Greg Collins, 1990

● 5 ☐ High Noon 11c ★★

Follow good edges and cracks just left of the prow/arête.
Drilled angles for pro should be scrutinized.
FA Greg Collins,1986

● 6 ☐ Ghetto Blaster 11a

This is the left-facing corner capped by a high roof. Gets
wide at the lip. *FA Greg Collins,1987*

● 7 ☐ The Defender (Open Project)

This takes a steep crack to a thin roof encounter, then
climbs into soft rock above. Should be good when it gets
clean. *Equipped Greg Collins*

● 8 ☐ Blasted Cactus 10c

A cool feature that's prettier to look at than to climb. Start
in the left crack of a box chimney. The crack gets thinner/
more pleasant as you climb higher. *FA Greg Collins, 1981*

○ 9 ☐ Dead Bird Crack 9

A nice hand crack turns ugly as you get higher.
FA Unknown 1970s

*These climbs are all on the beautiful wall right of Dead Bird
Crack. This is arguably the best sandstone in Sinks. Bolted
anchors protect these routes. Access them by scrambling up
from the right. Climbs listed left-to-right. FA (All Routes) Tom
Walter, Greg Collins, mid 1980s*

● 10 ☐ Gold Plated #1 12aTR

● 11 ☐ Gold Plated #2 12bTR

● 12 ☐ Gold Plated #3 11dTR

● 13 ☐ Gold Plated #4 11bTR

● 14 ☐ Gold Plated #5 11cTR

○ 15 ☐ Gold Plated #6 9TR

Lindsey Stevens **NO NAME CRACK** 7

GRADE II WALL

10AM-PM   15m   Vertical

5 7 2 1 0 0

The Grade II Wall faces north and sits directly across the canyon from the Rise Wall. To reach this wall, park at the Rise parking lot, cross the dry (except in June) riverbed, and hike up the short hill to the base of the wall. For routes 1-4, one can scramble up left of the cliff to gain the belay ledge between pitches one and two, identified by a band of limestone that splits the cliff.

Routes are listed from left to right.

● 1 ☐ Waiting For George, Left 10b

Climb either a nasty 5.7 slot or scramble up a left-leaning gully to gain the limestone band ledge. Move right and then up to a good, right-leaning corner. Take this past ledges, and up a nice section of stone, finishing on a good ledge. Rap off or continue to the top on sketchy 5.9 terrain. *FA Unknown*

○ 2 ☐ Waiting For George, Right 5

This climb takes the same start as Waiting For George, Left. From the limestone band, follow the same initial corner as the previous route, but go right where the crack splits at ledges. Above, you'll want to move back left and finish up blocky terrain (5.9) or rap off. *FA Unknown*

○ 3 ☐ Amanitas 9 ★★

Start as for Waiting for George or traverse in along the ledge. This is a left-facing corner to a roof to a great crack. From the second ledge, you can climb a scary 5.9 pitch straight above or traverse left or right to adjacent routes. Most climbers do only pitch two of this route. *FA G Heath and Wes Crouse, 1967*

● 4 ☐ Belladonna 10 ★★

Climb any number of crack/face options to reach the limestone band, or traverse in from the left. Lieback up a right-facing corner (9-) to the second ledge and a bolted belay. The third pitch moves right and then attacks the cool roof above, the route's crux. Standard Rack and small cams. Rappel descent via Ego Tripper. *FA Geoff Heath, 1967*

○5 ☐ **Ego Tripper 8 ★★**

This is the major corner system left of a big blank section of wall. This three pitch climb starts about 50 feet left of the obvious right-facing flake corner at the base. A short face climbing section with a bolt leads to an easy crack, which takes you to the ledge. Climb through the limestone band just right of two large bushes, and up a right-facing corner with a fist-sized crack. Belay at a block-covered ledge. Easier climbing up cracks and ledges leads to the summit. You can descend by rappelling the route.

●6 ☐ **Genius of Horror 11cX**

A crazy man's route. Just right of a big right-facing flake/corner, this is a slab to a skinnier right-facing corner. The corner becomes a roof near its top. Follow the roof right and escape onto the ledge above. Small cams make this more protectable than it was during the first ascent, but it's still very serious. *FA Greg Collins, 1983*

●7 ☐ **Fear and Loathing 12a ★**

Pitch one of this climb starts up low-angled rock, and is protected by a couple of old bolts. From the ledge at the limestone band, climb up into a right-facing flake. Follow this up and through a small overhsang to a nice belay below a rounded crack. Climb this crack, that goes from easy to very hard in a hurry. After the steep finger/hand section that makes up the crux of the climb, plan on a short section of wide crack to earn the top of the wall. *FA Jason Stephens, Scott Howard, 2007*

●8 ☐ **Avalanche 11bR**

This serious outing starts with a 5.8 slab just right of a hanging flake. Belay at the limestone band. Above, thin crack climbing with challenging pro takes you up a right-facing corner, past a small ledge and to a belay at an alcove. Above, the line steepens, and the crack becomes a hard-to-protect flare. Follow this to a ledge/slab with a tree. From here, pick any of the short cracks above to exit the wall. *FA Greg Collins, George Flam, Reave Castenholz, 1981*

●9 ☐ **Unemployment Line 10c**

Climb up a low-angle slab to a ledge with a small bush below the limestone band. Follow bolts through the band to a right-facing corner/flake system. After about 60 feet, the corner leans right and eventually hits a small roof. Before reaching the roof, move left on face moves to rounded ledges. Continue to traverse left to a right-facing corner which you can take to the top. *FA Unknown 1970s*

● 10 ☐ Four Dead Aliens 10d ★

This route takes a left facing corner about 30 feet left of the Mitten. Climb up on thin cam placements, widening as you go. A right exit near the belay is the more pleasant finish. 70 feet. *FA Greg Collins, Tom Daughton, 1984*

● 11 ☐ Mitten, Left Side 10b ★★

Pitch one takes a left-facing overlap that tends to be damp early season and tends to be wide and difficult year-round. Belay at the limestone band at the base of the Mitten flake. More awkward, yet clean, climbing takes you to the top of the flake. Traverse right to belay. Above, climb a short bolted slab, then move right on ledges to an easy left-facing corner.
FA Don Peterson,1978

○ 12 ☐ Mitten, Right Side 8R

Pitch one is an easy approach ramp from the right. Above, climb up crack to gain the chimney, a sporty, sandy affair. At the top of the flake, the route continues up a slab on bolts, then right and up an easy corner.
FA Rick Horn, 1967

● 13 ☐ The Boxer 10b ★

This is a fun variation to the Mitten, Right Side. Climb a steep crack in a right-leaning corner to join the Mitten halfway up its second pitch. *FA Unknown, 1970s*

● 14 ☐ Hooter's Holiday 10aR

This climb is at the far right end of the Grade II Wall. Start in right-facing cracks, moving left at the limestone band and up a right-facing feature to a big ledge (5.8) The serious second pitch takes a thin crack up to a difficult face move, steps slightly right, and up a right-facing dihedral. Standard rack with extra micro cams.
FA Jim Howe and Tommy Howe, 1985

○ 15 ☐ Royal Edge 7 ★★

This three (or two) pitch route doesn't get the attention it deserves. Start up right-facing cracks, belaying at a large ledge after about 80 feet. The second pitch takes the corner system above, passing several nice stances, around 100 feet. Pitch three moves left and up to the top on liebacks and good jams. One can also move right into the next corner to finish the climb. This alternate third pitch is also 5.7. Standard Rack. Descend via rappels to climbers' right. *FA Geoff Heath and Jeb Schenck, 1974*

SHADY**SIDE**

photo: Kyle Duba

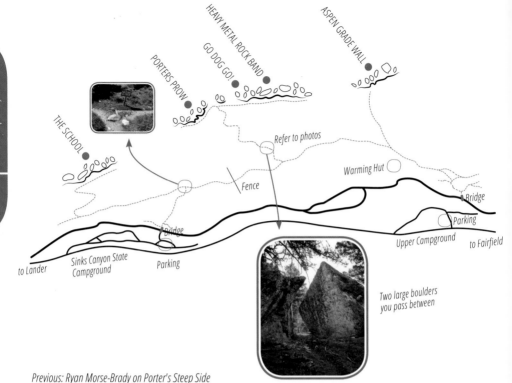

THE SCHOOL

PORTERS PROW

GO DOG GO!

HEAVY METAL ROCK BAND

ASPEN GRADE WALL

Refer to photos

Warming Hut

Bridge

Fence

Parking

Bridge

Upper Campground

to Fairfield

Sinks Canyon State Campground

Parking

to Lander

Two large boulders
you pass between

Previous: Ryan Morse-Brady on Porter's Steep Side
Photo: Kyle Duba

SHADY**SIDE**

The sunny walls of Fairfield Hill and the Main Wall are the crags that bring climbers to the canyon, but the south side of the canyon has several worthwhile crags, as well. On the tree-covered northfacing side of the road, three nice crags have been developed, allowing for a respite from the summer heat.

Starting across the river from the Sinks Canyon State Park Campground, there are four major outcrops. From left to right, they are The School, Porter's Prow, The Heavy Metal Rock Band, and The Slab Buttress, AKA "The Aspen Grade Wall." This wall has been renamed because of the popular trail below it, with no regard for the fact that Aspen Grade and Aspen Glade might be confusing to climbers.

The Aspen Grade and the right end of the Heavy Metal Rock Band can be approached from the upper campground. All other climbing should be approached from the lower "swinging bridge" approach noted below.

Approach: Each area has a slightly different approach they are all described in the beginning of each section.

CLASSICS

Grand Adventure P1 (p.194)
K-School (p.194)
Banish Misfortune P1 (p.194)

Imaginary Fans (p.194)
Ice Cream for Crow (p.200)

Spinal Tap (p.198)
The 11th Hour (p.195)
Grand Adventure P3 (p.194)

Goodnight Moon (p.197)
Goodnight Gorilla (p.197)

18
9
21
6
0
2

10AM-PM

20m

Vertical

THE**SCHOOL**

☼ 3PM-PM | 🚶 15m | ▦ Vertical

(7) (4) (6) (1) (0) (0)

Also known as the "Cool Crag" or the "Shady Side," this wall was first explored by Kirk Billings in the mid 1990s . A couple of great community efforts have been made to stabilize the hillside below the cliff and preserve vegetation, so please do your part to minimize impact in this area. There are many great moderates here that can be enjoyed all summer long.

Approach: *Park at the Popo Agie Campground, and hike across the swinging bridge over the Popo Agie River. On the far side of the bridge, the trail splits. You'll want to go straight ahead and up some short steps on a trail heading toward the cliffs on the hill above. After about 3-4 minutes on this trail, it forks. For The School go left, hiking another 3-4 minutes to another fork. Take the right fork at a sign that indicates you're headed for "climbing." Follow this trail uphill to the cliff.*

Routes are listed from left to right.

● 1 ☐ **Ms. Carmels 12a** ★
Starts at the left end of the Cool Whip ledge. Climb up through a small overhang and up the nice wall above.
FA Steven Vedder and Jake Dickerson, 2017

● 2 ☐ **Cool Whip 11a** ★
This climb is approached by walking left and downhill from where the trail meets the wall. After about 50 yards, you go uphill again, and then walk back right along a large ledge. Both this route and Ice Cream take nice lines above this ledge. 40' *FA Greg Collins and Sue Miller, 1993*

● 3 ☐ **Ice Cream 11d** ★
Just Right of Cool Whip. Nice rock. 40'
FA Greg Collins and Sue Miller, 1993

● 4 ☐ **Sorting Hat Left 10a**
This is the leftmost route on the low-angle wall where the trail reaches the cliff. Starts near a tree, climbing on big holds to a thinner finish. 55'. 10 bolts
FA Bob Branscomb, 2004

● 5 ☐ **Sorting Hat Right 10a** ★
This climb takes the middle line up the slab, reaching the same anchors as Sorting Hat Left. 55'. 10 bolts
FA Bob Branscomb, 2004

○ 6 ☐ **C'est Fini 9** ★
The right line on the slab. 60 feet, 10 bolts
FA Bob Branscomb, 2007

○7 □ Finish Your Homework 9 ★★

This climb and The Grand Adventure have been errone-
ously referred to as Ice Cream and Cool Whip for years.
This climb is on the wall right of where the trail meets
the wall. There is a big, dirty corner right of C'est Fini.
This climb is about 15 feet right of that. The bottom wall
is mostly jugs, with an anchor at a small ledge about 40'
Above, the route works left and up on more difficult rock.
FA Kirk Billings, 1996 Jim Ratz, 1999 (first anchors)

●8 □ + Finish Your Homework 11a ★★

Above P1, the route works left and up on more difficult
rock. FA *Jim Ratz, 1999 (complete route)*

○9 □ The Grand Adventure 8 ★★

This route has almost as many anchors as protection
bolts. The first "pitch" is an excellent moderate at 5.8.
FA Kirk Billings, 1996 (to first anchors)

●10 □ + The Grand Adventure 11a ★★

Above, the route climbs a difficult slab to another set of
anchors (11a). *FA Jim Ratz, 1999 (complete route)*

●11 □ + The Grand Adventure 11b ★★

Continuing through the roof above leads to the route's
crux, and a third set of anchors.
FA Jim Ratz, 1999 (complete route)

○12 □ The Big So So 7 ★★

Climb up nice rock to an anchor at a break.
FA Bob Branscomb, 2015

●13 □ + The Big So So 11c ★★

Continue up through a bulge to a thin edging finish.
FA Bob Branscomb, 2015

○14 □ Banish Misfortune 6 ★

Uphill and right of the previous route, this climb takes a
crack system (5.6) to a mid-way anchor 60'. 12 bolts
FA Bob Branscomb, 2005

●15 □ + Banish Misfortune 10a ★

Climb past mid way anchors and finish on a steeper wall.
60' *FA Bob Branscomb, 2005*

○16 □ Imaginary Fans 8 ★★

Fifteen feet right of Banish Misfortune.
FA Bob Branscomb, 2004

●17 □ + Imaginary Fans 10c ★★

Finish on slightly harder terrain above.
FA Bob Branscomb, 2004

○18 □ K-School 8

A variation to Imaginary Fans, this route jogs right from
the first set of anchors on that route. 60'
FA Bob Branscomb, 2004

PORTER'S
PROW

| 3PM-PM | 15m | Vertical |

0 0 7 0 0 0 0

This is a series of nice-looking gold corners above the Sinks Canyon nature trails. This small crag has just five routes, but is a nice respite from the summer's heat.

Approach: *(For Both Porter's and Heavy Metal Rock Band): Park at the Popo Agie Campground, and hike across the swinging bridge over the Popo Agie River. On the far side of the bridge, the trail splits. You'll want to go straight ahead and up some short steps on a trail heading toward the cliffs on the hill above. After about 3-4 minutes on this trail, it forks. Go right, following the path until you hit a buck-and-rail fence. Shortly after you pass the fence you will see a trail that breaks off to your left heading up hill marked by a blue diamond on a tree "see photo above". On this trail you will pass two house size boulders up to a drainage that will put you right between Porters Prow and Heavy Metal Rock Band. As the angle steepens and the gully narrows, a faint climbers' trail breaks left and over to Porter's. The crag is visible at this junction and should be easy to find. To access the Heavy Metal Rock Band, continue uphill and trend right another 3-4 minutes.*

Routes are listed from left to right.

●1 ☐ The Jazz Singer 11c

Left of the major prow, this climb takes low-angle rock up a black streaked wall just right of a corner system with several prominent flakes. 85' *FA Tricia Stetson, 1996*

●2 ☐ Porter's Prow Left 11d ★

This route has tan pained hangers and starts 6 feet right of Jazz Singer. Follow a line just right of the main prow to anchors visible on the skyline. 75' *FA Porter Jarrard, 1991*

●3 ☐ Porter's Prow 11c ★★

This is the central prow line. 70' *FA Porter Jarrard, 1991*

●4 ☐ Porter's Steep Side 11c ★★

This climb takes steep stone just right of the main prow. *FA Porter Jarrard, 1991*

●5 ☐ Dancing With Godzilla 11b

This is the rightmost route on the cliff. It takes the cleanest section of the not-so-clean face right of the main prow. 75' *FA Michael Lindsey, 1993*

The following two routes are uphill and right of Porter's Prow.

●6 ☐ The 11th Hour 11b ★★

This nice climb and the following are on a wall about 4 minutes uphill from the bulk of the Porter's Prow routes, and both are close to the access trail for the Heavy Metal Rock Band. *FA Christian Gauderer, 2016*

●7 ☐ 12 Hours To Live 11d ★★

This climb is a steep sprint on generally good holds. *FA Christian Gauderer, 2016*

PORTER'S STEEP SIDE 11c   Jessie Morse-Brady

HEAVY METAL
ROCK BAND

| 3PM-PM | 15m | Vertical |

5 **3** **5** **5** **0** **2**

This is the third dolomite crag on the shady side as you head up canyon. This is the widest of the walls, and has the most potential for great new routes. Many of the climbs here were established relatively "late" in the history of Sinks. The crag was first developed by Dennis Vandenbos and Jacques Ruschtmann, who lamented the sparely protected sport climbs at many crags they visited. At this cliff, they decided, there would be no such behavior...they would fill it with "heavy metal."

Approach: (For Both Porter's and Heavy Metal Rock Band): Park at the Popo Agie Campground, and hike across the swinging bridge over the Popo Agie River. On the far side of the bridge, the trail splits. You'll want to go straight ahead and up some short steps on a trail heading toward the cliffs on the hill above. After about 3-4 minutes on this trail, it forks. Go right, following the path until you hit a buck-and-rail fence. Shortly after you pass the fence you will see a trail that breaks off to your left heading up hill marked by a blue diamond on a tree "see photo above". On this trail you will pass two house size boulders up to a drainage that will put you right between Porters Prow and Heavy Metal Rock Band. At the top of the gully break right and follow a trail heading up traversing the cliff. Follow this trail for about 5 minitues and you will arive at Heavy Metal Rock Band.

Routes are listed from left to right.

●1 ☐ **Go Dog Go! 11b** ★
This route about 50 yards from the left end of the cliffband. The first part of this route follows a left-leaning seam, then tackles good climbing above. The seam catches some run-off so can be a bit dirty. 70'
FA Paul Piana, 2001

●2 ☐ **Goodnight Gorilla 12b** ★★
Climb up nice moves to a low roof, then right and up to a vertical wall with hard-to-see pockets. 5 bolts 50'
FA Paul Piana, 2001

●3 ☐ **Animal Sounds 12b** ★
Similar to Goodnight Gorilla, but without the roof. Feels more tenuous than it is. 7 bolts 55' *FA Paul Piana, 2001*

●4 ☐ **Goodnight Moon 12c** ★★
A crazy and cool set of moves. Starts in small corner under a high roof, then moves left to a prow and up to end near the left edge of the roof. 5 bolts 40'
FA Paul Piana, 2001

The following routes are 100 ft right of Good Night Moon, dubbed the Easy Listening Wall.

○5 ☐ **Kenny G's Amphitheater 8** ★
Start with stemming and move onto face with large pockets. 7 Bolts, 65' *FA Brian Fabel, 2014*

○6 ☐ **Smooth Jazz 7**
5 bolts 40' *FA Mandy Fabel, 2014*

○7 ☐ **Two-Finger Pocket Strum 9** ★
Thin start to longer moves on large pockets 4 bolts 40 feet. *FA Brian Fabel, 2014*

8 ☐ **Surround Sound 10a ★★**
The steepest of the routes on this wall with good pockets and fun climbing. *FA Brian Fabel, 2014*

○**9** ☐ **Promenade 8 ★**
Go through the tunnel right of Surround Sound. This climb takes big holds up the wall above, and is very fun up high. *FA Bob Branscomb, 2016*

10 ☐ **Spinal Tap 11c ★★**
This is the leftmost line on the tall, clean central wall. 70'
FA Dennis Vandenbos, 1999

11 ☐ **The Amp That Goes to 11 12a ★**
The next route left, up thin pockets on an ever-steepening wall. 70' *FA Steve Bechtel, 2010*

12 ☐ **When The Levee Breaks 12b ★★**
The right route on the wall, best identified by the large hueco at bolt 2. 75' *FA Jesse Brown, 2010*

13 ☐ **Dennis and Jacques' Excellent Adventure 11a ★★**
This is a fun route that climbs up a short wall, then over a small overlap to a steeper headwall. 7 bolts, 60'
FA Dennis Vandenbos and Jacques Rutschmann, 1997

14 ☐ **Route variation to D and J 11a**
This route is close to, and shares holds with Dennis and Jacques. The upper wall was bolted at the time of the *FA This variation to the start (which now makes an independent line) was done in 2010. FA Fritz Mercer, 2010*

15 ☐ **Stairway to Heaven 11a**
This is a long prow route, which makes an interesting and engaging ramble. *FA Jesse Brown, 2010*

○**16** ☐ **Paula's Arête 6 ★**
One of the better dolomite moderates, this climb is slightly hidden partway up a large gully, about 50 yards right of Stairway to Heaven.
FA Dennis Vandenbos, 2000

17 ☐ **Styff Kittens (Open Project)**
Steep wall just left of the very prominent arête. 50'
Equipped Steve Bechtel

18 ☐ **SB Route (Open Project)**
Leftmost line on the pretty golden wall. 50'
Equipped Steve Bechtel

● 19 ☐ George's Last Stand 10d ★

This is a pretty nice climb. Heads up the center of the gold wall to anchors below crappy rock. 65'
FA Dennis Vandenbos, D Newton, 1997

● 20 ☐ Indian Summer 10c

This climb is the rightmost route on the yellow-orange wall at the right end of the cliff. A small square-cut roof identifies the start of this climb. 7 bolts, 60'
FA Dennis Vandenbos, M Young, 1997

WHEN THE LEVEE BREAKS 12b — Blaine Limpus photo Matt Enlow

ASPEN **GRADE**

| 3PM-PM | 20m | Vertical |

(6) (2) **3** **0** **0** **0**

This wall is the rightmost of the Shady Side dolomite crags in Sinks Canyon.

Approach: From the Sinks Canyon Campground, across from the Main Wall parking area. After crossing the bridge, hang left and follow good trails heading down canyon, and diagonalling up toward the cliffs visible above. There are some trails breaking left and right as you pass through sage and grassy meadows, but use your intuition and aim for the cliffs. As the trail gains altitique and you get into denser trees, you'll hit a fork. Take a right and head up the "Aspen Grade" trail. Follow this trail for a short distance, and keep your eyes out for a small cairn and climbers' path heading left and up to the cliff. Take this path for about 5 minutes to reach the rock. Total approach time is around 20 minutes.

Routes are listed from left to right.

○ **1** ☐ **Celine's Cat 8**
Follow a crack feature to a break with an anchor and then up the long face above. *FA Bob Branscomb, 2017*

● **2** ☐ + **Celine's Cat 11b** ★
After the break continue up the long feature above. *FA Bob Branscomb, 2017*

● **3** ☐ **New Pony 10c** ★
Take a 10c face the the ledge/break, then continue up the shared finish above. *FA Bob Branscomb, 2016*

● **4** ☐ **Stone Moses 11c**
Thin climbing to an anchor at the ledge, with an optional extension up the finish that is shared with the routes left and right. *FA Bob Branscomb and Kristy Stouffer, 2017*

● **5** ☐ **Ice Cream for Crow 10b** ★★
A nice, long climb with an optional mid-way anchor. *FA Bob Branscomb and Mark Watkins, 2016*

○ **6** ☐ **True Sailing is Dead 8** ★
A full-value pitch at nearly 30 meters. *FA Bob Branscomb and Kristy Stouffer, 2017*

○ **7** ☐ **BF$ Route 7**
A decent route, but still a bit dirty. *FA Brian Fabel, 2015*

○ **8** ☐ **BF$ Route 7**
A chossy corner with some potential for being less chossy. *FA Brian Fabel, 2015*

○ **9** ☐ **BF$ Route 8**
This takes the longer corner to the right. *FA Brian Fabel, 2015*

○ **10** ☐ **Surfing for Perverts 5** ★
Easy climbing leads to the first anchor. *FA Bob Branscomb and Mark Watkins, 2016*

● **11** ☐ + **Surfing for Perverts 11a**
Climb the clean harder face above. *FA Bob Branscomb and Mark Watkins ,2016*

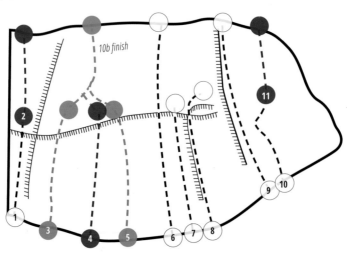

10b finish

GOODNIGHT MOON 12c

photo: Kyle Duba

MAIN **WALL**

WILDS
ACHIN FOR BOOTY
PURPLE GALAXY
MOSS CAVE
FACE DANCER
HARDWARE
CITADEL

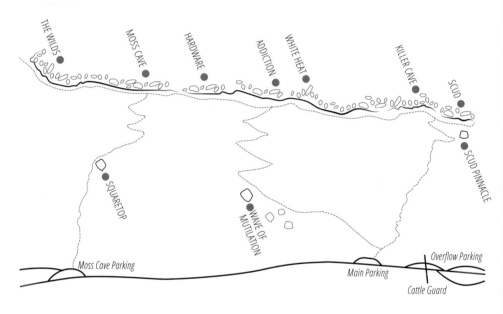

THE WILDS
MOSS CAVE
HARDWARE
ADDICTION
WHITE HEAT
KILLER CAVE
SCUD
SCUD PINNACLE
SQUARETOP
WAVE OF MUTILATION
Moss Cave Parking
Main Parking
Overflow Parking
Cattle Guard

Previous: Devlin Junker on Nirvana
Photo: Kyle Duba

MAIN **WALL**

To think that one of the best winter crags in the country is in the middle of Wyoming takes a little belief, but strangely enough, the Main Wall of Sinks is that crag. With a great southerly aspect, a clear hillside, and an inversion that keeps the canyon warmer than the valley below, one can climb here many days each week of the winter. If it's sunny and calm, even if it's below zero in town, you'll have good conditions at the wall.

In the summer, the sun rises high in the sky and the wall stays cooler. Sinks Main Wall is not Lander's best summer crag, but it can be OK even in mid-summer. The crag now features the highest concentration of routes in the area - as of this writing, there are close to 300 climbs on the wall from 5.5 to 5.14c.

Later in the season (May thru September) keep your eyes open for rattlesnakes and poison ivy. During the winter months neither is an issue. In 2012 there was a wildfire that burned much of the area above and below the crag. A few routes suffered damage from the fire, and might feature some sections of loose, "spalled" rock. Additionally, the fire has caused increased erosion above the crag, resulting in substantially increased rockfall. Be especially aware in the Harvest Moon and Whippery areas.

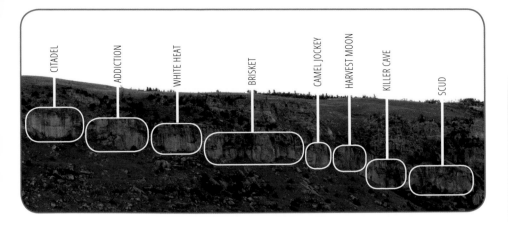

Before about 1990, the climbing at the Main Wall was very sporadic, with a few cracks and corners being climbed. With the advent of sport climbing worldwide, the climbers of Lander began looking at the crag in a different light - instead of looking for weaknesses in the band, Greg Collins and friends started admiring the crag for its strengths. Soon the clean, steep walls and roofs were home to new, hard, and modern climbs. The Main Wall is located 2.6 miles from the entrance to the canyon, with the primary parking being on the right side of the road, approximately 100 yards past a cattle guard. Additional parking is available down canyon 1/4 mile on the south side of the road.

Dogs Must Be Leashed in Sinks Canyon State Park. There is really only one rule at the Sinks Main Wall and it is this: leash your dog if you are in Sinks Canyon State Park. The state park includes all climbs from No Self Control to Left Out. The park line is clearly marked near the trail ta the base of the crag. Dogs should also be leashed if you approach via the Killer Cave Trail. Not only is there a possibility of receiving a ticket for ignoring this law, your actions can affect everyone's access to the crag. There are more than 1500 routes in the Lander area where your dog does not have to be leashed. If you can't follow this simple rule, choose to climb one of them instead of the ones in the park.

Approach: The trail leaves the parking lot from its right corner, and splits after just a few feet at the trail-head sign. For access to Citadel, and walls to the left of Addiction take The left trail (Addiction Trail) , while White heat, and walls to the right are best approached on the right trail, (The Killer Cave Trail).If you are accessing the routes of the Moss Cave or further left, you can park at the Fairfield Hill road (.4 mile further upcanyon) and hike up via the trail that passes Squaretop. Climbs xx to xx are located on large boulders below the cliffs. The Squaretop boulder is best reached via parking at the Fairfield Hill road and walking striaght uphill toward the cliff on a well-worn trail(.4 miles past the main parking area). The Wave of Mutilation can be reached by walking the Addiction trail to the first switchback, then angling downhill straight toward the road and around to the south face of the large boulder.

CLASSICS

 40

 10AM-PM

Go West Young Man (p.227)
Duck Soup (p.248) 65
Put Down Your Ducky (p.236)

Action Candy (p.245) 85
Smithereens (p.248)   20m
Sandman (p.206) 88

Bust a Nut (p.209)   67
Face Dancer (p.219) Winter
Heaven Can Wait (p.223) 8

Purple Galaxy (p.212)
Citadel of Hope (p.226)
Addiction (p.227)

The Throne (p.241)
Confessions of a Mask (p.217)
Pretty Hate Machine (p.228)

THE **WILDS**

11AM-PM | 15m | Vertical | Winter

③ ⑧ ③ ③ ③ ❶

The Wilds sits at the westernmost end of the Main Wall. This section of cliff has a more southwesterly aspect than the rest of the crag, and can be nice and cool on hot mornings, as well as very warm on cold afternoons. Many of the best 5.10 and 5.11 routes in the canyon are on this section of wall. The first 5.13 in Sinks, Savages, was established here in 1989.

Routes are listed from left to right.

● **1** ☐ **The Royal We 11b**
This climb is on the small buttress of rock 100 yards left of Earth AD. *FA Christian Gauderer, 2016*

○ **2** ☐ **Earth A.D. 9** ★★
Nice route at the very left end of cliff. A hard start leads to fun pulls between big holds. 40' *FA Vance White, 2007*

● **3** ☐ **Candyman 11a** ★
Climb up an easy left-facing corner/flake system to an anchor below a ledge (5.5), then up the steep wall above. 60' *FA Jeff Leafgreen, 1996*

● **4** ☐ **Ankle Biter 10d**
Up low angle rock to rightward traverse near top. 50' *FA Vance White, 2000*

● **5** ☐ **Tooth Fairy 10d** ★
Techy face climbing, starting in a small groove. Continuous and challenging pulls. 50' *FA Jim Ratz, 1995*

● **6** ☐ **Sandman 10c** ★★
Up thin right-facing flake system and then through a series of good pockets an anchor just above a horizontal break. 50' *FA Jim Ratz, 1995*

● **7** ☐ **Get on With It 12c** ★
Hard, thin climbing up a nice clean face. This route shares anchors with "The Wilds". 50' *FA Greg Collins, 1996*

● 13 ☐ Riff Raff 10d
A bouldery start gains the fractured flake system to face above. *FA Scott Robertson, 2015*

● 14 ☐ Blue Collar 10d
Ten feet right if Riff Raff. Scramble up slab then surmount bulge. Consistent climbing throughout leads to steep finish. *FA Jared Spaulding and Scott Robertson, 2015*

● 15 ☐ Desk Jockey 11a
Stem corner through bulge down low then step out onto the face. Pockets and side pulls lead to through crux bulge above.
FA Graham Kolb, Jared Spaulding, and Scott Robertson, 2015

● 16 ☐ Snap Back Relax 13a
Boulder problem start to easier moves. 50'
FA Greg Collins, 2000

● 17 ☐ The Physical 12c ★
Hard moves to groove, continuing difficulty, steep top out. 50' *FA Vance White, 2000*

○ 18 ☐ Where the Wild Things Are 8 ★
Climb the right wall of a big corner on face holds or climb the arete. 50' *FA Evan Horn, 2012*

● 19 ☐ Wild Child 10d
Climb up the same crack as "Blammo", but traverse left onto the arete and follow 4 bolts to the top. 50'
FA Evan Horn, 2012

● 20 ☐ Blammo 10c ★
This climb takes an obvious crack feature 20 feet left of the double cracks of Combustification. 50'
FA Evan Horn, 2012

● 21 ☐ Combustification 10c ★
This climb follows nice double cracks past a couple of cruxes. 55' *FA Joe Wall, 2007*

● 8 ☐ The Wilds 12a ★★
Start up small leftfacing corner to a good stance, then up hard moves above. 50' *FA Greg Collins, 1993*

● 9 ☐ TS Route (Closed Project)
Just left of Savages, climbs blank looking face.
Equipped Tony Stark

● 10 ☐ Savages 13a ★★
Good thin climbing up nice wall, just left of the obvious hueco. 50' *FA Greg Collins, 1989*

● 11 ☐ Aggressive Perfector 13b
Boulder up hard moves to the big hueco, then step right and up 5.12 terrain to the top. 60' *FA Vance White, 2010*

○ 12 ☐ Wicked Garden 9 ★
This route was really weedy and loose at the time of the first ascent. It has since cleaned up into a nice corner climb with a crux right at the end. 55' *FA Vance White, 2007*

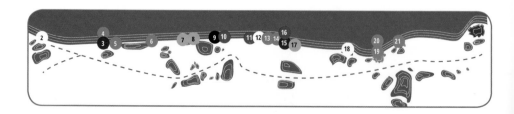

ACHIN' FOR
BOOTY

|
10AM-PM |
15m |
Slight |
Winter |

③ ① ⑧ ⑤ ① ⓪

The Achin' For Bootie sector is a great place for getting a pump, with half-a-dozen climbs that are 90 feet long and overhang 20 feet. This area can be windier than the rest of the crag, but catches late afternoon sun.

Routes are listed from left to right.

●**1** ☐ **Spragglepuss 10c**
Low angle climbing behind a large burned up tree.
Techy. 45' *FA Vance White, 1999*

●**2** ☐ **Bump N' Grind 12a** ★
Follows a deceptive prow to anchors below large square-cut roof. 50' *FA Keith Lennard, 1999*

●**3** ☐ **Mumble Pants 11c** ★★
Move up a good corner and through a small bulge then to anchors below the roof. *FA Scott Robertson 2016*

●**4** ☐ **Bust A Nut 11c** ★★
Climb up small a pillar to discontinuous cracks. Follow cracks and good moves to an anchor just below the large squarecut roof. 50' *FA Vance White, 2000*

○**5** ☐ **Dark Days 8** ★
This climb is just right of Bust a Nut. Climbs a corner past three bolts, then traverses right onto the face.
FA Jared Spaulding and Scott Robertson, 2015

●**6** ☐ **Hope Springs Eternal 11b** ★★
A nice climb up the clean face right of Dark Days. Shares the anchor with that route.
FA Scott Robertson and Jared Spaulding , 2015

●**7** ☐ **Winter Solstice 11a**
An awkward face climb 10 feet right of Hope Springs Eternal. *FA Scott Robertson and Jared Spaulding, 2015*

○**8** ☐ **Mega Beaver Moon 8**
Just left of New Age Gal (and right of Winter Solstice), stem up the corner until it makes sense to step left onto the face and then up to anchor. *FA Scott Robertson, 2016*

○**9** ☐ **New Age Gal 8** ★
Formerly Renaissance Man, the original line was un-cleaned and poorly protected. Scott Robertson contacted the original ascensionist and asked about rebolting the climb. Ed DeLong gave his blessing and suggested giving it a new name when the work was done.
FA (original) Ed DeLong 1994, (new) Anna Hagel, 2015

●**10** ☐ **Opal 12a**
Up the face just left of a small corner, then through a mini roof to an anchor on the arête above. 65'
FA Pete Absolon, 2004

ACHIN' FOR BOOTY 12a Jake Perkinson

photo Kyle Duba

●11 ☐ BrrAvery 12b

Up righttrending seam to "bling" chain anchor. 65'
FA Pete Absolon, 2004

●12 ☐ ApPetence 11c ★★

Named in memory of Pete Absolon who put up and
named the neighboring BrrAvery after his daughter.
Pete balanced being a great dad with his appetence for
climbing. *FA Scott Robertson, 2016*

●13 ☐ Ride the Apocalypse 13a

Climb up blocky rock to a very hard move, followed by
5.10 climbing to the anchors. This route used to be a
one move 12b, with a major hold break it is now much
harder and not very fun. 70' *FA Vance White, 2001*

●14 ☐ Picture of Industry 12a ★

Climb a crack feature up to a bulge, rest at a sandy
hueco, then tackle a hard crux. Continue up a nice finish
to anchors at a good horizontal. 85' *FA Mark Howe, 2002*

●15 ☐ Cavity Search 11d ★

Slab to lieback crack, then through a good and hard
bulge before the headwall. Many redpoint attempts end
near the last bolt of this one. 90' *FA Mark Howe, 2002*

●16 ☐ Achin' for Booty 12a ★★★

Climb up a rightfacing corner to a small ledge with a bolt.
Move straight up the center of the face to a rest, then
tackle a high crux. 95' *FA Unknown, 1992*

●17 ☐ Smell My Finger 11d ★★

Climbs face right of Achin' up to crack feature at top.
Similar to the latter. Pumpy. 90'
FA Mark Howe, 2002

●18 ☐ Waiting on a Friend 11b ★★

A difficult entry move leads to fun jug pulling and a small
bulge above. 80' *FA Mike Lindsey, 2003*

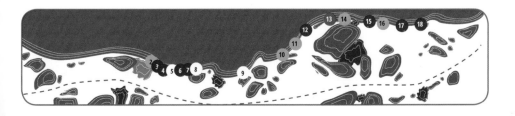

PURPLE **GALAXY**

10AM-PM | 15m | Vertical | Winter

The Purple Galaxy area covers everything between the steep wall of Achin' for Booty and the Moss Cave. For the most part, the routes here are vertical, featuring crimps and pockets. There are several 5.11 and 5.12 routes here that should not be missed.

Routes are listed from left to right.

●1 ☐ Parts and Labor 11b

Take the looseseeming slab up to steeper climbing, then through a small roof at the top. Bolts every 2 feet through the roof. 80' *FA Jim Ratz, 1999*

●2 ☐ Grabbing Greta 11c ★

Starts in a leftfacing corner, moves left to difficult moves on a slab, then climbs through a bulge near the top. A good route. 80' *FA Jeff Wendt, 2003*

●3 ☐ Gongoozled 11d ★★

Continuous tricky moves, then through a hard bulge at the top. 85' *FA Dave Doll, 2005*

●4 ☐ Blood Moon 11c ★★

Excellent climbing starting in a right-facing feature to the left of the big Aqualung corner. Long and varied, it keeps you interested the whole way. 90' *FA Scott Robertson, 2015*

●5 ☐ Aqualung 11c

This route climbs a big leftfacing corner and up the face above. 60' *FA Jim Ratz, 1998*

●6 ☐ TS Route (Open Project)

The short arête. A baffling prow.

●7 ☐ Purple Galaxy 12a ★★★

A hard opening sequence leads to a good rest, then up tough moves to a horizontal. Either lower from anchors here (80') or continue 3 more bolts to the top. 100'
FA Paul Piana, 1997

●8 ☐ Galactic Tactic 11c ★

Right of Purple Galaxy, this route climbs on crimps and good holds to a high anchor. Only marred by some "trouty" damp rock at the bottom. *FA Griffin Heydt, 2011*

●9 ☐ Krymptonite 11d ★★

A nice route that follows crimps and pockets up a mostly vertical wall. This route is about 15 feet right of Purple Galaxy. *FA Evan Horn, 2012*

●10 ☐ Cold Moon 11c ★★

Start on a big jug then climb up and slightly right on pockets along a seam feature. 60' *FA Scott Robertson, 2016*

●11 ☐ Dog Star 11b ★★

Starting just behind a large burned juniper, the route tackles a slight bulge on good pockets.
FA Scott Robertson, 2016

Big Agnes

STEAMBOAT SPRINGS, CO

● **12** ☐ **Cheese Wheel 13a**
This vertical route was hit very hard by the 2013 fire and has not been climbed since. 50' *FA Scott Cole, 1993*

● **13** ☐ **Monkey in the White House 12b**
This route, too, was badly burned in 2013. Many spalled flakes will make for different climbing. 45'
FA Scott Cole, 1995

● **14** ☐ **Ain't No Mercy 11b ★★**
This climb takes mostly big holds along a seam to the right of Monkey in the White House. 50'
FA Scott Robertson, 2015

● **15** ☐ **Sweet Begiulin' 11b ★**
Thin crimps on a vertical wall lead to easier climbing in a high corner. 50' *FA Scott Robertson, 2015*

● **16** ☐ **Diamonds in the Moonlight 10a ★★**
This route follows big holds and flakes 20 feet left of Southpaw. 50' *FA Scott Robertson, 2015*

● **17** ☐ **Southpaw 10c ★★**
Climb a leftleaning undercling crack, exiting onto face above. 50' *FA Tom Hargis, 2000*

The following 4 routes are on a pretty and clean wall.

● **18** ☐ **Macumba 11d**
Thin and sharp face, just right of Southpaw crack. 50'
FA Scott Cole, 1990

● **19** ☐ **Crowheart 12b ★★**
Good route up center of wall. Shares anchors with Macumba. 50' *FA Paul Piana, 2002*

● **20** ☐ **Bush Fire 12a ★**
This is a good climb up a rustcolored streak on the right side of the wall. 50' *FA Scott Cole, 1990*

○ **21** ☐ **Buzz Worm 9 ★★**
Climbing above a nice platform, follow the arete/cracks. 40' *FA Scott Robertson, 2015*

The following three routes are on a short wall right of the obvious arete Buzz Worm.

● **22** ☐ **Kickin' Turtles 10c ★**
Short excursion with interesting bulge.
FA Scott Robertson, 2016

● **23** ☐ **Bunky 10a ★**
Short warm up in the middle of this wall.
FA Scott Robertson, 2016

● **24** ☐ **Tyco 10d ★**
Bouldery start. *FA Scott Robertson, 2016*

The following routes start on a large ledge some 25 feet above the base of the cliff. They are accessed via an easy 3 bolt climb in the corner just right and uphill from Tyco. There are rap anchors for descent installed at the base of this wall.

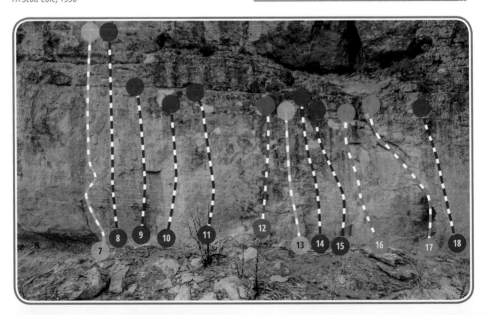

●25 ☐ **Jungle Gym 11b**
Leftmost climb. *FA Scott Robertson, 2016*

●26 ☐ **Red Rover 11a**
8' right of Jungle Gym. *FA Scott Robertson, 2016*

●27 ☐ **Monkey Bars 10c ★**
8' right of Red Rover and right of tree.
FA Scott Robertson, 2016

○28 ☐ **Slip n' Slide 8**
Right of second tree. Follow face to obvious left leaning
ramp. *FA Scott Robertson, 2016*

●29 ☐ **Tether Ball 10c**
Shares start with Slip n' Slide but goes straight up steep
face at the beginning of the left leaning ramp.
FA Scott Robertson, 2016

●30 ☐ **Hop Scotch 10b ★★**
Good thin face climbing right of the Slip n' slide start.
FA Scott Robertson, 2016

○31 ☐ **Four Square 8 ★**
25' right of Hop Scotch. Good beginner route. Bottom
anchor installed for belayer. *FA Scott Robertson, 2016*

○32 ☐ **Time Out 7**
Just right of Four Square. Another good beginner route.
FA Scott Robertson, 2016

───────────────────────────

○33 ☐ **Summer Solstice 8 ★★**
Bring 17-18 quickdraws plus anchor. This is the left of the
two routes on the large slabby wall left of Touchy Feely.
After moving through overlap down low this route follows
lots of good pockets to interesting slab up high.
FA Scott Robertson, 2016

○34 ☐ **Strawberry Moon 9 ★**
Another long route just right of the previous route.
Breaks right down low through pockets. One delicate
move on upper slab. *FA Scott Robertson, 2016*

●35 ☐ **Touchy Feely 11d**
Climb up the left side of a white streak, about 50' after
the trail exits the small "forest" at the end of the Moss
Cave. As far as dirty slabs go, this is a pretty good one.
70' *FA Scott Cole, 1990*

SCOTT
ROBERTSON

Scott first started climbing in Sinks Canyon in
the early 1990s, having begun climbing a few
years earlier in Maine. After taking a NOLS
course, he later moved to Lander full-time.
He has worked for the National Outdoor
Leadership School for years and was happy
to spend much of his early time in Lander
simply repeating routes put up by others.
More recently, though, Scott thought both
of contributing to the crag, and to opening
routes of a variety of grades to provide a better experience for all climbers. Over the past
few years, he added so many new routes
to the left end of the Main Wall that many
climbers refer to it as "Scott's Area."

His favorite crag is the Sinks Main Wall, but
he has been active throughout the area doing
first ascents. Scott is also an active member
of the CWCA board of directors and is a
regular at trail day events.

In Scott's words: "I used to walk under the
bands of dolomite pondering various unde-
veloped lines. Over the years, I was happy to
see that many of these lines were developed
by others. I finally decided that I wanted to
make a contribution as well. I wanted to have
new climbs available for locals...I figure that
I've climbed some of the Sinks routes hundreds of times. Also, I wanted to engage my
climbing brain in a different way. Visualizing
and developing new routes is a wonderful
puzzle process. It's an embarrassing amount
of work that goes into doing it well. The re-
ward comes when you watch people having
fun on it when you're done."

MOSS CAVE

10AM-PM | 15m | Steep | Winter

0 0 0 2 15 1

The Moss Cave is a beautiful wall that is mostly a seeping mess of choss. The right side, however, is often dry enough to climb and offers a great number of hard powerendurance type routes. There are many linkups of the six or so main lines, which make for a good variety of climbing.

Routes are listed from left to right.

● 1 ☐ 🔗 **Project**

This is the steep line just right of the wet rock that finishes up the high rightfacing corner. *Equipped Todd Skinner*

● 2 ☐ **Feed the Need 14c** ★

This climb is indicated in the picture on page 209 as #14 (Double Down), left of Good Luck Mr. Gorsky. Double Down is correct in the description starting at #16 and ending on #11. *FA BJ Tilden, 2016*

● 3 ☐ **Good Luck Mr. Gorsky 13c** ★★

Hard pulls on a nice continuously steep wall. The joke goes that these were the last words spoken by Neil Armstrong during his visit to the moon. Look it up. 70' *FA Paul Piana, 2004*

● 4 ☐ 🔗 **Aces Wild 13c** ★

Climb the first four bolts of Good Luck Mr. Gorsky, breaking right at the undercling and finishing the top of Pogey Bait. 75' *FA Kyle Vassilopoulos, 2009*

● 5 ☐ 🔗 **Taking the Pythons for a Walk 13c** ★

The opposite of Aces Wild. Start Pogey Bait, then traverse the undercling to finish Gorsky. Takes the crux of both routes. 75' *FA Kyle Vassilopoulos, 2009*

● 6 ☐ **Pogey Bait 13d** ★

Third line from the left. A bouldery opening leads to 5.12 climbing near the top. The name is worth Googling. 70' *FA BJ Tilden, 2008*

● 7 ☐ 🔗 **Undertow 14a** ★

Start at the Confession of a Mask tram start. Traverse left along the undercling crack to finish on Gorsky. 85' *FA BJ Tilden, 2012*

● 8 ☐ 🔗 **The Abortionist 13c**

Tram to the start of Confession, traverse left and finish up Pogey Bait. 75' *FA Matt Wendling, 2009*

● 9 ☐ 🔗 **Confession of Gorsky 13b** ★

Climb Confession of a Mask to the jug rest at bolt 6, then traverse way left to finish Gorsky. *FA BJ Tilden, 2011*

● 10 ☐ 🔗 **Maskabait 12d** ★

Climb Confession of a Mask to the jug rest at bolt 6, then traverse left and finish Pogey Bait. Probably slightly easier than Confession of a Mask, skipping Confession's hardest section. 70' *FA Vance White, 2009*

● 11 ☐ **Confession of a Mask 13a** ★★★

A0 Tram start leads to long moves between generally good holds. Very nice movement, and a great route despite the winch start. 65' *FA Paul Piana, 2004*

● 12 ☐ **Dealer Calls 14a** ★

This is the next straightup line right of Confession. Winch to a bolt near an obvious spike undercling. Hard from the getgo. 55' *FA BJ Tilden, 2009*

● 13 ☐ 🔗 **Snake Eyes 13d** ★

Start Dealer Calls, then move right past 2 bolts to join the top of Smoke Shapes. 50' *FA Zack Rudy, 2012*

● 14 ☐ 🔗 **Traveling Menagerie 14b** ★

Do the hard low traverse off the Smoke Shapes start all the way into Confession. 75' *FA Kyle Vassilopoulos, 2009*

Zack Rudy

CONFESSION OF A MASK 13a

● 15 ☐ ✏ Double Down 14c ★
Start at the bottom of Smoke Shapes, then do the low traverse into the start of Dealer Calls. This is the hardest route in Sinks Canyon. *FA BJ Tilden, 2014*

● 16 ☐ ✏ Shape Shifter 14a ★★
This route starts Smoke Shapes, then moves left after two bolts to finish on Dealer Calls. *FA BJ Tilden, 2014*

● 17 ☐ Smoke Shapes 13d ★★
Jump / cheater stone start to monos up streak. 55'
FA Matt Lund, 1998

● 18 ☐ Skinny Fat Man 12d ★
Takes the gray steak on the rightmost side of the Moss Cave. Technical. 6B 65' *FA Unknown, 1992*

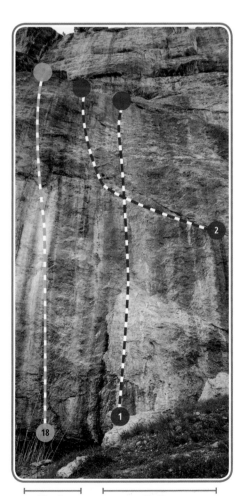

Moss Cave | Face Dancer

FACE **DANCER**

| 10AM-PM | 15m | Vertical | Winter |

1 5 7 0 0 0

The Face Dancer wall is a tall vertical section of crag with more than a dozen good 5.10 and 5.11 routes. This wall can get a bit dusty from runoff, but is climbed clean soon after any storms.

Routes are listed from left to right.

● 1 ☐ Calling Saint Fiacre 11c ★
Climb a small pillar/corner just at the end of the Moss Cave overhang. This leads to hard moves that join the end of Stone Seed after 4 bolts. 60' *FA Dave Doll, 2004*

● 2 ☐ Stone Seed 11d ★
(2 short pitches) Hard moves off pointy flakes at the bottom to a rail, then traverse left and up to anchors. A second, easier, pitch leads higher. This route occasionally gets dirty from run off, but is good climbing.
FA Greg Collins, 1995

● 3 ☐ Blessed Saint Yabo 11c ★★
Begins with the same bouldery move as Stone Seed, but moves straight up where Stone Seed traverses left. 50'
FA Todd Skinner, 2004

● 4 ☐ Diemos 10d ★★
Up gray slab, then through fun moves to a rightfacing corner near the top. 85' *FA Tom Hargis, 2001*

● 5 ☐ Winds of War 10c ★★
Start up ramp, then follow sustained moves to anchors. 85' *FA Mike Lindsey, 2002*

● 6 ☐ Face Dancer 11b ★★★
This popular route leads up big flake/slab to vertical wall with glassy pockets. 85' *FA Joe Desimone, 1993*

● 7 ☐ Eros 10d ★★
Climb up and right on rails and pockets. Nice climbing leads to an anchor above a good horizontal. 85'
FA Tom Hargis, 2001

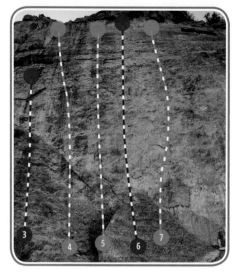

● 8 □ **Wicker Man 11b** ★
Sharp climbing with weirdly placed bolts. Pretty good stone. Go right at top. 75′ *FA Scott Cole, 1990*

● 9 □ **Wind River Rose 11a** ★
Begins just above jumbled boulders, a bit dirty after run offs, this is actually a decent climb. 70′ *FA Steve Scott, 1991*

● 10 □ **Fallen Idol 11b**
A tricky crux at the bottom leads to lower angled climbing on big holds. 65′ *FA Greg Collins, 1990*

● 11 □ **No More Heroes 10c**
This was once one of the more popular 5.10s in the canyon. A hardtoread crux takes you to a good stance, then easier rock above. 60′ *FA Greg Collins, 1990*

● 12 □ **Kamiakin 10b** ★
Start on a blocky ledge just left of the leaning pillar. A stinger first move is the crux. 65′
FA Dennis VanDenbos, 1995

○ 13 □ **Billie Idol 9** ★★
Climbs up the easy south face of the pillar, then up good pockets above. This route was hit hard by the 2013 fire, so expect some spalling and loose rock on the pillar face. 75′ *FA Jeff Leafgreen, 2002*

HARDWARE

| 11AM-PM | 15m | Vertical | Winter |

① ③ ⑦ ⑩ ⑧ ❶

Many of the climbs on this wall were established during a short period in 1991 by Porter Jarrard and friends. Many of the route names, such as Jill, Angry Bob, and The Zone, come from the scifi film Hardware.

Routes are listed from left to right.

● 1 □ **Apple City QuickStep 11b**
Up slab to interesting roof. 65′ *FA Dave Doll, 1998*

● 2 □ **Ambrosia Kills 12b** ★
This climb takes the small overhang and face left of Whipperly, then breaks through the big part of the high roof. 60′ *FA Sam Lightner, 2013*

● 3 □ **Whipperly Wamberly Walk 11b** ★
Scramble up ledges to a small bulge with a boulder problem, then up easier ground to the roof. A few powerful moves take you to the anchor. *FA Porter Jarrard, 1992*

● 4 □ **No Left Ear 10d** ★★
Up well protected juggy face to anchors. This is a popular climb. One can continue through the roof above, but it's not recommended. 70′ *FA Steve Bechtel, 1996*

● 5 □ **+No Left Ear 11d**
Up well protected juggy face to anchors. This is a popular climb. One can continue through the roof above, but it's not recommended. 70′ *FA Steve Bechtel, 1996*

Face Dancer   Hardware

6 ☐ **Unbreakable 10d ★**
This climb takes thin holds up to a bulge, then bigger holds to an anchor just below the large roof.
FA Ben Sears, 2015

7 ☐ **Fluffy Bagel 9 ★**
15' right of Unbreakable, this climb follows thin moves down low to easy pockets.
FA Anne Peick & Scott Robertson, 2017

8 ☐ **The Toaster 10d ★**
Thin climbing through a bulge down low then up along a broken flake to the anchor.
FA Anne Peick & Scott Robertson 2017

9 ☐ **SR Route (Closed Project)**
Long line right of The Toaster. *Equipped Scott Robertson*

10 ☐ **The Evil One 13a ★**
Climb right on "ramp" hold, then past savage crimp moves up the blank face to the anchor. 60'
FA Greg Collins, 1997

11 ☐ **Milkman 13a ★★**
Bouldery movement on edges and small pockets. Starts behind some bushes at the base of the wall. 60'
FA Vance White, 1999

12 ☐ **Slippery People 12b**
Poor. "Trouty" damp rock makes for a disappointing climb. 60' *FA Porter Jarrard, 1992*

13 ☐ **The Zone 13b ★**
This is the hardest of the Hardware routes. Crimp your way to the top. 60' *FA Frank Dusl, 1991*

14 ☐ **Shades 12d ★★**
Steep small crimps, continuous. 60' *FA Frank Dusl, 1992*

15 ☐ **Moe 12b ★★**
Begin in a leftfacing lieback. Large crimps and jugs. Very fun, but with a couple of somewhat greasy holds at the top. Very chalky. 60' *FA Porter Jarrard, 1992*

16 ☐ **Jill 12d ★**
A desperate crimp move leads to easier climbing above.
65' *FA Porter Jarrard, 1992*

17 ☐ **Hardware 12a ★★**
Climb up a thin crack to a crux move at bolt 3. A rightward traverse to jugs leads to easier climbing to top. Chalked sidepulls mark the start. 65' *FA Frank Dusl, 1991*

18 ☐ **Software 12c**
A direct start to the top of Hardware, this is usually a bit damp. 65' *FA Paul Piana, 1996*

19 ☐ **Mark 13 13a ★★**
Follows seams to long reaches between crimps. 70'
FA Porter Jarrard, 1991

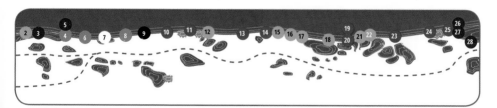

MOE 12b Sophia Kim

●20 ☐ **Upheaval 13b** ★★
Long pulls lead up and right toward Angry Bob. 70'
FA Greg Collins, 1999

●21 ☐ **Angry Bob 12d**
Crimp up the gold streak. A recently broken hold has
made this route harder. *FA Porter Jarrard, 1992*

●22 ☐ **Murgatroid 12a** ★★
This climb starts on a blocky "ledge" area right of the
main Hardware Wall. Hard edge climbing leads to a
good rest in a scoop, followed by easier but continuous
climbing above. 80' *FA Paul Piana, 1996*

●23 ☐ **First Responder 13b** ★★
Thin climbing up to the scoop, then up, up, up to a high
crux. 90' *FA Ty Mack, 2004*

●24 ☐ **Summon the Han 13d**
This route takes the long face right of First Responder.
FA BJ Tilden, 2016

●25 ☐ **The Heavens 13b** ★
Just right of a large bush on the wall. Hard moves lead to
a good rest, then 5.11 climbing to the top. 75'
FA Greg Collins, 1992

●26 ☐ **Heaven Can Wait 11c** ★★
Climb a chimney to a leftward traverse to join "Heavens"
after 4 bolts. One can climb inside the chimney, or face
climb the pillar, though the former makes it easier to clip
the bolts. 75' *FA Gary Wilmot, 1994*

●27 ☐ **Mutt and Jeff 11b** ★★
Shares the start chimney of Heaven Can Wait, then
moves right and up wellprotected face above. 80'
FA Mike Lindsey, 2002

●28 ☐ **Postcards From the Edge 11d**
Follow a short arête on the detached block to anchors.
Techy and thin. 30' *FA Richard Collins, 1989*

●29 ☐ **Hell Yes 11d**
Climb up right facing flake to a black headwall. Hueco
features up top. High crux. 75' *FA Vance White, 2014*

●30 ☐ **Value Pack 12b**
Climbs up ledge systems to a high crux on wall right of
the Postcards flake. 80' *FA Greg Collins, 1997*

VANCE **WHITE**

Vance "Victor Blanco" White moved to Lander in the late nineties and became a fixture of the local scene almost at once. Vance's first years in Lander were spent repeating most of the 5.12 and 5.13 routes in the area. Over the years, his ubiquitous presence and gregarious personality earned him the unofficial title of Mayor of Sinks. Whether it was just a friendly hello, an offered belay, or a full day's tour of the crag, Vance made everyone feel welcome at the cliff.

Victor has continued to climb in the years since his near-daily residence at Sinks, but has turned his focus to developing new routes at outlying crags. Over the past 15 years, Vance has helped establish multiple routes at Fairfield Hill, Sinks Main Wall, Wolf Point, and has led the charge in developing the Wolf Pup area. Among his many contributions are the very popular Earth A.D. and Bust a Nut at the Wilds area, Pitch Black near the Killer Cave, and Flight Club at Fairfield Hill.

Now in his forties, Vance spends more time at work and at home than at the crag, but still finds time to make it out every week. He still climbs as hard as ever, still puts in new routes whenever he can, but puts most of his energy into sharing this wonderful area with his daughter Andi.

CITADEL

| 11AM-PM | 15m | Vertical | Winter |

0 · 2 · 4 · 10 · 1 · 1

The Citadel wall is a pretty, vertical wall broken at half height by a horizontal band. Most routes here feature techy crimpy climbing.

Routes are listed from left to right.

●1 ☐ Fat Boys Skip School 11a
Begins on a ledge system reached by scrambling up from right. Climbs up flakes and pockets to a high crux. 45'
FA Mike Lindsey, 1994

●2 ☐ Biltong Rides Tornado 10c ★★
Just right of Fat Boys, fun climbing up a vertical wall. 50'
FA Biltong Murray, 1994

●3 ☐ Pick Apart The Day 11d ★★
Takes a vertical wall on large pockets to a steeper section of thin holds. 10' right of Biltong Rides Tornado.
FA Ben Sears, 2016

●4 ☐ Alley Cat Aggression 12b ★★
The next route right of Pick Apart The Day, features good pockets and a confounding crux. *FA Ben Sears, 2016*

●5 ☐ Lab Rat on the Run 12b ★★
This route sits right where the trail meets the wall. Climb up on relatively easy rock to some reachy moves at mid height. A punchy finish awaits. *FA Ben Sears, 2016*

●6 ☐ Fun Planet 10a ★
Follows the slab to a high rightfacing dihedral. Starts off the ledgy feature to the left of Blood Brother. 70'
FA Georgie Stanley, 1992

●7 ☐ Wide Awake Zombie 12b
Climbs the face just left of Blood Brother. It feels contrived to stay left of Blood Brother at crux, so most climbers join that route for a move or two. 75'
FA Heidi Badaracco, 1995

photo Kyle Duba

DIVINE INTERVENTION 13b

Jordan Jack

● 8 ☐ **Blood Brother 11a** ★★
Climb the groove/ramp to a vertical face that leads to a slightly overhanging seam. Full value! 75'
 FA Sue Miller, 1991

● 9 ☐ **Funk Soul Brother 12a** ★
This takes the left of two climbs behind the large juniper. Vertical 5.11 climbing leads to a rest, then a short crux before easy terrain takes you to the top. 65'
FA Mark Howe, 2002

● 10 ☐ **Right About Now 11c** ★★
This is just right of Funk Soul Brother, and can be identified by the big hueco at half height. Hard face climbing to a BIG jug, then up a steep wall to an easy slab finish. 70'
FA Mark Howe, 2002

● 11 ☐ **Tel Aviv Miracle 12b** ★★
Hard crimping leads to a good rest, then a tricky finishing move. 50' *FA Greg Collins, 1991*

● 12 ☐ **Paladin 12a** ★
Stout crimping leads to long headwall moves. 75'
FA John Warning, 1997

● 13 ☐ **West of Hell 12d** ★★
Loweranglaed face climbing takes you to the horizontal, then it's on to the crimpy headwall. 75' *FA BJ Tilden, 2006*

● 14 ☐ **Divine Intervention 13b** ★
Climb Citadel to the horizontal, then up and left on very small holds. 75' *FA Frank Dusl, 1994*

● 15 ☐ **The Citadel of Hope 12c** ★★★
Climb up and right on good holds to the horizontal (11a), then up through twisty, fun moves to a hard exit. 75'
FA Greg Collins, 1990

● 16 ☐ **The Stronghold of Decay 12c** ★★★
Work up thin, sometimes dirty moves, past a few really cool holds. 75' *FA Greg Collins, 1991*

● 17 ☐ **The Earth Died Screaming 12b**
Easier climbing low leads to long hard headwall moves. 75' *FA Heidi Badaracco, 1994*

● 18 ☐ **SL Route (Closed Project)**
This is the furthest right route on the wall.
Equipped Sam Lightner

ADDICTION

10AM-PM	15m	Slight	Winter

3 · 0 · 4 · 8 · 4 · 0

The Addiction Wall sits right at the top of the Addiction approach trail. The wall is characterized by shorter, slightly overhanging routes. Many routes feature big moves on good holds.

Routes are listed from left to right.

●1 ☐ Black Celebration 11b
On high wall above and left of "Addiction" wall. This follows a prominent black streak. Strangely, this was one of the first routes done at this section of the wall. 30'
FA Joe Motherway, 1993

○2 ☐ A Beautiful Life 9 ★★
Follow flakes and a seam up a vertical wall to a slab. Named in memory of Jim Ratz. 45' *FA Tom Hargis, 2005*

○3 ☐ Soup Sandwich 8 ★
This starts in the right crack, climbing up and right, then moving back left onto a less than vertical face to finish at the Go West anchors. 40'. *FA Steve Bechtel, 2006*

○4 ☐ Go West, Young Man 7 ★★★
Climb the leftarcing crack. Certainly the most popular route at the Addiction Wall, it was one of the last established. 45' *FA Kirk Billings, 2001*

●5 ☐ Mezzmerie 12c
Climbs up the Soul Finger seam to the small ledge, then out left onto face. 45' *FA Paul Piana, 1996*

●6 ☐ Soul Finger 11a ★
Starts up blocks and flakes, following the crack into a dihedral at the top. Very techy and footworkintensive. 55'
FA Steve Bechtel, 2006

●7 ☐ The Road to Dushanbe 12a ★★
This route also takes the Soul Finger crack for the first 3 bolts, but moves right once you hit the bottom of the corner. Nice moves on good edges and pockets take you to an exit crux. In case you didn't know, Dushanbe is the capital of Tajikistan. 55' *FA Sam Lightner, 2014*

●8 ☐ Surplus Fusion Reaction 13a ★★
Up the steep face just left of Addiction. Climb crimps and small pockets in nice, continuous sequences. The name comes from a misquoted line from an old Simpsons episode. 65' *FA Frank Dusl, 1994*

●9 ☐ Addiction 12c ★★★
Climb up and right on crimpy crux moves to a good rail, then up long moves to a final engaging slab. One of the alltime classics. 60' *FA Frank Dusl, 1991*

●10 ☐ **Dogs of War 13a** ★★
Hard barndoor moves take you to a good rest, followed by a thin crimp crux. After the crux this route joins the top of Pretty Hate Machine. 65' *FA Frank Dusl, 1992*

●11 ☐ **Pretty Hate Machine 13c** ★★★
Directly behind the big tree, every move of this thing is full value. 75' *FA Frank Dusl, 1991*

●12 ☐ **The Gathering 13c** ★★
Steep climbing on crimps. This starts at the right end of the tree, just left of the seam that marks the start of Public Enemy. 60' *FA Frank Dusl, 1992*

●13 ☐ **Public Enemy 12c** ★
Climb up the thin seam to a good rest after bolt 3, then through a short crux that ends at a big rail. 5.11 climbing takes you to the top. 60' *FA Gary Wilmot, 1992*

●14 ☐ ✎ **Drug Enemy 12a** ★★
Climbs Corner Drug to third bolt, then traverses left on a jug rail to finish on Public Enemy. 60' *FA Greg Collins, 1997*

●15 ☐ **I Want A New Drug 12c** ★
Climb Corner Drug to the third bolt, then step left and climb the steep face between Corner Drug and Public Enemy. 55' *FA Vance White, 2011*

●16 ☐ **Corner Drug 11a** ★★
The chalked up corner climb. Pumpy. 55'
FA Greg Collins, 1997

●17 ☐ **White Dwarf 12c** ★
Continuous hard moves up bulging wall. 45'
FA Greg Collins, 1997

●18 ☐ **The Black Hole 12d**
Hard steep moves past an obvious "black hole" pocket. 35' *FA Greg Collins, 1992*

●19 ☐ **Dewalt's Challenge 11d**
Steep climbing up flakes and edges. Tends to collect a bit of dirt from runoff. This route was named for the first ascentionist's difficulty in drilling the route with a cordless Dewalt screw gun. 30' *FA Trey Warren, 1997*

WHITE **HEAT**

10AM-PM | 15m | Vertical | Winter

① ⑤ ⑩ ⑦ ④ ②

This wall marks the midsection of the cliff, and is easily identified from the parking lot by it eponymous white streak. This wall's main routes tend to be very technical, but shorter than much of the rest of the crag. The right end of the wall features longer, easier routes.

Routes are listed from left to right.

●1 ☐ **Velvet Sea 10a** ★
A short route on the left side of the Shortie Sortie wall.
FA Ben Sears, 2016

●2 ☐ **Shortie Sortie 10c**
This climb goes up the center of a slab on the next section of wall right of the Addiciton wall. 40'
FA Greg Collins, 1990

●3 ☐ **Divided Sky 11c** ★
A technical face climb just right of Shortie Sortie. Stick clipping is a good idea. *FA Ben Sears, 2016*

●4 ☐ **Wind Blows High 11b** ★
The longest route on the face, this climb starts behind the left end of the big tree, off the right end of a low flake/ledge. Shares anchors with Divided Sky.
FA Ben Sears, 2016

●6 ☐ **Anarchist's Lament 11a** ★★
Scramble up the same start as Fun, Fun, Joy, Joy. Start the same crack, but clip the bolts on the left wall. Move up and left after 3 bolts then to a good rest followed by a final bulge. *FA Ryan and Jesse Morse-Brady, 2017*

●5 ☐ **Fun, Fun, Joy, Joy 10b** ★
Climbs up a corner just right of a large juniper then out onto a nice face to the right. 50' *FA Ken Trout, 1993*

Addiction

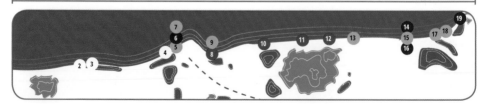

●7 ☐ Rat Scat Fever (Open Project)

This route starts off with a hard boulder problem, and then followed by engaging thin climbing. Estimated to be mid 13. Stick clipping 2nd bolt is recommended. *Equipped Ben Sears*

●8 ☐ Dime Time 13a

Hateful crimps up vertical wall. 50' *FA Greg Collins, 1992*

●9 ☐ Mono a Mono 13a ★

Long moves between...monos! 50' *FA Paul Piana, 1992*

●10 ☐ Acid Ranger (Open Project)

Looks really hard. Thin crimps, long moves. Estimated to be around 14+. 50' *Equipped, Greg Collins*

●11 ☐ White Heat 12d ★★

Start in the small leftfacing corner, the up and left to huecos. Hard moves from these lead to easier climbing. 55' *FA Greg Collins, 1990*

●12 ☐ Blushing Crow 12c ★★

Shares the same desperate start with "White Heat" but moves right at bolt 2 and up long moves between good pockets. 55' *FA Paul Piana, 1993*

●13 ☐ War Party 12b

Follow a seam past 2 bolts then up easier climbing above. 50' *FA Greg Collins, 1990*

●14 ☐ The Sting 14a

This thin longstanding project stood unclimbed for nearly 25 years. *FA BJ Tilden, 2016*

●15 ☐ Consumption 12b ★

Continuously difficult moves between small holds. 50' *FA Greg Collins, 1990*

●16 ☐ Searching for Blanton's 12b ★★

A nice route on a very clean section of the wall, just left of Central Pillar. *FA Sam Lightner, 2014*

●17 ☐ Central Pillar 11a ★

Climb up tall "pillar", then past thin moves into leftfacing corner feature. Up past the ledge to fun headwall. 80' *FA Gary Wilmot, 1993*

●18 ☐ Searching for Jose Cuervo 12b ★★

Climb up a tricky slab to the bulge, through the bulge on thin pockets, then up a fun headwall. 80' *FA Craig Reason, 1991*

●19 ☐ No Impact 11d ★★
Hard slab climbing leads to big moves through the bulge.
50' *FA Greg Collins, 1989*

●20 ☐ Spike In Vein 11c ★★★
Similar to "No Impact" but with an easier slab and easier
bulge. 50' *FA Greg Collins, 1994*

○21 ☐ Storm Warning 9 ★★
Climb up ledges and seams to right side of bulge, pass
bulge high on the right, up past ledge to high crux. 80'
FA Greg Collins, 1998

●22 ☐ Hale Bopp 10d
Climbs lowangle face to progressively steeper wall.
Baffling crux at top. 80' *FA John Warning, 1997*

●23 ☐ Peter Bopp 11a
Up face/seam to hard headwall. 80'
FA John Warning, 1997

●24 ☐ Little Creatures 11c ★★
Traverse ledge right to the beginning of this route, just
past a small tree. Hard thin moves lead to fun, pumpy
climbing above. Be careful lowering off if your rope is
less than 60M. 85' *FA Jim Howe, 1991*

●25 ☐ Tiny Creatures 10a
This climb starts down and right of Little Creatures, ending at the ledge that Little Creatures starts on. It follows a
leftfacing corner past 3 bolts. *FA Liz Lightner, 2014*

●26 ☐ Titanic 11b ★★
Climbs a leftfacing corner to the ledge, then through a
nice bulge and up the long face above. 100'
FA Greg Collins, 1998

●27 ☐ Pocket Full of Kryptonite 13b
Hard thin vertical climbing leads to a crux bulge. 60'
FA Frank Dusl, 1993

●28 ☐ Guardian Angel 12a
Thin face moves on a wall left of the big corner lead to a
fun headwall above. 75' *FA Dave Doll, 1998*

●29 ☐ Angel of Mercy 11a ★
This route follows the big corner crack, then moves left to
share the last half with Guardian Angel. 75'
FA Dave Doll, 2001

photo Kyle Duba

Sam Lightner **NO IMPACT** 11d

BRISKET

10AM-PM 15m Vertical Winter

1 | 4 | 0 | 2 | 0 | 0

The Brisket area is the short, broken section of cliff right of White Heat. The area's namesake route is a powerful climb, supposedly named after the ripped physique of Rob Hess.

Routes are listed from left to right.

●1 □The Brisket 12c
Very bouldery climbing up a seam, then left and up a tricky face. This route was named after the impressive lats of Rob Hess. 45' *FA Greg Collins, 1990*

●2 □Fine Dining 12b ★
Seams and thin edges right of The Brisket. 45'
FA Greg Collins, 1998

●3 □The Guyver 10b ★★
Follow a thin seam and face to anchors near a small roof.
40' *FA Jeff Leafgreen, 2005*

○4 □Rokai Corner 8 ★
Fun, easy climbing up a polished corner. 40'
FA Vance White, 2007

●5 □Praying to the Aliens 10b ★
Climbs an awkward crack system to anchors just below big ledge. 35' *FA Ed Delong, 1993*

●6 □Caught Stealing 10c
A hard, poorly protected move leads to a runout to the anchors. 30' *FA Chris Stover, 1991*

●7 □Pigs in Zen 10c
A Wandery short red slab. 30' *FA Chris Stover, 1991*

White Heat | Brisket

White Heat | Brisket

HAPPY **WHEEL**

10AM-PM | 15m | Vertical | Winter

2 5 4 4 1 0

One of the last developed walls in the area, this sector has produced some really good routes. A good variety of grades and a nice base area makes this a great location for many climbers.

Routes are listed from left to right.

● **1** ☐ **Pet Arête 10d**
Climb a balancey arête to a spicy rightward traverse at top. Shares Yellow Cake anchors. 50′
FA Kristen Kremer, 2000

● **2** ☐ **Yellow Cake 12b**
Thin moves lead to a hard mono move and an easier top. 50′ *FA Greg Collins, 2000*

● **3** ☐ **Cloud Calling 12b** ★
Climb the dark streak up a gently overhanging wall on engaging moves and hard to see monos. 50′
FA Greg Collins, 2000

● **4** ☐ **Where They Gonna Run When Destruction Comes? 12c** ★
Up the difficult face just left of Happy Wheel to a hard high bulge. 70′ *FA Greg Collins, 2000*

● **5** ☐ **Happy Wheel 10a** ★
Start in a wellprotected corner, then move out of corner to the right and up a thin face. 45′
FA Heidi Badaracco, 1999

● **6** ☐ **Twice Baked 11c**
Takes the prow right of Happy Wheel. 50′
FA Rick Thompson, 1998

● **7** ☐ **White Lotus 13c** ★
Climbs steep rock on offbalance moves just right of Twice Baked. 45′ *FA Leif Gasch, 2006*

● **8** ☐ **Wild Flower Royale 12b** ★
This climb takes a bulge and righttrending corner feature 20 feet right of White Lotus. 45′ *FA Jeremy Rowen, 2011*

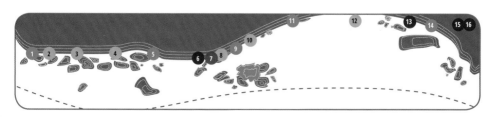

PET ARETE 10d — Ifrane Brennan | photo Kyle Duba

CAMEL JOCKEY

| 10AM-PM | 15m | Vertical | Winter |

6 **2** **4** **5** **1** **1**

The big dihedral a hundred yards left of the Killer Cave marks the Camel Jockey area. More Funky Than Gunky is the the area's most popular 5.9, while climbs like Sand Digger don't get the attention they deserve based on location. This area is nice on windy days.

Routes are listed from left to right.

●**1 ☐ No Self Control 10c**
Thin slab climbing on the left of the arch. 45'
FA Dave Brinda, 1994

●**2 ☐ Straight Up Crew 11c ★**
Up the right side of the small arch, then through the bulge to a good slab. 50' *FA Greg Collins, 1996*

●**3 ☐ GC Route**
2 bolts and anchors have been placed. Probably will be 5.12. *Equipped Greg Collins*

●**4 ☐ Wammoe 12b**
Continuously hard moves up a vertical wall. 60'
FA Greg Collins, 1997

●**5 ☐ Sand Digger 12b ★★**
Start on a hard boulder problem into a short crack, then up a steep face on neat moves to hard exit moves. 65'
FA Hassan Saab, 1990

●**6 ☐ Camel Jockey 13b ★**
Up the center of the pretty wall on long moves. 60'
FA Hassan Saab, 1990

○**7 ☐ More Funky Than Gunky 9 ★★**
Very popular crack in corner then up through a small roof. It's noted by some climbers that this route could be led on gear instead of bolts...of course, the same could be said of all the climbs at Sinks. 70' *FA John Hauf, 1980*

●**8 ☐ Child's Play 10c ★**
Flakes to a thin crux, then up and right to anchors. 55'
FA Dave Brinda, 1991

●**9 ☐ Passion Party 10c**
This is the first route on the wall as the hill inclines to the right. 40' *FA Vance White, 2011*

○**10 ☐ ZBoys 8 ★★**
Follows fun flakes up a lowangle wall. 50'
FA Vance White, 2007

●**11 ☐ Dreaming of the Rasta Bus 10a ★★**
Fun climbing on a slab takes you to bigger pockets high. 40' *FA Bob Branscomb, 2010*

○**12 ☐ Dogtown 9 ★★**
Climb a rightfacing corner to big holds. 45'
FA Vance White, 2007

●**13 ☐ Hunger Force 11c**
Climb off flake into hard crux, then up easier moves to top. Sharp. 45' *FA Vance White, 2007*

●**14 ☐ Bones Brigade 10a**
Climb up face into lefttrending corner. 65'
FA Vance White, 2007

●**15 ☐ Spent Rods 11b**
This route and "Bad Milk" begin on the ledge up behind "No Self Control". Climb up gully to left to reach the ledge. 35' *FA Gary Wilmot, 1992*

●**16 ☐ Bad Milk 11a**
The right route on the upper ledge, this climb is the better of the two. 35' *FA Chris Walberg, 1994*

MORE FUNKY THAN GUNKY 9 Liz Schmol

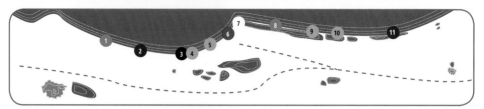

●9 ☐ Lost Boy 12d
Burly thin climbing. 50' *FA Bj Tilden, 1997*

●10 ☐ Steel Rain 12b ★
This climb takes the slightly overhanging face 10 feet left of Red Light Love. *FA Sam Lightner, 2015*

●11 ☐ Red Light Love 11c ★
Start on flakes, up right through a techy move, then past fun moves to anchor. 65' *FA Scott VanOrman, 1998*

●12 ☐ The Ogre 11a
Short route just right of a small gully. 30'
FA Tim Hampton, 1991

○13 ☐ Doodles 6 ★
Face climb uphill and left of Zozo's Dance.
FA Dennis VanDenbos, 2016

○14 ☐ Zozo's Dance 7 ★★
The long face climb, ending in a high corner left of Put Down Your Ducky. Starts in a seam. *FA Lightners ,2015*

○15 ☐ Put Down Your Ducky 8 ★★
An exceedingly popular slab route, look for a small shelf at the base, and a well worn belay area. 80'
FA Dave Doll, 1999

○16 ☐ Beware the Foosa 7 ★★
The blocky corner right of Put Down Your Ducky.
FA Dave Doll, 2015

●17 ☐ Dutch Rudder 12a ★
This climb takes thin holds through a bulge to a vertical wall above. If you'd like to know the origin of the name, stop by the Wild Iris store and ask Jeremy! 50'
FA Jeremy Rowan, 2009

○18 ☐ Frogger 8 ★★
Climb the left side of the huge flake right of Dutch Rudder, then up the face above. *FA Lightners, 2015*

●19 ☐ Berzerk 11a ★
The face of the flake, joins Frogger at the top of the flake.
FA Lightners, 2015

HARVEST MOON

10AM-PM	10m	Vertical	Winter

1 **4** **6** **4** **1** **0**

The Harvest Moon area is the traditional warmup area for the climbs of the Killer Cave. There are a high number of very good 5.10 and 5.11 routes on this section of wall. The area between Pocket Calculator and Global WarmUp is a major rockfall zone. This is not a good place to hang out between climbs. Better to set your packs down near Harvest Moon or around by Dutch Rudder.

Routes are listed from left to right.

●1 ☐ **Global WarmUp 10c** ★★
Begin in a small corner, and move up to less steep terrain. 6 bolts 45' *FA Ellen Bechtel, 2007*

○2 ☐ **Sam I Am 9** ★★
Start at the high point of the hill, just right of what's left of a large bush. Climb the corner, then left and up a juggy face. 50' *FA Steve Bechtel, 2008*

●3 ☐ **Pocket Calculator 12b** ★
Starts just right of a large bush, up thin pockets to long easier wall above. 60' *FA Greg Collins, 1998*

●4 ☐ **Elmo's Fish 10d** ★★
Climb up a shallow rightfacing corner to an obvious undercling and up the steep face. 60'
FA Heidi Badaracco, 2000

●5 ☐ **Firecracker Kid 10b** ★★
Up lieback flake to a ledge, then to corner climbing. 55'
FA Tim Rawson, 1984

●6 ☐ **Sun Spot 11d** ★
Climb up slick crimps and small pockets to good holds near the top. 45' *FA Sue Miller, 1991*

●7 ☐ **Harvest Moon 11a** ★★
Start up rightward undercling, then straight up on glassy holds. Features ringtype bolts. Continuous. 55'
FA Richard Collins, 1989

●8 ☐ **After the Goldrush 11c** ★★
Climbs a thin face to easier pocketed headwall. An alternate start traverses in from Harvest Moon at 5.10b (Harvest Rush). 7 bolts 60' *FA Steve Bechtel, 2006*

●9 ☐ **Powderfinger 10c** ★★
Follow a seam to a big flake undercling, then up and over to jugs above. 6 bolts 50' *FA Steve Bechtel, 2007*

●10 ☐ **Sign of the Times 11b**
Technical climbing up and left to a chain anchor. 50'
FA Frank Dusl, 1992

Harvest Moon   Cave Left

KILLER CAVE **LEFT**

10AM-PM   10m   Steep   Winter

0 **0** **1** **6** **12** **0**

This famed section of wall is host to dozens of 5.13 and 5.14 routes, including some of the best routes of those grades anywhere. The steep climbing, relaxed atmosphere, and shelter from the elements make this an ideal crag. The rotten nature of the rock near the bottom of the cliff limits the number of independent starts, so expect many climbs to share the same first few bolts. This crag is sunny all winter, and is steep enough to catch shade much of the day during the summer.

●11 ☐+ Sign of the Times 13a ★
Up the black streak in the headwall above the anchors for pitch 1. Total length is 95' *FA Frank Dusl, 1992*

●12 ☐+ Hypernova 12b ★★★
From the end of Sign of the Times (p1), climb up and right to the roof then over and up shallow corner. Use caution when lowering! 105' *FA Steve Bechtel, 1999*

●13 ☐+ Black Dynamite 12b
Climb either Sign of the Times or Powderfinger, then continue up the wall above, trending right of Hypernova. Follow black hangers to a black streak through the roof. Crank some hard moves, then up the vertical wall above. Use caution when lowering. 105' *FA Vance White, 2013*

●14 ☐ Whirling Disease 11a ★
This climb takes damp rock through the small bulge left of Brown Trout. *FA Lightners, 2015*

●15 ☐ Brown Trout 11c
Unfortunately a little trouty, but good climbing through diagonalling roof. 85' *FA Greg Collins, 1992*

●16 ☐+ Pitch Black 12c
From the anchors of Brown Trout, climb straight up a black streak. This takes an arete, then moves up technical terrain to a vertical wall above. Requires a rope longer than 60 meters to lower off. *FA Vance White, 2012*

Routes are listed from left to right.

●1 ☐+ Cutthroat 11d
The big leaning corner above Brown Trout. Use care in lowering if climbing this route from the ground, a 60 meter rope will barely get you down. 110'
FA Paul Piana, 2000

●2 ☐+ To the Moon, Alice 12b ★
Continue straight up the wall above Blue Moon, heading for the top of Cutthroat. This is a very high route, use care in lowering! 110' *FA Paul Piana, 2000*

●3 ☐ Blue Moon 12a ★★
Great climbing up big flake and thru overhanging terrain above. This route originally went to the top of the cliff, but is now done to anchors after bolt 7. 70'
FA Keith Lennard, 1990

●4 ☐+ Full Moon 12a
Climb Blue Moon, then move up and left to finish with an additional 70 feet of 5.11 climbing. Use caution when lowering. 110' *FA Keith Lennard, 1990*

●5 ☐ Moonstone 13b ★★
Climb up hard moves to a great jug, past more hard moves, and up easier terrain. This climb follows a beautiful golden streak. 70' *FA Greg Collins, 1992*

photo Kyle Duba

Vance White

BUSH DOCTOR 12a

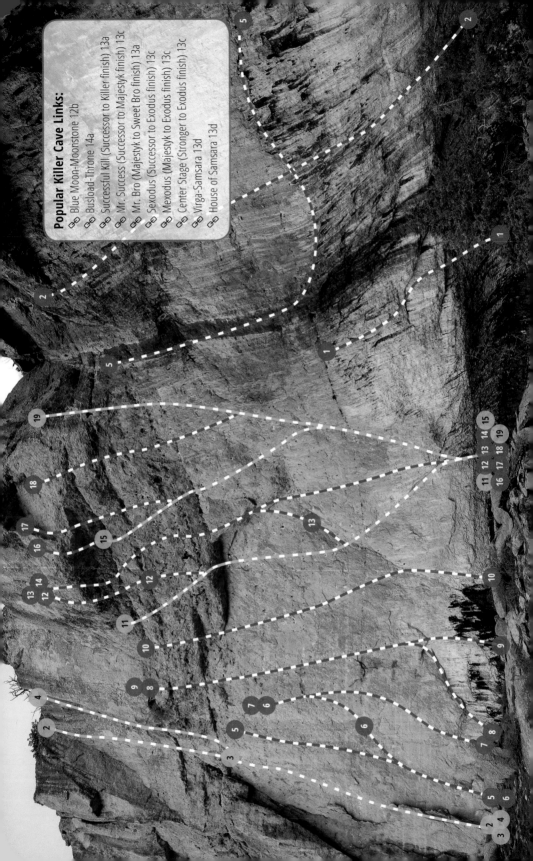

Popular Killer Cave Links:

- Blue Moon–Moonstone 12b
- Busload–Throne 14a
- Successful Kill (Successor to Killer finish) 13a
- Mr. Success (Successor to Majestyk finish) 13c
- Mr. Bro (Majestyk to Sweet Bro finish) 13a
- Sexodus (Successor to Exodus finish) 13c
- Mexodus (Majestyk to Exodus finish) 13c
- Center Stage (Stronger to Exodus finish) 13c
- Virga–Samsara 13d
- House of Samsara 13d

● 18 □ **Nirvana 13a** ★★
Same start as Cartoon, but continue right where Cartoon goes straight up. Long moves up a continuously steep wall. 85' *FA George Squibb, 1992*

● 19 □ **Kingdom of Jah 12d** ★★
Shares start with Cartoon, but traverse even further right than Nirvana, then up good pockets to anchors just left of the black streak. 75' *FA Greg Collins, 1998*

KILLER CAVE RIGHT

10AM-PM | 10m | Steep | Winter

1 4 2 11 14 0

Routes are listed from left to right.

● 1 □ **Virga 13c** ★
Tram start. Short route that moves past hard pulls, ending at anchor near the horizontal band of pockets. 4 bolts 35' *FA Matt Lund, 1998*

● 2 □ **Organic 14b** ★
Start in underclings, moving left and up steep wall to horizontal band. Join Basra to the top. *FA BJ Tilden, 2003*

● 6 □ ✎ **Sister Ray 13a**
Start as for Moonstone, but head right and join the upper section of Busload of Faith. 60' *FA Greg Collins, 1991*

● 7 □ ✎ **Busload of Faith 14a** ★★
Hard moves from the getgo, starting off a small block and moving right. 60' *FA Frank Dusl, 1993*

● 8 □ **Wield the Scepter 13b** ★
Starts just right of Busload, traverses a hard undercling arch into The Throne, then up that route. 85' *FA Ty Mack, 2004*

● 9 □ **The Throne 13b** ★★★
Hard crimping leads to an undercling, then long moves up an easier headwall. 80' *FA Greg Collins, 1991*

● 10 □ **The Successor 13b** ★★
Thin moves up a righttrending seam feature, then up continuous difficulties to surmount a roof at the top. *FA Greg Collins, 1994*

● 11 □ **Killer 12c** ★★
Start with A0 start (usually a fixed aider on bolt 1) to gain a leftleaning seam, follow it left and up to a juggy wall and roof above. 80' *FA Greg Collins, 1990*

● 12 □ **Sweet Bro 13a** ★
Takes Killer to just above the roof, then moves right and up hard long moves, then over another small roof at top. 90' *FA Steve Babits, 2003*

● 13 □ **Mr. Majestyk 13b** ★★★
Up Killer to the end of the seam, then right through a 12a crux (usually a fixed long draw here), up corner to good rest. Punch it thru steep climbing to a horizontal, and up left through the roof to share the Sweet Bro anchors. Mrs. Majestyk is a 12d variation that traverses right to the Cartoon Graveyard anchors before the crux lip moves. 90' *FA Steve Bechtel, 1997*

● 14 □ **Stronger Than Reason 13c** ★
Hard thin pockets straight up from the Killer start bolt. Joins Mr. Majestyk at high horizontal. Only 13b if you stop at Cartoon's anchors. 90' *FA Matt Lund, 1997*

● 15 □ **Cartoon Graveyard 12d** ★★★
A0 start (at ring bolt and standard hanger) to an undercling, then up right through a low crux. After the rest at bolt 5, go straight up to anchors below the 6' roof. The extension through the roof is Exodus. 80' *FA Paul Piana, 1997*

● 16 □ + **Exodus 13c** ★★
A 3 bolt extension to Cartoon Graveyard that adds substantially to the difficulty. 90' *FA Vance White, 2006*

● 17 □ **Samsara 13a** ★★★
Climb Cartoon Graveyard to the horizontal rest, then up and right through the roof. Full value crux at the end. 90' *FA Kirk Billings, 2002*

●3 ☐ **Shao Lin Shadow Boxing 13b**
Hard pulls between positive holds. Join Baghdad to finish. 80' *FA Geoff Sluyter? 1999*

●4 ☐ **Shaolin Degree 13d**
Start on Shaolin Shadowboxing and finish the Zero Degrees roof. 80' *FA BJ Tilden, 2008*

●5 ☐ **House of God 13a**
Start in Baghdad's leftfacing corner, up to horizontal pocket band, then L all the way to black streak and up. 100' *FA Greg Collins, 1992*

●6 ☐ **Basra 12c**
Start as for Baghdad, but continue left along horizontal to next line of bolts. Climb up and through steeps above. 80' *FA Greg Collins, 1993*

●7 ☐ + **Baghdad 12d** ★
Climb leftfacing corner to horizontal, traverse left and up good holds through steep wall above. 75'
FA Greg Collins, 1990

●8 ☐ + **Deadman's Reach 12d** ★
Do the shared Baghdad start, up past the big flake as for Zero Degrees, but splits left and up overhanging rock to the roof. Break the roof with a big move, then finish the same as Cannonball. *FA Steve Bechtel, 2009*

●9 ☐ + **Cannonball 12d** ★★
Climb the Baghdad start corner, then up to the big roof above, as for Zero Degrees. At the rings below the roof, split left and up the roof past 3 bolts to finish on Deadman's Reach. *FA Steve Bechtel, 2009*

●10 ☐ + **Zero Degrees 13c** ★
Climbs up Baghdad start corner, then straight up and out the big roof above. 75' *FA BJ TIlden, 2008*

●11 ☐ **Less Than Zero 11d** ★
This is Zero Degrees to the anchors below the roof. The boulder problem at the start makes this feel pretty hard. 70' *FA BJ Tilden, 2008*

●12 ☐ **Shark Bait 13b**
Climb the first four bolts of the Urchin then trend left up overhanging prow. *FA Chris Marley, 2013*

●13 ☐ **The Urchin 13a** ★★
Short and powerful route, starts in undercling /lieback corner, up and over the bulge to an anchor on the slab above. *FA Greg Collins, 1994*

●14 ☐ **Ring of Fire 12b** ★★
Shares the Bush Doctor start, but moves left after bolt 6, through the small roof and up a steep prow. 75'
FA Pete Absolon, 2004

●15 ☐ **Bush Doctor 12a** ★★
Start in a major corner above a big boulder. If the start is done from the ground (sans cheater blocks/log) this route is 12b. Climb up corner, thru bulge, then straight up after bolt 6. This is the middle line of bolts on the wall above the shared start.75' *FA Trey Warren, 1999*

●16 ☐ **Bloodline 12a** ★★
Same as Bush Doctor, but traverses right to a big dihedral after bolt 6. (This route actually is a combo of Bush Doctor and Clown Stabber.) 75' *FA Heidi Badaracco, 2000*

●17 ✇ ☐ **Bloody Endeavor 12b** ★
Climb Bloodline to the base of the corner, then traverse onto the top of Endeavor to finish. Rope drag can be a bummer on this one. *FA Vance White, 2010*

●18 ☐ **Clown Stabber 12d** ★
Same start as Bush Doctor, then right into bulge after bolt 3. Long moves to easy corner above. Variations include Clown Doctor (12d), and Clown of Fire (13a, traversing high and avoiding the corner rest) 75'
FA Paul Piana, 2000

Nate Drolet **MOONSTONE** 13b

●19 ☐ Jimmy Wings Not Included 12c ★★
Again, the same start as Bush Doctor. After bolt 3, traverse right along the undercling, crossing Endeavor and turning to the right side of the prow. Up face and through a small roof. Not as contrived as it sounds, and pretty fun. 70' *FA Paul Piana, 2001*

●20 ☐ Dr. Endeavor 13a ★★
Climb Bush Doctor to bolt 3, then traverse right out the undercling and finish on Endeavor. *FA Unknown*

●21 ☐ Endeavor to Persevere 13c ★★★
Climb up the center of the belly, starting on the big boulder. The hard bit is just getting to the undercling crack, then it's just some enduro 13a climbing to the anchors. 75' *FA Craig Reason, 1991*

●22 ☐ Endeavor to Stab Bush 13c
This hybrid links the Endeavor start to the cruxes of Clown Stabber and Bush Doctor. Endeavor to Stab Fire is a slightly harder variation. 75' *FA Leif Gasch, 2005*

●23 ☐ Love Endeavor 13c ★
Climb the start of One Love, then traverse left past 2 bolts to finish Endeavor. *FA BJ Tilden, 2013*

●24 ☐ One Love 13c ★★
Hard mono pulls through a low bulge, then up vertical wall to another hard roof at the top. 65'
FA Greg Collins, 1997

●25 ☐ Comin' Home Curly 14a ★
Starts as One Love, but breaks right at bolt 3. Hard monos. 65' *FA Todd Skinner, 1999*

●26 ☐ Spook Eyes 12b
Start on right end of the big bulge, just behind the big tree. Very powerful start leads to fun, easier climbing to the top. 60' *FA Paul Piana, 1999*

●27 ☐ Second Hand Nova 10d ★★
Start on thin crimps, moving up and left to a seam. Up face above to small roof. 55' *FA Jeff Leafgreen, 1999*

●28 ☐ Backup Binkie 11c
Hard bouldery start leads to easy slab, then up to anchors. 60' *FA Jeff Leafgreen 1999*

●29 ☐ King of Hearts 10d ★
Hard moves low to easy climbing, then thru tricky bulge and up slab above. 80' *FA Tricia Stetson, 1997*

●30 ☐ Action Candy 10a ★★
Long route with many bolts, continuous moderate moves. 80' *FA Heidi Badaracco, 1997*

●31 ☐ Make Sinks Great Again 10b ★
A long face climb up through the high bulge right of Action Candy. *FA Sam Lightner, 2017*

○32 ☐ A Very Good Place To Start 7 ★
A nice route just right of Make Sinks Great Again. *FA Sam Lightner, 2017*

GREG **COLLINS**

Greg is the "invisible man" of Wyoming climbing. From the time of his arrival in Lander in the early 1980s until the mid 2000s, Greg was at the forefront of rote development in the Lander area. From 5.13 sport routes, to cracks just as hard, to some of the Wind Rivers' hardest climbs, Greg's name is synonymous with hard, high quality lines.

Among Greg's best known routes are Cranner Roof (5.13a, likely Wyoming's first 5.13, at Cranner Rock),

Killer (5.12c, Sinks Main Wall), Citadel of Hope (5.12b, Sinks Main Wall), The Giant's Bite (5.9, Leg Lake Cirque), and Full Tilt (5.13a, The Joint). Between hard sends at the crag, Greg made innumerable trips to the big mountains, including the Alaska Range and the Karakoram.

Dividing his time between instructing for NOLS, guiding for Jackson Hole Mountain Guides, and writing no fewer than ten editions of guidebooks for the Lander area climbing, Greg still found plenty of time to put in routes. No one knows for sure (not even Greg) how many new routes he did during his years in Lander, but there is no doubt he established more lines than any other climber.

Greg's focus the last few years has turned more toward skiing near his home in Victor, Idaho, but he still finds time to climb, and climb well. Recently, he managed a free ascent of the Moonlight Buttress in Zion (V, 5.12d)... thirty years after he brought the 5.13 grade to Wyoming.

Steve Babbits

CARTOON GRAVEYARD 12d

SCUD **WALL**

| 10AM-PM | 10m | Vertical | Winter |

8 12 1 0 0 0

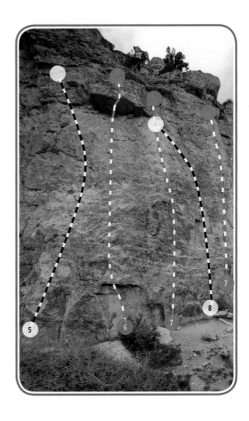

This is by far the most popular crag in Sinks Canyon, featuring a big concentration of moderate routes with a nice base area. When using this area, please stay on established trails, avoid damaging plants and trees, and use your own hardware for toproping routes.

Routes are listed from left to right.

○1 □ **Doggin' Dude 8** ★
This is the first climb after the trail dips away from the wall beyond Action Candy. Climb up seam feature to slab above. 50' *FA Jeff Leafgreen, 1998*

●2 □ **Leave it to Bieber 10b** ★★
Takes the black streak right if Doggin' Dude.
FA Rick Guerrieri and Steven Vedder, 2016

●3 □ **Banoffee 10a** ★★
Continuous slabby face. 50' *FA Jeff Leafgreen, 2000*

●4 □ **Smithereens 10b** ★★★
A low-angled face leads to a corner, then an arete feature, ending in wild and exposed steep moves.
FA Kyle Duba, 2016

○5 □ **Duck Soup 9** ★★★
This route is the first you reach after dropping down the hill from Banoffee. Climbs up flakes to steeper wall above. 50' *FA Dave Doll, 1999*

●6 □ **Stud Alert 10c** ★★
Move through a low overhang to easier slab, then through a 3' roof at the top. 50' *FA Dave Doll, 1997*

●7 □ **Climb Like a Girl 10a** ★
Thin crimps and longer moves, then through small roof above. 50' *FA Jeff Leafgreen, 2000*

○8 □ **Atta Boy, Girl 9** ★
Up pockets and seam to a leftward traverse that ends sharing the Climb Like a Girl anchors. 50'
FA Mark Howe, 2002

●9 □ **Boy, I Gotta Go 10a** ★★
This is the very popular prow route. 45'
FA Jeff Leafgreen, 2000

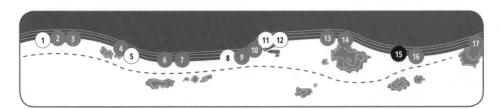

10 ☐ You Go, Girl 10d

Start in a corner, then move out onto the prow to join Boy, I Gotta Go. *FA Heidi Badaracco, 1997*

11 ☐ Mei Day 6

Up corner and low angle face. 60'
FA Mei and Jim Ratz, 1997

12 ☐ Girls' Day Out 6

Face climbing and ledge mantling. 60'
FA Mike and Laura Lindsey, 1997

13 ☐ Bombs Over Crag Bag 10b ★★

Rails and lieback to fun jug climbing. 10 bolts, 65'.
FA Mandy Fabel Brian Fabel, 2014

14 ☐ Iron Dome 10d ★

Starts behind the large tree at the base of the Scud Wall. Climbs up and passes a large flake (solid) to the flakes right. 7 bolts, 65' *FA Sam and Liz Lightner, 2014*

15 ☐ Rubber Soul 11a ★

Easy climbing to tricky bulge. 55' *FA Jim Ratz, 1997*

16 ☐ Storm of the Century 10d ★★

Hard start leads to very good headwall climbing. 55'
FA Mike Lindsey, 1996

17 ☐ Scud Alert 10a

Good pockets up short wall. Left and right variations have been equipped with 23 bolts, both are silly. 40'
FA Greg Collins, 1990

To the Politically Correct Wall: From #14, contour 200 yards east to the next rock band. Climbs located on the far right of the wall. (not pictured)

---

18 ☐ Justified 8 ★★

Slab to steeper corner. 50' *FA Dave Doll, 2014*

19 ☐ A Firm Shake 9 ★

Climb face to arete. 4 bolts 35' *FA Brian Fabel, 2014*

20 ☐ Right Side of History 10b ★★

Climb flakes to long moves through a buldge 7 bolts, 50'
FA Brian Fabel, 2014

21 ☐ Left Out 8

Lieback to face climbing. 5 bolts. 40' *FA Brian Fabel, 2014*

SCUD PINNACLE

10AM-PM · 10m · Vertical · Winter

Routes are listed from left to right.

1 ☐ West Ridge 5

(requires gear) Climb 50' prow to the summit.
FA Unknown, 1970s?

2 ☐ Spank the Monkey 11d ★

A decent climb up the south side arête. 50'
FA Eric Ming, 1995

3 ☐ Monkeys on the Moon 11c

Takes the center of the steep southeast side. 45'
FA Jim Ratz, 1993

4 ☐ Monkey Man 10c ★

Climb up off block along seams to a high anchor. 45'
FA Mike Lindsey, 1993

5 ☐ Monkey Wrench 9 ★★

This climb takes steep rock on the north side (facing the cliff) of the pinnacle. 40' *FA Jeff Leafgreen, 2007*

WAVE OF
MUTILATION

| 10AM-PM | 5m | Vertical | Winter |

0 0 0 0 2 0

Routes are listed from left to right.

● **1** ☐ **Monkey Gone To Heaven 14b** ★★

The left route on the Wave of Mutilation boulder. Monos, etc. 25' *FA BJ Tilden, 2005*

● **2** ☐ **Wave of Mutilation 13c** ★★

Long moves between good pockets. Steep! 30'
FA Frank Dusl, 1994

photo Kyle Duba

Zack Rudy

WAVE OF MUTILATION 13c

Jill Hunter

BURLY 11d

SQUARETOP

12AM-PM | 5m | Vertical | Winter

Routes are listed from left to right.

●1 ☐ **German Girl 12a** ★★
The steep and cool looking overhanging arête. 40'
FA Unknown, 1992

●2 ☐ **American Man Meat 12a** ★
Climb one bolt up on German Girl, then move right and finish on cool holds through a small overhang. 40'
FA Jesse Brown, 2011

●3 ☐ **Burly 11d** ★★
A semiclassic. Jug haul it up the west face right of the arête. 40' *FA Greg Collins, 1991*

●4 ☐ **Hurly 12a** ★★
The cleanest of the west face lines, straight up the face left of Boys From Brazil. 40' *FA Sam Lightner, 2014*

●5 ☐ **Boys From Brazil 11c**
Steep corner and face in the center of the west wall. 40'
FA Jim Ratz, 1995

●8 ☐ **Lunch Break 11a** ★★
This is the face just right of Boys From Brazil. Good moves on nice holds make this the best 5.11 on the boulder.
FA Mike Lilygren, 2015

●6 ☐ **Isolate and Dominate 11a**
This is the rightmost route on the face, ending in a small corner at the top. 35' *FA Brian Dunnohew, 2010*

●9 ☐ **Walk The Line 11c** ★
This climb takes the arete feature between Isolate and Dominate and Full Irations. *FA Sam Lightner, 2015*

●7 ☐ **Full Irations 12a** ★★
The left route on the southeast face, start off flat boulder to reachy moves. 35' *FA Greg Collins, 1999*

●8 ☐ **Zion Train 12b** ★★
Good pockets up center of face. 35' *FA Greg Collins, 1999*

●9 ☐ **Steel Pulse 11a**
A nice wall, but in need of some more cleaning. 35'
FA Vance White, 2010

●10 ☐ **EZ Up 10c**
Hard start leads to easy climbing above. 40'
FA Unknown, 1990s

●11 ☐ **When I Hang My Boots to Rest 12b**
Face left of the Original Route dihedral. 30'
FA Kyle Rowden, 2010

○12 ☐ **Original Route 9** ★★
Bolted corner on north side. 35' *FA Unknown, 1970s*

●13 ☐ **Crack Fox 11a** ★
Face just right of the Original Route. *FA Vance White, 2010*

●14 ☐ **Jesse's Girl 13a** ★★
Cool, techy route just left of the German Girl arete. 40'
FA BJ Tilden, 2011

FAIRFIELD **HILL**

photo: Kyle Duba

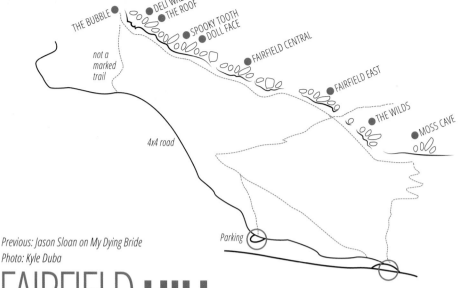

not a marked trail

THE BUBBLE
DELI WALL
THE ROOF
SPOOKY TOOTH
DOLL FACE
FAIRFIELD CENTRAL
FAIRFIELD EAST
THE WILDS
MOSS CAVE

4x4 road

Parking

Previous: Jason Sloan on My Dying Bride
Photo: Kyle Duba

FAIRFIELD **HILL**

The Fairfield Hill cliff is the western-most developed dolomite cliff in Sinks Canyon. Fairfield has always been the black sheep of Sinks Canyon climbing. Although climbing here has paralleled that of the Main Wall, it has received only a fraction the traffic. Development here has included several climbers, but well over half of the 100+ climbs were established by Bob Branscomb. His efforts, and the efforts of Ed Delong, Paul Piana, Dave Doll, and a few others have created one of the finest crags in Wyoming.

Directions: Drive up canyon 3 miles from the "entering Sinks Canyon State Park sign", and take the two-track on the right. If you have a low clearance vehicle, it may be best to park just off the pavement and walk. Follow this road for 3/4 mile and park. Walk up the very rough 4WD road above for about 400 yards to a righthand trail marked by two largecairns. Follow this long diagonal all the way to the right end of the Fairfield Hill cliff. From here a climbers' trail leads back west (left) along the base.

This is also a good approach trail for the left end of the Sinks Main Wall. An obvious trail connects the Fairfield and Main Walls near the top of the long diagonal of the Fairfield approach trail.

Routes are described left to right, and are divided into three main sectors: Fairfield West, Fairfield Central, and Fairfield East.

CLASSICS

Teenagers From Mars (p.260)
Hi Ho Silver Away (p.262)

Blah Blah Blah (p.261)
Chainsaw Willie (p.267)
Second Helping (p.269)

Don Ho (p.257)
Incombustible (p.262)
American Nightmare (p.267)

My Dying Bride (p.265)
Dream of Least Weasels (p.264)

29
35
32
22
4
4

10AM-PM

30m

Vertical

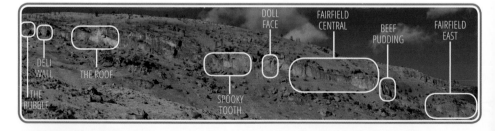

DELI WALL
THE ROOF
THE BUBBLE
SPOOKY TOOTH
DOLL FACE
FAIRFIELD CENTRAL
BEEF PUDDING
FAIRFIELD EAST

THE **BUBBLE**

| 10AM-PM | 30m | Vertical | Winter |

1 3 1 3 1 0

Routes are listed from left to right.

● **1** ☐ **Afternoon Delight 12b**
The leftmost route on the Bubble, featuring bouldery moves through the bulge. *FA Jesse Brown, 2010*

● **2** ☐ **Don Ho 11d** ★★★
One of the best in the whole area. Takes the left side of the main bulge. 50' *FA Todd Skinner, 2002*

● **3** ☐ **Sheepeater 12d** ★★
The main line through the center of the bulge.
FA Todd Skinner, 2002

● **4** ☐ **Fizzle Doubt 12c** ★★
The route right of Sheepeater, this is a good one.
FA Paul Piana, 2002

● **5** ☐ **Blessed Black Wings 13a** ★
The longest route at the bubble, this follows a black streak on the right side of the feature.
FA Vance White, 2010

THE DELI WALL

This wall is located in an alcove of sorts, a couple hundred feet right of the Bubble.

● **6** ☐ **Prickled Pickle 10d** ★
Climb up a small corner system, then move left. Finish on a prickly bulge. *FA Steven Vedder and Will Balis, 2017*

● **7** ☐ **Fist Full of Meat 10a** ★★
The next route right of Prickled Pickle, big holds through a bulge. *FA Will Balis and Steven Vedder, 2017*

● **8** ☐ **Belly Full of Meat 10a** ★★
Just left of a right-leaning crack, this climb takes sidpulls and underclings through a steeper start, finishing on low-angled terrain. *FA Steven Vedder, 2017*

○ **9** ☐ **Hot Pastrami 6** ★★
Just left of a leaning pillar, this climb takes a featured wall and ends in a section of cool black rock.
FA Libby Vedder, 2017

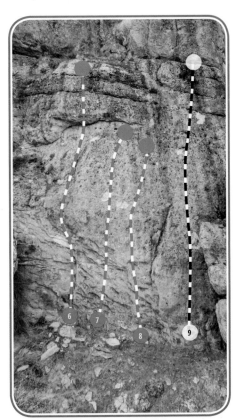

photo Kyle Duba

BLESSED BLACK WINGS 13a Vance White

THE **ROOF**

10AM-PM | 30m | Vertical | Winter

   5 6 7 4 1 1

Routes are listed from left to right.

●1 ☐ **Something Like Another Chance 10a**
This is the leftmost climb on a short wall about 150 feet right of The Bubble, and about the same distance left of the Roof. This and the following three routes are all close together on the same nice wall. *FA Bob Branscomb, 2011*

●2 ☐ **The Hundredth Monkey 10a ★**
The next route right, this is a slightly thinner outing.
FA Bob Branscomb, 2011

○3 ☐ **Only As Pretty As You Feel 9 ★**
Another short climb, this one is fun.
FA Bob Branscomb, 2011

○4 ☐ **Wyoming Hair Disaster 8 ★**
Climb this route, if only for the name!
FA Bob Branscomb, 2011

●5 ☐ **Sensor 11c**
About fifty feet down the wall from Wyoming Hair Disaster, This is a thin slab / prow route on a dark wall.
FA Richard Collins, 1989

●6 ☐ **Locust Invasion 11c ★★**
This route takes the thin seam and face just left of The Plague. *FA Steven Vedder and Rick Guerrieri, 2018*

●7 ☐ **The Plague 12d**
This route climbs a clean short face just right of very red stone. One of the first hard sport routes in the area.
FA Greg Collins, 1989

●8 ☐ **Grin Face 11a ★★**
The first route right of the Plague, this route is clean and has good movement.
FA Steven Vedder and Rick Guerrieri, 2018

●9 ☐ **Knock the Smerk Off 10a ★★**
Just right of Grin Face.
FA Steven Vedder and Rick Guerrieri, 2018

○10 ☐ **Teenagers From Mars 8 ★★**
This climb takes a rounded prow feature. Fun.
FA Vance White, 2008

○11 ☐ **Devil Lock 6 ★**
This route takes the corner and face left of Teenagers From Mars. *FA Vance White, 2008*

● **12 ☐ Blah, Blah, Blah 10d ★★**
This climb takes a corner to an undercling traverse right, then up the face above. Full value. *FA Vance White, 2008*

● **13 ☐ Biggie Smalls 12a ★★**
Up the face right of Blah, Blah, Blah. A fire victim, so watch for broken rock. 40' *FA Sophia Kim, 2012.*

● **14 ☐ Estimated Prophet 11a ★**
This route is in the center of the wall between Blah, Blah, Blah and the Brotherhood. Start on a little pillar and climb the nice face above. *FA Bob Branscomb, 2013*

● **15 ☐ The Brotherhood 12a ★★★**
This climb takes an open-book feature above two cool leaning flakes to the left of the roof. Rest your way to a high crux. *FA Vance White, 2011*

● **16 ☐ Flight Club 13a ★★**
Just left of the huge roof feature and identified by the large hueco. Just to the right of "Brotherhood".
FA Vance White, 2011

● **17 ☐ Open Project**
 Roof Projects The huge roof right of the Brotherhood has been explored sporadically for climbing, but the great lines have yet to be done. This 15-20 foot roof will offer top-end routes, but will require a lot of brushing.

○ **18 ☐ Zeb 9**
This is a left-arching crack under the roof that ends at anchors where the feature changes to horizontal. 40'
FA Vance White, 2009

● **19 ☐ The Abortion 11d**
This route takes thin moves up a vertical wall to take on the very right side of the roof. *FA Keith Lennard, 1990*

● **20 ☐ Driller's Delight 11d ★**
Taking the black streak just right of the roof (start in a left-trending crack feature), this is a continuous and technical climb. *FA Greg Collins, 1989*

● **21 ☐ Swift 11a**
Another techy route, this route is the left one on the streaked face right of the roof. *FA Sue Miller, 1989*

● **22 ☐ More Cowbell 10b ★**
This climb is just right of Swift. Jump to start (stick clip recommended) then climb easier moves above.
FA Vance White, 2010

● **23 ☐ Liquid Swords 12a ★**
Techy grey streak just left of Black Sunday.
FA Vance White, 2012

● **24 ☐ Black Sunday 10c**
This is a red and black streaked crack.
FA Vance White, 2009

SPOOKY **TOOTH**

10AM-PM 30m Vertical Winter

9 3 4 4 1 0

Routes are listed from left to right.

○1 ☐ Revolution is Evolution 7 ★★

This route is on the next section of wall right of the black and red streaked wall holding the previous three climbs. Layback up a flake and then step on to the face above. Short, but fun. *FA Bob Branscomb and Kristi Stouffer, 2010*

○2 ☐ Take Some Petrol, Darling 8 ★

This is the face right of Revolution is Evolution's flake. Nice pockets and fun climbing. *FA Bob Branscomb, 2010*

●3 ☐ Hand on the Torch 10b ★

The right route on this section, a techy start leads to easier climbing. Hit by the 2013 fire, this climb is slightly harder than it originally was.
FA Bob Branscomb and Kristi Stouffer, 2010

○4 ☐ Hi Ho Silver Away 7 ★★★

A fun route with the hardest part in the upper third, a lower angle 5.7 small hold/smearing face on nice rock. Easy and fun pocket pulling to there. Well protected. *FA Bob Branscomb and Mark Watkins, 2012*

●5 ☐ Incombustible 11c ★★★

This climb is on a prow feature left of a large rightfacing corner. Climb a flake/crack and then over a bulge. *FA Steven Vedder and Rick Guerrieri, 2018*

○6 ☐ Sugar Mountain 8 ★★

A long route (130ft) starting on a block left of some trees. Crux is from bolts 2-4 with an interesting steep pocket pulling section above the first ledge and a strange mantel near the top. Perhaps the longest easy sport route in Sinks. *FA Bob Branscomb, 2011*

○7 ☐ Scenic Cruise 8 ★

Shares same start with Sugar Mountain. At the 3rd bolt, traverse right and then straight up. Pocket pull the steep wall above the first ledge. From anchor on second ledge, traverse up and right to a cool, steep, knobby finish to the anchor. *FA Bob Branscomb, 2012*

○8 ☐ Spooky Tooth Left 6

Up the left side of the flake. Protect this route with gear or TR from the anchors atop the flake after climbing the right side. *FA Bob Branscomb, 2010*

INCOMBUSTIBLE 11c Steve Vedder

9 ☐ Spooky Tooth Right 7 ★★
This is a fun flake, lieback climb. Just don't pull out too hard! 50' *FA Bob Branscomb, 2010*

10 ☐ The Great Deceiver 11b ★★
This is a very technical route up a pretty, reddish face, right of the Spooky Tooth. *FA Scott Cole, 1990*

11 ☐ New World Odor 7 ★
This is the corner climb. *FA Vance White, 2009*

12 ☐ Moveable Feast 9 ★
Lieback up the wide crack feature right of New World Odor. *FA Bob Branscomb, 1994*

13 ☐ Weasels Ripped My Flesh 12b ★
About 30 feet right of Moveable Feast, this is the left of three short routes on a clean wall. A hard start leads to nice jugs along a black streak. *FA Bob Branscomb, 1992*

14 ☐ Axis of Weasel 12a ★★
Another hard start leads to great climbing above. *FA Paul Piana, 2004*

15 ☐ Manifest Destiny 10a ★★
A short climb on the right side of this clean wall. *FA Ed DeLong, 1999*

16 ☐ Shadowline 11b ★
This rounded prow right of Manifest Destiny offers up techy and tricky climbing. *FA Bob Branscomb, 2004*

17 ☐ Save A Prayer For Lefty 13b ★
Follow a left-leaning flake to high hard face moves. *FA Todd Skinner, 2004*

18 ☐ A Dream of Least Weasels 12b ★★
This is the center route in the nice clean wall down right of Manifest Destiny. Thin holds on great rock. *FA Dave Doll, 2004*

19 ☐ Viatameen H 12d ★★
This is a full-power prow route, on the wall just right of A Dream of Least Weasels. Named for the way in which Todd's daughter, Hannah, said the word "vitamin". *FA Todd Skinner, 2004*

20 ☐ Kashmir 11a ★
This route takes the arete/prow feature to anchors at about 50 feet. Thin to start. *FA Bob Branscomb, 1999*

21 ☐ Cheaper Than Religion 10b ★★
Just right of Kashmir, this climb takes a low crux bulge to continuously engaging climbing above. 100' *FA Bob Branscomb, 2008*

DOLL FACE

10AM-PM | **30m** | **Vertical** | **Winter**

2 0 1 2 1 0

Routes are listed from left to right.

○1 ☐ **Tweedle Dee 5**
This and the next route are on a short wall that sits slightly higher up the hill to the left of the Doll Face prow. This is the left climb. *FA Bob Branscomb, 1991*

○2 ☐ **Tweedle Dum 6**
The right route, slightly harder. 25'
FA Bob Branscomb, 1991

●3 ☐ **My Dying Bride 12d ★★★**
This route is the left climb on the steep prow called "Doll Face". Start up technical moves, then through sweeping moves over a bulge. One of the best of its grade in the area. *FA Paul Piana, 1996*

●4 ☐ **Doll Face 13b ★**
This climb is on the right side of the steep wall. Curves right on technical moves before the pumpy finish.
FA Paul Piana, 2004

●5 ☐ **Doll Parts 11d ★**
Climb up a neat face ending left of the corner. 70'
FA Heidi Badaracco and Paul Piana, 1996

●6 ☐ **Our Barbies, Ourselves 12a ★**
This line takes the clean bulge right of the main Doll Face. Really great moves and an exciting finish. 70'
FA Paul Piana, 1996

photo Kyle Duba

MY DYING BRIDE 12d — Jason Sloan

Daniel Mock

CHAINSAW WILLY 10d

FAIRFIELD
CENTRAL

 10AM-PM   30m   Vertical   Winter

4 11 7 3 0 2

Routes are listed from left to right.

●1 ☐ **Diluted in Lime Light (Open Project)**
This climb takes the low-angle face up to and through the hard squarecut roof. Estimated to be 5.13.
Equipped Ben Sears, 2017

●2 ☐ **American Nightmare 11d** ★★
Climb up tricky seams and corners just to the right of the large roof. *FA Ben Sears, 2017*

●3 ☐ **BS Route (Closed Project)**
This climb goes up a clean vertical wall just right of the previous climb. *Equipped Ben Sears, 2017*

●4 ☐**Saucerful of Secrets 11d** ★★
Recleaned 2017. Climb the vertical wall just left of a dead bush up continious and demanding moves. 60'
FA Bob Branscomb, 1996

●5 ☐ **Bound to a Stencil 11d** ★★
This climb goes up a clean vertical wall just right of the Saucerful of Secerets. *FA Ben Sears, 2017*

●6 ☐**Alan Shepard Goes to Space 11b** ★
This climb is right of Saucerful of Secrets and starts in a small overlap. *FA Bob Branscomb, 1996*

●7 ☐**Touch of Gray 10c** ★★
This is a well-protected and nice climb on the left side of a small prow. *FA Bob Branscomb, 1998*

●8 ☐**Chainsaw Willy 10d** ★★
Climb a left leaning crack, then exit onto the face above. Good climbing. *FA Bob Branscomb, 1993*

●9 ☐**Screaming Trees 11a** ★
This climb is right of Chainsaw Willy, and is directly behind an aptly named burned-up "screaming" tree. A low crux leads to sportier easy climbing above.
FA Bob Branscomb and Jack Kay, 1992

●10 ☐**Born X-Eyed 10a** ★
This climb is just right of Screaming Trees and shares its anchor. This climb was a classic, but was affected by the 2013 fire. Much spalling has occurred and the grade might have changed. *FA Bob Branscomb, 2002*

○11 ☐**Youth Culture Killed My Dog 9** ★★
This is a fun face climb right of Born X-Eyed.
FA Bob Branscomb and Kristi Stouffer, 1993

○12 ☐ **Uncle Meat 8**
A sporty route with fun moves just right of Youth Culture Killed My Dog. *FA Bob Branscomb and Jack Kay, 1990*

● 13 ☐ **Slave to History 10a** ★
A shorter route, this one is on very good rock, starting a little higher than Uncle Meat.
FA Bob Branscomb and Kristi Stouffer, 2005

● 14 ☐ **Make Peas Great Again 10c** ★
Takes the face 15 feet left of Coyote Delight, ending near a diagonal crack. *FA Ryan and Jesse Morse-Brady, 2016*

○15 ☐ **Coyote Delight 7**
Another clean wall, follow nice moves to an anchor at 40'
FA Bob Branscomb, 1992

○16 ☐ **Last Trip to Tulsa 8** ★
This is a black streak near where the wall curves into a big corner. Fun, but short.
FA Bob Branscomb and Kristi Stouffer, 1995

● 17 ☐ **Visualize Whirled Peas 10b** ★★
 Another shorty, but really good. Just right of Last Trip to Tulsa, and shares its anchors.
FA Bob Branscomb and Kristi Stouffer, 1995

● 18 ☐ **Have Mercy 10c** ★
On the wall right of a right-facing corner. A tricky start leads to fun moves high.
FA Bob Branscomb and Kristi Stouffer, 1994

● 19 ☐ **Jump Jim Crow 11b** ★
A continuous and thin route. *FA Bob Branscomb, 1996*

● 20 ☐ **Atom Tan 10c** ★
The middle route on the clean wall right of Have Mercy, and a good one. *FA Bob Branscomb, 1996*

● 21 ☐ **I Wish I Was A Catfish 10c** ★★
The rightmost route, and probably best of the three.
FA Bob Branscomb and Kristi Stouffer, 1996

● 22 ☐ **Nobody's Fault But Mine 10b**
This climb takes a short reddish face on the high point of the hill about halfway between I Wish I Was A Catfish and Hellzapoppin. *FA Bob Branscomb, 1993*

● 23 ☐ **Hellzapoppin 11d** ★★
To the right of Nobody's Fault But Mine, the walls get a bit taller, steeper, and cleaner. This climb starts in a right facing corner and takes the face all the way up through bulges at the top. *FA Paul Piana, 1996*

● 24 ☐ **Electric Fence 12b** ★
Not too far right of Hellzapoppin, Electric Fence climbs a clean face and also breaks the roofs up high.
FA Paul Piana, 1996

● 25 ☐ **Exile on Main Street 12a** ★
About 100 feet right of Electric Fence, this climb takes a sustained crimpy face. *FA Bob Branscomb, 1993*

● 26 ☐ **Tiger Style 12c** ★
About 100 feet right of Electric Fence, this climb takes a sustained crimpy face. *FA Christian Gauderer, 1993*

● 27 ☐ **Straight, No Chaser 10b**
This route takes a long arete / flake feature near where the wall forms a large prow. *FA Ed Delong, 1992*

BEEF **PUDDING**

Routes are listed from left to right.

●1 ☐ Zebra Cakes 12b ★★

Right of Straight, No Chaser, there are a few hundred feet of not-so-appealing rock. However, to the right of this, there is a very clean east-facing wall that sits on top of a big, low ledge. Zebra Cakes takes the left line off this ledge. *FA Paul Piana, 2001*

●2 ☐ Beef Pudding 12c ★

This is the right climb off the ledge. *FA Paul Piana, 2001*

○3 ☐ Unnamed 9

This route takes the clean corner to less clean rock at the top. *FA Unknown*

●4 ☐ Brave Like Old John Wayne 11d ★

Right of the block, there is a vertical wall with three routes. This is the left line and features fun moves on small holds. *FA Bob Branscomb, 1995*

FAIRFIELD **EAST**

10AM-PM · 30m · Vertical

7 · 12 · 11 · 4 · 0 · 1

Routes are listed from left to right.

●1 ☐ Hanoi Jane's Video Workout 11a

The center line on the wall, worth doing for the name alone! *FA Bob Branscomb, 1995*

●2 ☐ World On A String 11b

The rightmost route on this wall, this is the third-best climb. *FA Bob Branscomb, 1991*

○3 ☐ Meadow Rock TRs

There is a small wall between the central and right sections of Fairfield. This nice little wall is short even by Fairfield standards, but features several toprope problems. You can access the top easily and there are bolted anchors.

○4 ☐ Rez Ride 8

This is the leftmost climb on the slabby wall at the left end of Fairfield East. *FA Ben Elzay, 2011.*

○5 ☐ L, L, and L 9 ★

Affected by the fire, this route is still very good. L L and L is an abbreviation for Lewd, Lecherous and Lascivious, reflecting Ed's view of the morons he had to work with in his job at the time. *FA Ed DeLong, 1995*

●6 ☐ Your Own Private Idaho 10c ★

Two slab routes head up to anchors below a big boulder at the rim. This is the left one. *FA Bob Branscomb, 1992*

●7 ☐ Physical Graffiti 11a ★

This tricky climb is the right one that heads up toward the boulder at the rim. *FA Bob Branscomb, 1992*

●8 ☐ Second Helping 10b ★★★

The best route on this section of cliff, suffered some fire damage. *FA Bob Branscomb, 2008*

●9 ☐ Houses of the Holy 10b ★

This route starts behind blackened stumps that once were junipers. Good climbing on techy moves. *FA Ed DeLong, 1992*

●10 ☐ Presence 10d ★
Another slab route, similar in movement and grade to the adjacent climbs. *FA Ed Delong, 1993*

●11 ☐ Nimrod 11a ★
Start in a small corner (crux) then move left and up good, sustained climbing. *FA Bob Branscomb, 2008*

●12 ☐ Devilution 12b
A low boulder problem leads to lower-angled climbing on pods. *FA Vance White, 2011*

●13 ☐ Pistol Whipped 12b
Right of a big burned up Juniper, this once-pretty route was scorched by the 2013 fire. *FA Vance White, 2011*

●14 ☐ SR Route (Closed Project)
Equipped Scott Robertson

●15 ☐ Restless Natives 12d ★
This climb is the dark streak right of some arches. Stick clip bolt 2, and climb right of the bolt line until at the 3rd bolt. Following the bolt line would be harder but seems contrived. Another burn victim, it's unlikely this has seen an ascent since the fire. *FA Vance White, 2011*

●16 ☐ Blind 11d ★★
This is one of the first routes established on dolomite in SInks Canyon...go figure. Not a bad line, but it's some-what nondescript. On the vertical face with big flakes left of the Big Bambu pillar. *FA Keith Lennard, 1989*

●17 ☐ Big Bambu 11b ★
This is a short, fun, overhanging climb on a detached pillar. *FA Bob Branscomb, 1998*

●18 ☐ Leslie's Arete 12a
This climb is on a blunt arete about 30 feet right of Big Bambu, and just left of the obvious corner of Sorta Maybe Kinda Wild. Short. *FA Vance White, 2008*

●19 ☐ Sorta Maybe Kinda Wild 10b ★★
This is a fun corner to an engaging rightward exit.
FA Bob Branscomb, 1999

●20 ☐ Leon Trotsky's Hair 11c ★★
This is a fun, sequence-heavy face right of the corner. The two share a finish. *FA Bob Branscomb, 2004*

●21 ☐ Che 11d ★
A bouldery start to much easier climbing.
FA Bob Branscomb, 2004

●22 ☐ A Piolet For Leon 10d ★
Another tricky start leads to a low-angled finish on a ramp. *FA Bob Branscomb, 2008*

●23 ☐ Say Hello to Geronimo 10b ★★
A nice climb stating below a small overhang. Continuous-ly steep and fun. *FA Bob Branscomb and Kristi Stouffer, 1994*

○24 ☐ **West of Venus 8** ★
A slab route with a seam start. Continuous challenges and good rock make for a nice climb.
FA Bob Branscomb, 1995

○25 ☐ **Realm of the Venusian Sex Pygmies 8**
This route is just right of West of Venus, and is another you should do just because of the name.
FA Bob Branscomb, 1993

○26 ☐ **Revenge of the Pygmy Sex God 8** ★
About 30 feet right of Realm..., this climb is fun, but too short. *FA Ed DeLong, 1992*

●27 ☐ **Treats 10a** ★
Next route left of Revenge..., this climb shares its first bolt with Apostrophe.
FA Bob Branscomb and Kristi Stouffer, 2005

●28 ☐ **Apostrophe 10a** ★
Same start as Treats, but moves right after bolt 1.
FA Bob Branscomb and Kristi Stouffer, 1993

●29 ☐ **Afterthought 10b**
Slab with chain anchor. *FA Bob Branscomb, 2010*

●30 ☐ **Con's West Left 10a**
At the high point on the wall, there are two short slabs. This is the left one. *FA Bob Branscomb, 1993*

○31 ☐ **Con's West Right 6**
This is the right slab. *FA Bob Branscomb, 1993*

●32 ☐ **They Shoot Horses 11b** ★
On the "pinnacle" at the right end of the wall, this climb takes the center of the main face. *FA Bob Branscomb, 1991*

●33 ☐ **Kissing Marilyn Monroe 11c**
This climb is just right of They Shoot Horses. Roughly follows the arete feature. *FA Bob Branscomb, 1992*

●34 ☐ **Hieroglyphic 11c** ★
This route is on the overhanging east side of the pinnacle, just right of Kissing Marilyn Monroe. Cool.
FA Bob Branscomb, 1992

●35 ☐ **French Blow 10c** ★
To the right of Hieroglyphic, this climb is a bit shorter and easier. This is the rightmost line on the Fairfield wall.
FA Jesse Brown, 2011

photo: David Lloyd

SINKS **GRANITE**

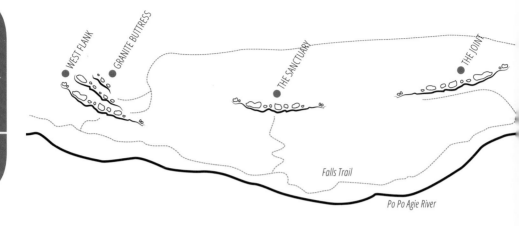

Previous: Tom Rangitsch on Rimfire
Photo: David Lloyd

SINKS
GRANITE

The granite crags of Sinks Canyon are a microscopic version of the Wind Rivers to the west. Climbers have long visited these cliffs, but only recently have they seen concentrated activity. As early as the 1950s, climbers were establishing lines on the Z-Crack Wall and the Granite Buttress. More recently, in the fall of 2010, the Lander Area's hardest boulder problem was established on a block at the base of these walls. The climbs here range from easy multi-pitch scrambles to 5.14 projects.

These crags are best in spring and fall, though their south-facing aspect makes many of the lines climbable in winter. Summer afternoons can be pleasant at the Joint and Sanctuary, as these walls start catching shade around 2pm.

The cliffs are described as you approach them from the Bruce's Parking Area. All three major areas are visible from the parking lot. The Joint is the steep and streaked wall closest to the road. The Granite Buttress is the huge rounded dome that sits a half-mile further up the trail. The Sanctuary is made up of the broken cliffs between.

CLASSICS

29
15
21
18
10
5

Secret Slab (p.279)
Willie's Corner (p.284)

Willie's Wall (p.284)
Good and Plenty (p.283)

Obscured by Clowns (p.275)
Mr. Big Shot (p.277)
Sportsline (p.283)

Foundation (p.279)
Empire (p.279)
The Lonely Town of Andersonville(p.286)

TS Arete (p.277)
Centerfire (p.279)

8AM-2PM

30m

Vertical

Winter

Routes are listed from right to left.

○1 ☐ **Moon Over Dog Street 8** ★
This is a short face climb to a splitter hand crack 50 feet right of 1000 Churches. You'll need quickdraws and one cam. 50' FA Steve Bechtel, 2009

●2 ☐ **1000 Churches 10d** ★
Seams and edges. 4B 40' *FA Steve Bechtel, 2006*

●3 ☐ **Ambro-agie 12a** ★★
This is a really nice arete feature with a baffling switch. 35' *FA Steve Bechtel, 2006*

●4 ☐ **Obscured by Clowns 11b** ★★
Beautiful smooth face with great edges. 40'
FA Ellen Bechtel, 2006

●5 ☐ **Slick Fifty 12a** ★
Arête on slick red rock. 45' *FA Steve Bechtel, 2006*

●6 ☐ **Ziggurat 12b** ★
Dihedral on slick rock to ledges. The first 10 feet are the whole business. 45' *FA Steve Bechtel, 2006*

to Fossil Hlll

THE **JOINT**

☀	🚶	▮	❄
8AM-2PM	15m	Vertical	Winter

(2) (3) (6) (9) (6) (3)

The Joint is the first of the granite crags along the Middle Fork Trail, about 10 minutes from Bruce's Parking Area. It is best recognized by the tall black-streaked wall that sits at the center of the crag. The main concentration of routes is on the steep, lower third of this wall. Routes exist both to the left and right of this main sector, and several potential lines exist on the upper reaches of the wall

The Joint is reached by parking at the "Bruce's Parking Area" just after the road crosses the river (4.2 miles from the canyon entrance). There are toilets at the Parking Area. Cross the road to the foot bridge and cross the river. Head up canyon about 5 minutes along the Middle Fork Trail. The cliff is visible for the entire approach. About 200 feet after passing the last electrical pole along the trail, angle up a long slope of large talus blocks that leads right of the cliff. Near the top of this talus, work left on a nice, established "trail" through the upper talus. Poison Ivy is present here, so stick to the rocks.

● 7 ☐ The Rift 12b ★
This route takes a cool shallow corner to ledgy climbing above. 45' FA Steve Bechtel, 2006

● 8 ☐ Bluebeard 11d ★★
White corner with roof to steep juggy climbing above. 5B 50' FA Steve Bechtel, 2006

● 9 ☐ Mr. Big Shot 11a ★★★
This steep wall follows a seam, but you're mostly on jugs and big edges. 50' FA Steve Bechtel, 2006

● 10 ☐ Stone Pulse 10d ★★
This climb takes the discontinuous cracks and corners on the right side of the big slot in the middle of the joint. FA Ben Venter, 2016

● 11 ☐ CG Route (Closed Project)
The vertical clean face right of the TS arete. Equipped Christian Gaudderer

● 12 ☐ TS Arete 13c ★★★
A super-cool arete on the left margin of the huge gully; the feature is broken into two sections. The last route that Todd bolted in the Lander area, this route was freed by Todd's friend BJ Tilden in summer of 2013. Scramble up easy terrain and belay from a ledge to start. 80' FA BJ Tilden, 2013

● 13 ☐ Project (Headwall)
Between the Arete and the Fun House. Equipped Tom Rangistch

● 14 ☐ The Fun House 12a ★★★
Starts on the ledge at 1/3 height, then climbs up to the summit. You could also start with either Big Smoke or Get Wacky. 100' FA Greg Collins, 1989

○ 15 ☐ Soft Option 9 ★
This is the rightmost route on the Full Tilt wall. Move up and right on easy ground to a ledge, then up a left facing corner above. 40' FA Steve Bechtel, 2006

● 16 ☐ Kid Gloves 11c ★
Up a hard face past small ledge to fun steep moves. Avoiding the corner to the right at the start makes this route 12a. 40' FA Steve Bechtel, 2006

● 17 ☐ Broken Heroes 13a ★
Small corner to bulge. 40' FA Steve Bechtel, 2007

● 18 ☐ Big Smoke 11c ★★
Liebacks and jugs lead to a hard rightward exit move. 40' FA Gary Wilmot, 1990

● 19 ☐ Get Wacky 12b ★
Seam climb on a black streak. 40' FA Rob Hess, 1989

● 20 ☐ Bad Brain 13c ★★
Hard bouldery moves with the famous undercling crimp. 45' FA BJ Tilden, 2006

● 21 ☐ ✎ Big Brain 13d ★★
Starts on Bad Brain, then traverses to Full Tilt at bolt 2, climbing the cruxes of both routes. FA Chris Marley, 2014

● 22 ☐ Full Tilt 13a ★★
Follows seam to hard top moves. 40' FA Greg Collins, 1989

● 23 ☐ BJ Route (Closed Project)
Equipped BJ Tilden

● 24 ☐ Kilodeer 10a ★
Up groove past 4 bolts to anchor at ledge. 40' The corner above is 5.11 and is protected with small cams and wires. FA Joe Wall, 2006

● 25 ☐ October Sky 13a ★
This is the big red arete left of Kilodeer. Start with the first 4 bolts of Kilodeer, then move left and up. 100' FA John Hennings, 2006

● 26 ☐ Feel the Bern 12a ★★
Great Arete climbing. 55' FA Christian Gauderer, 2016

● 27 ☐ I'm Ron Burgundy? 12a ★
Climb an overhanging wall on large holds to a hard move at the top. 55' FA Steve Bechtel, 2006

● 28 ☐ Twelfth Labor 11c ★
Corner with seam to steep headwall. 55' FA Steve Bechtel, 2006

● 29 ☐ Oral History 12a ★
50'. Start up difficult arête, then turn a tricky roof before hitting the easy climbing. 50' FA Steve Babits, 2006

THE SANCTUARY

This is the nice group of buttresses between the Joint Wall and the main Granite Buttress. Although this area has seen sporadic use from climbers for several years, it wasn't until 2006 that routes were developed in earnest by John Hennings. Following in John's footsteps, Tom Rangitsch and BJ Tilden led the charge for new routes in this area. A sanctuary from both the occasional wind and from the relentless pockets of the dolomite, this is a great alternative to Lander's other crags.

Approach: *The Sanctuary is reached by parking at the "Bruce's Parking Area" just after the road crosses the river (4.2 miles from the canyon entrance). There are toilets at the Parking Area. Cross the road to the foot bridge and cross the river. Head up canyon about 10 minutes along the Middle Fork Trail. After passing the Joint and the major boulder field below it, the trail leads into and open, sage-covered field. Walk through this field for a very short distance, then angle uphill toward the crag. This is the first section of cliff past the Joint, and is only separated from that crag by a few hundred feet of broken rock and gullies.*

Routes are listed from left to right.

UPPER TIER

●1 ☐ Smirk 11d ★
This route is the leftmost on the wall. Start just left of a low roof. 45' *FA John Hennings, 2006*

●2 ☐ Stiff Upper Lip 13a ★★
Share start with Smirk. Climb up and right through a small roof and then along a seam. 45' *FA John Hennings, 2006*

●3 ☐ The Brown Arête 11b
Third route from the left, the name says it all. 50' *FA John Hennings, 2006*

●4 ☐ Backbone of the West 12b ★★
This black-and-white arête is left-facing. Really fun. 45' *FA John Hennings, 2006*

●5 ☐ No Name Crack 11b ★★
This is the splitter crack. The 5.11 ends at a ledge with a bolt. The roof above might or might not have been done at 5.12. 35' small cams and wires. *FA unknown*

○6 ☐ Remember a Day 8
This is the dark, wide crack to the right. As recommendable as a Susan Sontag novel. 60' *FA Branscomb and Bill Hunt, 2001*

○7 ☐ **Big Pink 8**
Another wide and fun adventure. Shares anchor with
Obscured by Cloud. 40'. *FA Bob Branscomb, 2003*

●8 ☐ **Obscured by Cloud / Nimbus 11c** ★★
This climb takes the west-facing wall, and features a
mid-point anchor (10b to here). A hard move above
leads to more 5.10 climbing, an extension originally
called Nimbus. One point of aid separated the two 5.10
sections until 2013. 60'
FA Branscomb 2003 (both sections) Bechtel 2013 full route

●9 ☐ **Time and Materials 12c** ★
This is the leftmost climb on the steep "Foundation Wall."
A low crux leads to long moves on easier ground. 45'
FA BJ Tilden, 2008

●10 ☐ **Foundation 12c** ★★★
The best route on this wall, considered to be one of the
best of the grade in the whole area. 45'
FA Tom Rangitsch, 2008

●11 ☐ **Empire 12b** ★★
Little brother to Foundation. *FA Tom Rangitsch, 2008*

●12 ☐ **The Seldon Plan 11b** ★★
On the right end of the main Foundation wall, just left of
broken rock. Bigger holds...the warm-up for the routes to
the left. 45' *FA Tom Rangitsch, 2008*

●13 ☐ **Terminus 12a** ★
This climb takes the black arête right of the previous wall.
FA Tom Rangitsch, 2008

●14 ☐ **The Left Jewel of Mr. Texas 11a** ★
A V3-ish move leads to 5.10 climbing. The leftmost route
on the cube-like Zirconia Boulder. This is up a wide ramp
about 200 feet right of the Foundation Wall.
FA John Hennings, 2006

●15 ☐ **The Right Jewel of Mr. Texas 10d** ★
The right-hand slab in the Zirconia Boulder's west face.
40' *FA John Hennings, 2006*

●16 ☐ **Rimfire 13b** ★★
This is the steep southwest arête on the Zirconia Boulder.
FA Tom Rangitsch, 2009

●17 ☐ **Centerfire 13d** ★★★
This is the overhanging center *FA BJ Tilden, 2008*

●18 ☐ **Cornered and Cleaved 12d** ★
Climb a corner, then traverse crack left to Centerfire
finish. *FA John Hennings, 2006*

●19 ☐ **Cock The Hammer 12b** ★
Just to the right of "Cornered and Cleaved", this climb
takes a corner, face and lieback moves to a finger crack
and face exit. *FA Vance White, 2012*

○20 ☐ **Gemini Cracks 8** ★
Parallel cracks on a small pillar feature about 75 feet
right of the Zirconia Boulder. 60' *FA Bob Branscomb, 1995*

●21 ☐ **Going, Going, Gone 11c**
Bolts and thin pro up a clean slab.
FA Bob Branscomb, 1995

●22 ☐ **Bullwinkle 10b** ★
Slab with bolts and thin pro. 45'
FA Bob Branscomb, 1995

LOWER TIER

●23 ☐ **Monument To What? 10a** ★
A short climb on a clean wall. *FA Bob Branscomb, 1996*

●24 ☐ **Pigs in Zen 10a** ★
This is a right-facing corner on clean stone. 40'
FA Bob Branscomb, 1996

○25 ☐ **Secret Slab 9** ★★
4 bolts plus gear to anchors. 40' *FA Branscomb 1996*

●26 ☐ **The Lathe of Heaven 12a** ★
About 150 feet right of the Secret Slab is a very obvious
overhanging arête feature. This is the route. This climb is
basically halfway between the Joint and Sanctuary.
FA Tom Rangitsch, 2010

Zach Alexander **LEFT JEWEL OF MR. TEXAS** 11a

GRANITE **BUTTRESS**

  10AM-PM | 25m | Vertical | Winter

 8 4 7 0 1 0

This buttress is the large dome-like feature seen up-canyon from Bruce's parking lot. This buttress consists of great Wind River granite, and is divided horizontally into three distinct tiers. In fact, the logical approach to most of the climbs takes a trail that leaves the Middle Fork Trail before reaching The Joint, and winds uphill above the crags. Climbers then descend to the second and third tiers to access the routes. The mass of routes are concentrated on the upper tiers, though some shorter crags lower on the buttress are also described. These small crags are best approached from below, via the Middle Fork Trail. Although it seems strange to describe upper pitches of multi-pitch climbs first, that's exactly what we're going to do. Because of the way you approach the cliff, we describe the Third Tier first, then the Second, and finally the lower part of the buttress and the lower crags.

Approach: The Granite Buttress is the huge dome-like crag that sits approximately one mile up canyon from the road. It is reached by parking at the "Bruce's Parking Area" just after the road crosses the river (4.2 miles from the canyon entrance). There are toilets at the Parking Area. Cross the road to the foot bridge and cross the river. Head up canyon about 3 minutes, looking for a faint climbers' path that heads uphill to the right before you reach the rocky outcrops east of the Joint. Follow this switchbacking path to the top of the hill, then take it west, above the crags of the Joint and Sanctuary. Once on top of the hill, the going is pretty easy.

After 15-20 minutes of hiking, small granite outcroppings will appear to your right (between you and the river). Walk toward these rocks on the climbers' path, and find a route down between a slab and a steep west-facing wall. There is a short, silly bolt ladder on this wall, which serves as a good point of reference. Hike down the gully at the base of this wall, looking to your right (west) for the "tier" of the Buttress you'd like to reach.

Routes are listed from left to right.

Sportsline 11d ★★
This is a bolted, right-facing corner on left end of ledge.
Originally led on gear, this route was bolted about
ten years after the first ascent by the first ascentionist.
Physical. *FA Greg Collins, 1988*

●2 ☐ **Sport Center 11c ★**
This climb takes the face right of Sportsline. A loose pillar
marks the start, and a tricky bulge marks the end.
FA Unknown

●3 ☐ **Willie's Wall, Pitch Two 10a ★**
Continuation of Willie's Wall from Tier 2. Takes an obvious crack system past a bush to a small overhang, then
moves left. *FA unknown*

●4 ☐ **Willie's Wall, Direct Variation 10b ★★**
This route takes the finger crack straight up at the end of
Willie's Wall. *FA Randy Cerf*

●5 ☐ **Megalomania 11a ★**
This route takes a crack system to ¾ height, then moves
left slightly to finish. *FA Mike Stern and Jeff Wilber, 1980*

●6 ☐ **Hargis Route, Pitch 3 11d ★★**
This bolted face route starts behind the large block left of
Black Water. *FA Hargis, 2007*

●7 ☐ **Hargis Route, Right 11a ★★**
This is the bolted face just left of Black Water. Climb
ledges rails past a few hard-to-read moves.
FA Hargis, 2007

○8 ☐ **Black Water 7**
This follows a left-facing corner in a black water streak.
You can exit left or right, the right being easier.
FA Unknown

Second Tier

Routes are listed from left to right.

○9 ☐ **The Chimney 5**
At the extreme left-end of the second tier. Scramble up
on a ledge, then around a corner into this non-appealing
slot. Chances are, yours will be the third ascent!
FA Unknown

○10 ☐ **The Ramp 7 ★**
This unique climb takes a left-trending ramp/crack
system that ends in a slot (crux). The squeeze chimney
just left is about 5.8. 60' *FA Unknown*

●11 ☐ **Good and Plenty 10a ★★**
This is a right facing corner climb with some zig-zags. It
sits just left of a diagonal black dike. *FA Unknown, 1960s*

●12 ☐ **Willie's Wall, Pitch One 10c** ★★★
This unique climb is one of the best in the whole canyon. Originally led on fixed pins and bad bolts, it's been rebolted and is now a safe lead.. 50'. *FA unknown, 1970s*

●13 ☐ **Instructor of the Future 13a** ★★
This climb takes the face right of a broad, rounded arête in the middle of the cliff. 5 bolts. 50' *FA Greg Collins, 1994*

○14 ☐ **Willie's Corner 5** ★★
This is a low-angle corner with several cracks working up it. 50' *FA Unknown*

○15 ☐ **Lead Wall 9** ★
Climb a crack system in the middle of the face right of Willie's Corner. Pass a small roof, then step left to join Willie's. A direct finish takes the seams straight above through steeper ground (10b). Anchors above this route allow for a good descent back to the base of the tier for many routes. *FA Unknown*

●16 ☐**Hargis Route, Pitch Two 11b** ★★
This climb follows the prow right of Lead Wall. 50, *FA Hargis, 2007*

○17 ☐ **Hanging Corner 8** ★
Start in a left-facing corner and then climb steeper cracks above, just left of a black streak. *FA Unknown*

○18 ☐ **Corner 6** ★
The climb starts just behind a big, leaning pillar. Climb the pillar, then follow a nice hand and fist crack to the top. *FA Unknown*

○19 ☐ **Arête 7**
Follow seams up to a dihedral on an arête. *FA Unknown*

First Tier

●20 ☐ **Hargis Route 11d** ★★★
This climb is a three pitch affair that climbs the entire height of the Granite Buttress. Pitch one follows low-angle corners, ending on the Second Tier just below Willie's Corner. Move right to a pitch up the prow right of Lead Wall, ending at a bolted anchor on the Third Tier. Pitch three starts behind a large block, and takes a bolted face two routes left of Black Water. One can rappel the route or walk off right.

GRANITE BUTTRESS
WEST FLANK

10AM-PM   25m   Vertical   Winter

⑤ ④ ① ⓪ ⓪ ②

The West Flank of the Granite Buttress has received sporadic attention for years, but other than a few old pitons and some brushed lichen, it's hard to tell what has been done. In the early 2000s Bob Branscomb and friends started exploring this area, and have established several routes. Bob readily suggests that many of these might not be first ascents, but we will give him credit until other information comes forward.

Approach: *via the Middle Fork Trail. Hike the trail past the Joint and Sanctuary, then continue along the Middle Fork Trail below the talus at the base of the Granite Buttress itself. As the trail ascends a steeper section of hill after dipping near the river, you'll pass a steep boulder with a small hole dug out near the base. Just after passing this boulder, leave the trail to the right and head up the hill. A few faint switchbacks will lead you through boulders toward the clean southwest facing slabs above.*

Routes are listed from left to right.

○1 ☐ **West Crack 6** ★
This is the leftmost crack on the wall. Takes wires and cams to #2 Camalot. *FA Unknown*

○2 ☐ **5.7 Crack 7** ★★★
This nice crack takes gear up to a #1 Camalot. *FA Unknown*

○3 ☐ **Nothing's Shocking 9** ★★
Climb a left-facing corner to a break, then step left and up the face past 2 bolts, finishing in a small crack. Wires up to mid-sized cams. *FA Bob Branscomb, 2013*

●4 ☐ **Stop Making Sense 10b** ★
Take the same start as Nothing's Shocking, but move right at the break. Continue past 4 bolts to the ledge.

●5 □ Lost Art 11a ★★

A right-facing corner leads to a clean face with 3 bolts. FInish in a left-trendingcrack at the top. This route had very old bolts on it, and was reequipped in 2013 by Bob Branscomb. It is not known if this climb had a free ascent before Bob's. *FA Unknown*

○6 □ Central Crack 9 ★

Cracks and right-facing features up the right-center portion of the wall. Gear to #3 Camalot. *FA Unknown*

●7 □ Barefoot Crow Left 10a ★★★

Start on a blocky feature, then move left and up to a small roof. Move right under the roof and up past 3 bolts to an anchor. *FA Bob Branscomb, 2013*

●8 □ Barefoot Crow Right 10a ★★★

Start of the same blocks as the previous climb. Move right and up the clean face past several bolts, finishing in a good crack. Small wires and Cams to 1.5". *FA Bob Branscomb, 2014*

○9 □ Mainsail 6 ★

This route takes the major right-facing corner just left of the big gully. Camalots to #2 plus some wires. *FA Paul Piana, 1982*

●10 □ The Past is Tense 10c ★★★

Right of the gully, scramble up to a ledge on the right to belay. Bring a wide variety of cams (to #4). Climb a crack to a ledge then up a clean face past a bolt. Step right and finish up nice, thin cracks at the top. *FA Bob Branscomb, 2014*

●11 □ BB Route (Closed Project)

Anchors only. *equipped Bob Branscomb*

●12 □ BB Route (Closed Project)

Anchors only. *equipped Bob Branscomb*

Z-CRACK BUTTRESS

| 10AM-PM | 30m | Vertical | Winter |

9 **0** **0** **0** **0** **0**

This cliff is at the right end and just below the "First Tier" of the Granite Buttress. These cracks and corners were well-traveled in the 1960s and 1970s, but have seen little activity in recent years. There is potential here for some really good sport routes.

Routes are listed from left to right.

○1 ☐ **Unnamed 8**
This climb takes a right-facing corner / chimney just right of a blank, clean wall. There is a large bush in the crack, but that doesn't tell you much...most of these routes have large bushes in them. Pass an overhang at the top by moving right. Have a nice grovel. *FA Unknown, 1960s*

○2 ☐ **Unnamed 6**
This climb takes a right-leaning, offset wide crack 10 feet right of a nice-looking arête. Ledges at the start give way to more strenuous climbing above. Gives an appreciation for how good most other climbs on Earth are.
FA Unknown 1960s

○3 ☐ **Z Crack Overhang 9 ★**
This is the best route on this cliff. A slightly-overhanging crack and face climb. After reaching the small ledge near the top, stay left to sustain the thrill. *FA Unknown 1960s*

○4 ☐ **Z Corner 8**
This climb is in a major corner. Climb up to a ledge at 1/3 height (with a big bush on it), then up a right-facing crack above. *FA Unknown, 1960s*

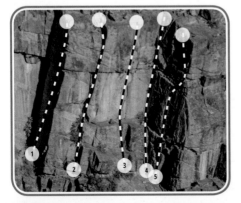

○5 ☐ **Z Crack 6 ★**
Climb up a nice crack to a horizontal with blocks on it, move left about 15 feet, up another crack to a big ledge, then left again and up to the top. *FA Unknown, 1960s*

Practice Walll sits just above the Middle Fork Trail. Approach it by wandering uphill just after passing a boulder that has a large overhang just above the trail. Most climbers don't ever climb here, but those who do usually top rope these 25-foot routes. Climbs are listed left-to-right. No photo.

○6 ☐ **Overlap Crack 9**

○7 ☐ **Sapper Face 9**

○8 ☐ **Sapper Corner 9**

○9 ☐ **Sapper Crack 8**

ANDERSONVILLE

| 8AM-2PM | 45m | Vertical | Winter |

1 **0** **0** **1** **0** **0**

This crag is another 15 minutes up the Middle Fork Trail from the Granite Buttress. Continue past the falls cutoff, and stay right at the fork in the trail beyond. A series of switchbacks leads into some granite. Beyond, the terrain levels out and a large cliff can be found just right of the trail. There are several cracks and slabs on this wall, but only two recorded climbs. No photo.

Routes are listed from left to right.

●2 ☐ **The Lonely Town of Andersonville 12b ★★★**
This is the overhanging hand-to-finger crack that splits the left side of the wall. Scramble to a small ledge to start. 60' *FA Dave Anderson, 2005*

○2 ☐ **An Unexpected Visitor 8 ★**
This route takes the next major crack system right of the obvious Lonely Town of Andersonville, and was established after Andersonville became a little less lonely. 70 '
FA Szu-ting Yi, 2012

Zack Nadiak **FOUNDATION** 12c

BALDWIN **CREEK**

photo: Kyle Duba

Previous: Tony Stark on Rain of Gold
Photo: Kyle Duba

BALDWIN **CREEK**

Baldwin Creek wall is one of the great limestone cliffs in the U.S. It is tall, clean, and nearly five miles long. In the early 90s, it was the hushed secret crag that everyone traveled to Lander to see. Despite the great rock, the excitement ebbed after just a few seasons. The rough road, long approach, and constant sun exposure make this a tough crag to visit regularly. Make no mistake: the road isn't that bad, the days can occasionally be cool, and the routes are fantastic. Plan to visit in the early days of June (the road usually opens around Memorial Day), or in late October or November. You'll almost assuredly be the only climbers at a great cliff in one of the prettiest valleys in Wyoming.

Getting There: From downtown (at Main and 5th streets) head west on Main toward the mountains. Just after 9th street, Main veers right, heading north. After about 1/4 mile there is a traffic light (Near ShopKo). Take a left here, on Baldwin Creek Road. Leave Lander going west on Baldwin Creek Road. Follow this paved road for 5.5 miles, until the paved road turns to the south (left) and it is possible to continue west on an improved dirt road. After .9 miles, the road splits, with the left fork heading into a ranch and the right fork taking you north along a big red butte to your right. This is Shoshone Lake Road. After passing the butte, you'll follow this road as it climbs up several switchbacks to the crest of a small hill (about 5 miles).

At the top of this hill is a parking area popular with ATV riders. From here on, the road is very rough and requires a high-clearance vehicle. Some desperate souls have parked here and walked the rest of the way to the crag. This is not recommended. The road continues up through meadows and aspen and can be very rough in spots.

After 10-15 minutes of slow going, you'll cross a yellow cattleguard and a "Entering Public Lands" sign, near the top of a hill. About 100 yards later, there is a clear area to park on the left, just before the road heads back downhill into a wooded drainage. This is the Baldwin Creek climbing area trailhead. This is 13.5 miles from Main Street in Lander.

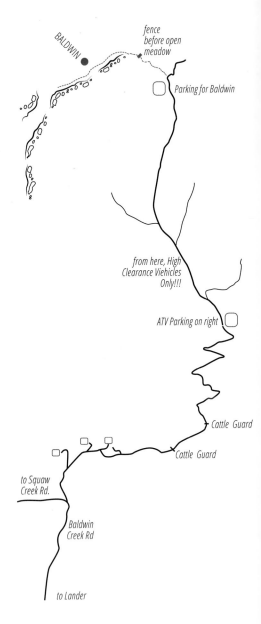

BALDWIN

fence
before open
meadow

Parking for Baldwin

from here, High
Clearance Viehicles
Only!!!

ATV Parking on right

Cattle Guard

Cattle Guard

to Squaw
Creek Rd.

Baldwin
Creek Rd

to Lander

photo Zach Snavley **ORANGE FOR ANGUISH** 14c Devlin Junker

The Approach: From the parking area, walk west up the road for about 200 feet. There is a faint trail heading left (south) from here, and past a BLM trail kiosk that is cleverly placed where no one will ever find it, 150 feet from the road. Follow a mostly flat path through a forest and over a small fence to an open meadow at the crest of a hill. This is a 12-15 minute walk so far.

Drop down the hill and follow faint switchbacks through a break in the cliff. Heading left as you go down the gully, you will find a footpath at the base of the cliff, taking you down the band, back to the east.

The first climbs you reach break through the obvious long, high horizontal roof, about 200 yards along the cliff from the descent gully. The bulk of the climbs, however, are another 3-5 minutes along. Look for the slightly over-hanging black wall of Brave Cowboy, and the lone "shade tree" against the wall near Amused to Death.

CLASSICS

Dinosaur Rock (p.297)

White Lightning (p.292)
Gimmie Shelter (p.297)

Brave Cowboy (p.295)
Piston Hurricane (p.297)
Tres Amigos (p.295)

Rain of Gold (p.297)
Skyliner (p.292)
Orange for Anguish (p.297)

0

1

9

26

17

7

 8AM-2PM

 30m

Vertical

BALDWIN **CREEK**

| 10AM-PM | 30m | Vertical | Slight |

Routes are listed from left to right.

●**1** □ **TS Route (Open Project)**
Through roof left of Skyliner. *Equipped Todd Skinner*

●**2** □ **Skyliner 13b** ★★
Mid 5.11 climbing takes you to an anchor atop a huge flake. Continue up to the roof and climb it just left of a seam feature. 100' *FA Todd Skinner, 1994*

●**3** □ **Magpies on an Afterbirth 12a**
Gold shuts on slab, diagonals right once you're over the bulge. *FA Ken Driese, 1994*

●**4** □ **TS Route (Open Project)**
Right of gold shuts, direct line through a low bulge to end of "Magpies" *Equipped Todd Skinner*

●**5** □ **Greased Lightning 12b** ★
Starts below the right end of a large bulge, climbs through the bulge on big moves, then finishes on a less-than vertical wall above. 75' *FA Will Hair, 1994*

●**6** □ **Space Brigade 12b** ★★
This climb follows cool flakes and underclings on an ever-steepening wall. 95' *FA Bj Tilden, 2006*

●**7** □ **Swiss Miss 5.13a** ★★
Techy climbing forever on a just less-than-vertical wall to anchors below square-cut roof. 90' *FA Sandra Studer 1994*

●**8** □ **White Lightning 11a** ★★
This is the big left-facing corner. Starts in a crack, then up right into the dihedral. 80' *FA Will Hair, 1994*

●**9** □ **Daybreaker 13b** ★
Hard start leads to tricky climbing on rounded prow. 65' *FA Todd Skinner, 1994*

●**10** □ **Troubleshooter 13a** ★★
This route takes small pockets through the really nice bulge right of Daybreaker. Shares anchors with Mask Without a Face. 45' *FA Todd Skinner, 1994*

●**11** □ **Mask Without a Face 12a** ★★★
Climb up to a nice horizontal band of big pockets, move slightly right, then up through a steep bulge using big pockets and big moves. One of the best around. 45' *FA Greg Collins, 1994*

●**12** □ **Hair Trigger 12b**
This climb is about 75 yards right of Mask. Starts on underclings and sidepulls, then through the left side of the roof on difficult moves. Finish on continuous vertical stone. 70' *FA Will Hair, 1994*

●**13** □ **Where There's A Will, There's A Way 12c**
Climb up the vertical face, then through the 3-foot black roof on hard moves. Easier (but not easy) climbing leads to anchors. 70' *FA Will Hair, 1994*

●**14** □ **Pizza Hut Girl 12b** ★★★
Named after the cutest girl in Lander in 1994. This route takes a small arête, then moves right along the lip of a big roof. After a short rightward traverse, head up a pumpy finish. 75' *FA Bobby Model, 1994*

●**15** □ **Sideshow Bob 13c** ★
Short, boulder-problem route right of the "Pizza Hut Girl" roof. 40'. *FA Todd Skinner, 1994*

●**16** □ **Beelzebubba 12a** ★
Climbs tricky right-facing corner to easier climbing above. Of historical interest this was the first routeTom Rangitsch established in Lander. 65' *FA Tom Rangitsch, 1994*

●17 ☐ Break Like The Wind 11d ★
Climbs up a seam to a vertical face above. 65'
FA Steve Bechtel, 1994

●18 ☐ I Am A Fat Man 12c ★
Right of Break Like the Wind, this climb takes tricky moves up a bulging wall. 65' *FA Steve Bechtel, 1994*

●19 ☐ Black Jaques Schellaque 13a
Twenty feet of tough climbing leads to a rest, followed by 5.12 climbing above. 70' *FA Scott Milton, 1994*

●20 ☐ Lucky Thirteen 12d
Tricky seam climbing to pumpy wall above. Technical. 80'
FA Steve Bechtel, 1994

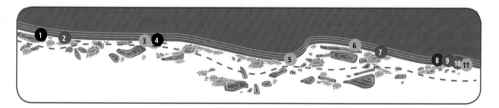

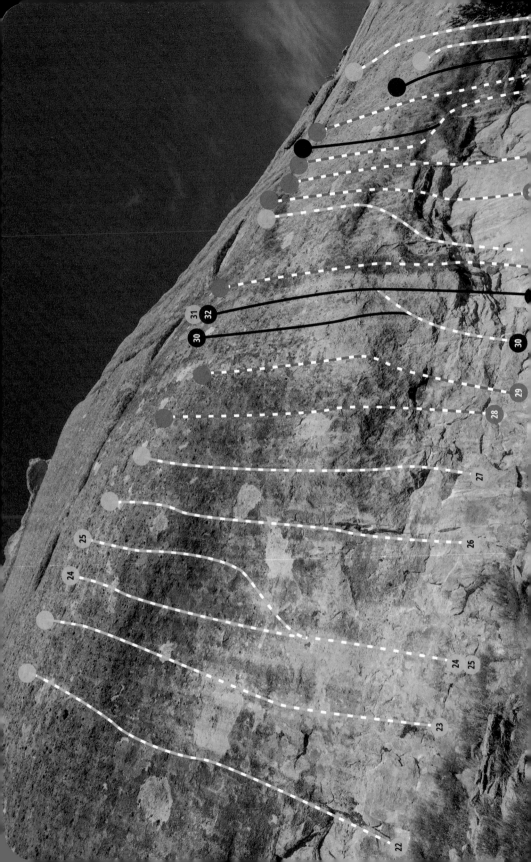

21 ☐ Mephisto 12c ★★

Long moves on generally good pockets. This route is really nice. 80' *FA Steve Bechtel, 1994*

22 ☐ Western Family 12d

Another tricky seam climb, this one gives away almost nothing. 75' *FA Gary Willmot, 1993*

23 ☐ Surfer Rosa 12c ★

Climb up pretty gold wall to high bulge 80'. *FA Frank Dusl, 1994*

24 ☐ Little Pedro's Mexican Tidal Wave 12b ★★

The crux is low, but the "tidal wave" above spits off most redpoint attempts. 80' *FA Greg Collins, 1993*

25 ☐ Barbarossa 12b ★

Shares the crux start with Little Pedro, then moves up right to hard steep climbing. Maybe slightly easier than the climb to the left. 80' *FA Frank Dusl, 1993*

26 ☐ Brave Cowboy 12a ★★★

An excellent route, starts in the shallow left-facing corner (usually with small bushes growing in it), then climbs through the hard steep wave. 80' *FA Frank Dusl, 1993*

27 ☐ Tres Amigos 12c ★★★

Hard low moves lead to a good rest, then a continuous hard headwall. 75' *FA Frank Dusl, 1993*

28 ☐ Viva Hate 13d ★★

Through steep moves to easier climbing at the top. 75' *FA Tommy Caldwell, 1998*

29 ☐ The Power of One 13a ★★

Hard mono moves lead to a gold streak. One of the prettiest stretches of limestone in the area. 80' *FA Frank Dusl, 1994*

30 ● No Cross, No Crown (Open Project)

No Cross, No Crown Splits left halfway up Last Chance for a Slow Dance. *Equipped Greg Collins*

31 ☐ Last Chance for a Slow Dance 12d ★

Climb up through the steep wave, then right and up a thin face above. 75' *FA Frank Dusl, 1994*

32 ● FD Route (Open Project)

Straight up into "Last Chance" finish. *Equipped Frank Dusl*

33 ☐ Burnout 13c ★

This takes the obvious black streak. One of the first routes bolted, it was one of the last done on the wall. *FA BJ Tilden, 2009*

34 ● Graffiti Man 12c ★★

Starts on a small prow, then up past some small roofs along crack. Move onto a good pocketed headwall when the crack runs out. Beware the "keeper mono". 60' *FA Frank Dusl, 1993*

35 ● Bittersweet 13c ★★

Very hard slab climbing leads up to the roof band, then through its center. 70' *FA Frank Dusl, 1993*

36 ● Supple Cowboy 13a ★

Climb a left-facing corner to the right side of the Bittersweet roof, then turn it to the right. Vertical 5.12 climbing takes you to the anchor. 60' *FA Frank Dusl, 1995*

37 ● Cowboy This 13d ★★

This is the left-trending line that roughly follows the arc of the bulge. 65 feet. *FA BJ Tilden, 2008*

38 ● Wishing Well (Open Project)

Wishing Well Starts Cowboy This, then moves straight up. *Equipped Frank Dusl*

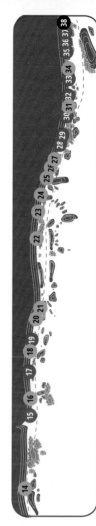

Ben Sears

BRAVE COWBOY 12a

●39 ☐ **Access Denied 13a** ★★
Monos and long moves lead through a black section of wall. *FA Frank Dusl, 1993*

●40 ☐ **TS Route (Open Project)**
Follows black hangers. *Equipped Todd Skinner*

●41 ☐ **State of Grace 12d** ★
Two routes left of the tree. Very powerful moves up underclings and small pockets. 55' *FA Frank Dusl, 1993*

●42 ☐ **Two Guys Names Festus 12d** ★★★
Climbs up long moves and thin pockets just left of the big tree. 65' *FA Frank Dusl, 1993*

●43 ☐ **Amused to Death 12a** ★★
Right of the big tree, climb up through the left side of the little arch roof to a spicy, yet easier, slab above. *FA Frank Dusl, 1993*

●44 ☐ **The Bravery of Being Out of Range 13a** ★★
Climbs a vertical face to the biggest part of roof (crux), then up easier face moves above. 80' *FA Frank Dusl, 1993*

●45 ☐ **Piston Hurricane 12b** ★★★
Up a good face to the roof, do a tenuous move, then climb 5.11 to the top. 80' *FA Steve Bechtel, 1994*

●46 ☐ **TKO 12b** ★★
Up the right side of arch, then thru roof and up a nice wall to anchors. 80' *FA Bobby Model, 1994*

●47 ☐ **Rapid Fire 12b** ★
Climbs the face just right of the arch. Continuous good moves. 75' *FA Bobby Model, 1994*

●48 ☐ **Losing Streak 12c** ★★★
A hard, beautiful grey streak. *FA Bobby Model, 1994*

●49 ☐ **Voodoo Chile 11c**
Starts on a flake, up hard moves to an easier slab above. *FA Mike Lindsey, 1994*

●50 ☐ **Gimmie Shelter 11b** ★★
Star left of large bush, climb up to undercling, over it, and up a good wall. 60' *FA Mike Lindsey, 1993*

●51 ☐ **Withering Heights 11a** ★
Hard start just right of the bush. Good pockets after the first bolt. *FA Aileen Brew ,1994*

●52 ☐ **One Trick Pony 11a**
This climb takes a nice section of wall. It tends to catch a little dust from runoff, so a brush might be nice to carry early season. *FA Jim Ratz, 1994*

●53 ☐ **Dinosaur Rock 10c** ★★
Starts on a grassy slope, climbs up past big pockets through small bulges. *FA Mike Lindsey, 1994*

●54 ☐ **Ticket To Ride 11c** ★
This route is about 100 yards past Dinosaur Rock. Good climbing on the vertical wall left of the Orange for Anguish Wave. *FA Mike Lindsey, 1995*

●55 ☐ **Sunshine Superman 11b** ★
Vertical, technical climbing. This is the middle route on the wall. 65' *FA Mike Lindsey, 1994*

●56 ☐ **Can't Always Get What You Want 11d** ★
Climb a prow to a slab at the top. This is the rightmost route on the vertical wall left of the wave, 65' *FA Frank Dusl, 1994*

●57 ☐ **Rain of Gold 13b** ★★★
Climb up the arête start to the steep face above. 75' *FA Sandra Studer, 1996*

●58 ☐ **Orange For Anguish 14c** ★★
Up the Rain of Gold arête, then right and through the center of the steep wave. 85' *FA BJ Tilden, 2008*

●59 ☐ **SL Route (Open Project)**
Right side of wave. *Equipped Sam Lightner*

●60 ☐ **A Bullet For Mr. Texas 13a** ★★
A nice route about 200 yards right of the wave. Walk on down there...you won't miss it. *FA Kirk BIllings, 1999*

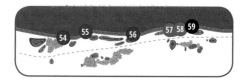

photo: Zach Buecker

SUICIDE **POINT**

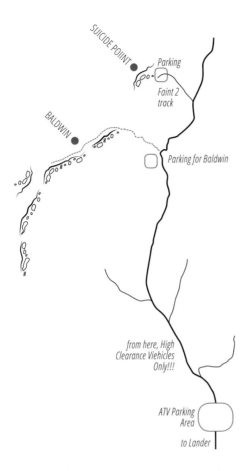

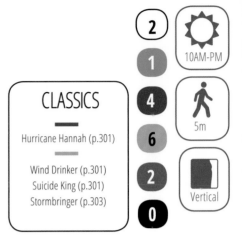

CLASSICS

—

Hurricane Hannah (p.301)

—

Wind Drinker (p.301)
Suicide King (p.301)
Stormbringer (p.303)

Previous: Kyle Duba on Wind Drinker
Photo: Zach Buecker

SUICIDE **POINT**

Suicide is Lander's most alpine sport climbing area. This crag is the western-most end of the mighty Baldwin Creek Wall, but is provided as a separate chapter since it is approached from a different parking area and is some three miles west of the bulk of the Baldwin Creek climbs.

The rock at Suicide is wind-weathered and is very angular. Many routes follow cracks, corners, and other distinct features. The 5.9 "Apocalyptic Lapse Rate" take natural gear so for this climb bring a few medium-sized cams. The rest are all bolted sport climbs in one of the most wild and beautiful crags you'll ever visit.

Directions: From downtown (at Main and 5th streets) head west on Main toward the mountains. Just after 9th street, Main veers right, heading north. After about ¼ mile there is a traffic light. Take a left here, on Baldwin Creek Road (at ShopKo). Leave Lander going west on Baldwin Creek Road. Follow this paved road for 5.5 miles, until the road turns to the south (left) at the top of a hill and it is possible to continue west on an improved dirt road. After 0.9 miles, the road splits, with the left fork heading into a ranch and the right fork taking you north along a big red butte. Once past the butte, the road turns left, and heads west up a hill. Follow this road as it climbs up several switchbacks to the crest of a small hill (about 5 miles).

At the top of this hill is a parking area popular with ATV riders. From here on up, the road is very rough and requires a high-clearance vehicle. The road continues up through meadows and aspen and can be very rough in spots for the next few miles.

Near the crest of a hill, you'll pass a cattle guard and an "Entering Public Lands" sign. About 100 yards later, there is a clear area to park on the left, just before the road heads back downhill into a wooded drainage. This is the Baldwin Creek climbing area trailhead. This is 13.5 miles from Main Street in Lander.

Continue on the two-track down the hill. The road gets rough again at the bottom, then heads into open fields soon after. Just over 1 mile past the Baldwin Creek parking area, you should be able to see Suicide Point on the ridge to your left. Take the faint road uphill and park on the ridge below the cliff.

SUICIDE **POINT**

10AM-PM | 5m | Vertical | Slight

2 1 4 6 2 0

A climber's path leads up to the huge prow (Wind Drinker). All described climbs are within two minutes of this prow. Climbs are described left-to-right.

Routes are listed from left to right.

●1 ☐ Hurricane Hannah 11b ★★
Start up arête below Wind Drinker (the VERY obvious prow), then move left around corner to steep face. This climb was done by Amy and Todd Skinner the summer after their first daughter, Hannah, was born. 80'
FA Todd Skinner, 1998

●2 ☐ Wind Drinker 12b ★★★
Climb up easy ground to an anchor (5.6), then out the wild "hatchet blade" prow. 70' *FA Todd Skinner, 1997*

●3 ☐ Suicide King 12c ★★★
Easy face climbing right of the arête leads to long pulls up overhanging rock. 80' *FA Steve Bechtel, 1998*

●4 ☐ Storm Chaser 11d ★
Starts in a crack, then up a steeper face above. Be careful to avoid climbing right to the Weeping Wrist anchors. 80'
FA Todd Skinner, 1996

●5 ☐ Weeping Wrist 11b ★
Thin face climbing leads through a bulge to an anchor in alcove. 65' *FA Steve Bechtel, 1998*

●6 ☐ A Cry for Help 10c
Up a slab to a horizontal, then up a short steep wall. Bolted by Dave Brinda way back in 1991 and then abandoned for the "more accessible" climbs of Baldwin Creek. 55' *FA Steve Bechtel, 1998*

●7 ☐ Blue Steel 11d ★
This climb is on the face adjacent to the "Hatchet Blade" climbs described above. Climb a vertical face to a short overhanging finish. *FA Aaron Steele, 2009*

●8 ☐ Flowers for a Dead Man 13b ★
Climb the center of the clean overhanging face left of the offwidth corner. There is a funny story associated with this route name, but it won't be told here. 60'
FA Todd Skinner, 1998

photo Kyle Duba

WIND DRINKER 12b Dave Goldman

○9 ☐ Painless 9 ★★

Climbs the steep offwidth corner. Fun. Mike Lilygren had a great habit of rolling in and snagging the classics at every new crag. 60' *FA Mike Lilygren, 1998*

●10 ☐ Nickel Winchester 12b ★★

This climbs the edgy overhanging face, finishing below the roof. 60' *FA Todd Skinner, 1999*

○11 ☐ Apocalyptic Lapse Rate 9

Climbs the dihedral with natural and fixed protection. Bring cams to 2". 80' *FA Michael Brown, 1996*

●12 ☐ Golden Ulric 12c ★★

Starts in corner, then climbs out a steep wall and through bulging rock above. 100' *FA Todd Skinner, 1998*

●13 ☐ Silver Nimschke 13b ★★

Climb up underclings through a bulge, then up through thin pockets. Named after the famed firearms engraver. 80' *FA Todd Skinner, 1998*

●14 ☐ Stormbringer 12d ★★★

 Up the huge corner to an anchor (5.9), then out a 20 foot horizontal roof. 75' *FA Steve Petro, 1998*

●15 ☐ Cloudwalker 12b ★★

This route shares the starting corner of Stormbringer, then breaks right out an easier section of the roof. 75' *FA Matt Wendling, 2008*

OTHER AREAS

(YOUNG MOUNTAIN)

This is the high crest of limestone that sits visibly on the skyline as you drive down into the valley from the Wild Iris area. A beautiful wall, route development has been thwarted by the terrible approach.

To access it via Pass Creek, drive to Limestone Mountain Road from Lander (approximately 24 miles south on WY 28), and follow that road past the Wild Iris turnoff (bear left at the fork) and down into the Pass Creek valley. You'll descend some switchbacks, and go past a left hand turn into the Pass Creek cabins, a group of private summer homes. After winding down a hill, and past some gentle curves, you'll hit a fork in the road near the base of Young Mountain. If you were to go right, you'd head for Wolf Point and Wolf Pup.

Head left and down a rough road, eventually paralleling Pass Creek. The road leads to a nice open area before crossing Pass Creek and the Little Popo Agie River. Park on the left side of the road in a meadow area before crossing Pass Creek.

To reach the crag, hike the road to the river crossing, and wade across. This can vary from very easy in late season, to very high and dangerous waters in May and June. Once across, follow the two-track for about 2 miles up through sage and timer until you're below the obvious south facing wall. The Missing Years is on the tallest and cleanest section of wall. If you have access to an ATV or have a truck you don't care too much about, you can drive the rough road through the Little Popo Agie, and on up to the hillside below the cliff. In this case, the hike is only about 10 minutes. There are two established routes here.

☐ The Missing Years 13a ★★
Takes the center line up the pretty and clean wall. Established on a massive four-wheel drive mission the same day as Truckin' back in 1992. 100' *FA Dusl, 1992.*

☐ Truckin' 12a ★
The other route at the crag. 60' *FA Greg Collins, 1992*

(STONE HORSE)

Stone Horse is a west-facing crag near Dickinson Park, northwest of Lander. Route development began on this wall in 1994, and it has seen sporadic visits since that time. The crag is accessed via the Shoshone Lake Road, which is on the Wind River Indian Reservation. Driving this road to the crag requires a Tribal Fishing Permit, which costs $80 for Wyoming residents and $120 for non-residents. The cliff sits right on the reservation boundary. The north half is on the reservation, the south half is on USFS land. Obviously climbing is only allowed on the south half of the crag. There are fewer than a dozen routes, all 5.11 to 5.13 at this cliff. There are also several small pinnacles and buttresses to the south of Stone Horse that have seen a little climbing action. The scenery here is spectacular, and the climbing will be fun.

(LOST CABIN)

Lost Cabin is a huge wall of dolomite in the North Fork drainage. It is accessed via the same road as Stone Horse, but you continue to drive north from that crag and then descend to the Lost Cabin wall from the top. Access to this crag from the canyon is not permitted.

The cliff is several miles long, and is as high as 350 feet in some places. It is futuristic and undeniably wild. There are maybe 5 established routes on the wall. Paul Piana's spectacular Yellow Boy (12b) is a rope-stretching arete. Arcanum is a three-pitch route featuring a great 5.11 first pitch, a wild 12c last pitch, and a 5.14 project for pitch two. Todd Skinner started bolting the unbelievably steep "Slant Project" - a wall that could one day host a 200'+ pitch at about 45 degrees overhang.

(YOUNG MOUNTAIN)

The south-facing cliff band on Young Mountain has not escaped the eyes of Lander's climbers. As one drives down into the Little Popo Agie drainage from Wild Iris, it's hard to miss. The western extension of this cliff, where it dips into the main Little Popo Agie canyon is where the Sweat Lodge and Ghost Town are located. The main band has been explored, but has not been the site of any climbing. The approach is long, and the cliff band nothing remarkable. However, the leftmost side of the wall has seen some action. In 2011, Vance White and friends made the hike and established two or three long, clean pitches on the tall southwest corner, facing the Strawberry Roan wall. No doubt there is much to do in this area, but the season is limited and there is a lot of rock much closer to the car.

5.9

5.10a

5.10b

5.10c

5.11b

5.11c

5.11d

5.12a

5.12b

5.13a

5.13b

5.13c

5.13d

STEVE BECHTEL

Steve is an author and climbing coach. A climber for more than 25 years, Steve previously published two editions of Lander Rock Climbs, as well as several other guidebooks. A Wyoming native, Steve started climbing in Lander in 1990. Since 2006 Steve has owned and operated Elemental Performance + Fitness, Lander's climbing gym and training center, with his wife Ellen. Steve also operates Climb Strong, the world's leading source on performance climbing information. A driven first ascentionist, Steve has established nearly 300 new climbs.

BEN SEARS

Ben is a graphic designer, tattoo artist, rock climber, and route developer. You can see Ben uitilizing his true passion at the Gannett Grill, flipping burgers and pouring beers. He moved here briefly in 2009 then again in 2012, and then again in 2019. In the last few years Ben has established over 50 routes, many of them being in the new area "Little Shady". He also was involved with "Bouldering in the Wind River Range". Ben plans of tattooing for the rest of his days in Lander so look him up @bensears.art or contact him for graphic design/tattoos at bsear945@gmail.com.

KYLE DUBA

Kyle Duba didn't plan to spend a decade in Lander when he first moved here in 2009, but it's easy for the days to slip away when so many of them are spent with nothing more important to do than go climbing with your friends and try to grab onto slightly smaller or slightly further apart holes in a rock. Having successfully joined the ranks of "ex-NOLS," Kyle now finds himself enjoying the hustle of freelance video production & photography—and, of course, still climbing rocks. Get in touch if you need something filmed, want to go climbing, or for fan mail kyleduba@gmail.com

FIND ALL THE CRAGS OF
LANDER ROCK CLIMBS
IN THE Vertical-Life App

DOWNLOAD NOW FOR FREE

Vertical-Life
climbing app

YOUR WORLDWIDE CLIMBING GUIDE